Critical Acclaim for
The Nudist on the Late Shift

"An entertaining and often dramatic account of frenetic and interlocking worlds. Rich in character and anecdote, *The Nudist on the Late Shift* conveys with unusual immediacy the volatility of an environment where billion-dollar ideas are a dime a dozen."

—*The New Yorker*

"A great chance to meet brainiacs, the geeks, the VCs, the driven, and the edgy who populate the Valley . . . Bronson's reports from the front lines give readers a sense of the absurd that seems to thrive in the Valley."

—*USA Today*

"A revealing profile of Valley culture . . . what really makes *The Nudist on the Late Shift* is Bronson's breezy, insightful writing."

—*Business Week*

"A java-fueled chronicle of the less-than-marquee but still pivotal figures of the digital future."

—*Details*

"An impressionistic work of art . . . a pastiche of keenly observed scenes and characterizations. Bronson hangs out with programmers, makes sales calls with salespeople, sits in on meetings between start-up entrepreneurs and venture capitalists, and captures it all with the same kind of breezy eloquence that makes his novels enjoyable reads. In his spot-on, inside account of what the process of going public is like, he describes the terrors of being beholden to the vagaries of the stock market with classic exuberance."

—*Salon*

"What *The Nudist on the Late Shift* tells us is the why of Silicon Valley. It tells us the how . . . it shows a true understanding of what life is like in the Valley. It's a look at who makes up the Valley culture and why they're there. It's about people with ideas who crave the challenge of finding answers, who can't bear to think of spending the rest of their lives counting numbers and collating papers."

—*San Diego Union-Tribune*

THE Nudist ON THE Late Shift

Po Bronson

Broadway Books New York

Visit our website at www.broadwaybooks.com
First Broadway Books trade paperback edition published 2000.

Designed by Barbara M. Bachman
Frontispiece photo of David Filo by Meri Simon

Library of Congress Cataloging-in-Publication Data Applied For

ISBN 0-7679-0603-9

00   01   02   03   04   10   9   8   7   6   5   4   3   2   1

THE AUTHOR WISHES TO THANK HIS EDITORS, PARTICULARLY

MARTHA BAER AND KATRINA HERON AT <u>WIRED</u> AND

JON KARP AND GEOFF MULLIGAN AT RANDOM HOUSE.

LEGAL NOTE

There are some people in this book who asked that their names be changed. They and their reasons for seeking pseudonymity are as follows:

The individual identified here as Michael Zilly was freely open and on the record about his unusual manner of funding his start-up venture—growing marijuana and selling it wholesale—until he got a job with a respectable corporation and did not want his background to catch up to him. His identifying details have been altered. The name and function of his product (now called the SupraNova) and the names of his business partners (identified here as Henry Silva, Jr., and Mark Conegan) are pseudonyms.

In a similar dynamic, the individual identified here as John/David Foster retroactively requested a pseudonym for himself and his employer only when the latter ran into unexpected financial difficulty. The names Kevin North, eFree, and eFree/Global are pseudonyms.

In exchange for pseudonymity, the Oracle salesperson identified as Mars Garro allowed me to pose as his assistant while we made his rounds without requesting permission from his superiors. In the same chapter, the "E-Shop Merchant System" is also a pseudonym.

The individual identified as Claudia Gomez asked for a pseudonym, since lying about one's identity in order to trick receptionists into giving out employee names might be viewed as fraudulent behavior. The individual identified as B., who had developed an intricate plan to murder one of his coworkers, asked that I not use his name for obvious reasons. The individual I call Noah Ames asked not to be identified because, at the time, he was attempting to keep his Internet telephony product under wraps until a formal public product launch. The final person in the book I name only as Luis to protect his father.

CONTENTS

The Nudist on
The Late Shift

WHEN YOU MEET a billionaire for the first time, you really want him to do something billionairish. You have no idea what being a billionaire might be like, but you can't help but be curious. What is it like? The billionaire is a little bit of a zoo animal for the public in this way. Particularly the instant billionaire. Because that's the public fantasy. Nobody's really all that fascinated anymore with fifty-five-year-old stone-hearted moguls who made their billions crushing little people for twenty-five years. It's so much more appealing to imagine being a billionaire when you're young enough to really enjoy it and you haven't had to be cruel to people to earn it. The Sub-35 Billionaire is really a new life-form, an economic mutation that emerged from this little pond of vigorous capitalist Darwinism. It's as if dinosaurs suddenly hatched again in the Alviso mudflats off San Jose. The Sub-35 Billionaire, this new species, captures the imagination not just like any zoo animal—he's a brontosaurus.

So when you meet your first Sub-35 Billionaire, you want to do it in his natural habitat, because that way you're that much more likely to catch him doing something bil-lionairish. You're not picky. You'll take just about any eccentric behavior as evidence of what Sub-35 Billionaires are like. Just as long as there's a sparkle in the moment, the light through the dia-mond, verifying that it's real.

It is in this manner, and with this purpose, that people who come to Yahoo!'s offices in Santa Clara for one reason or another take a little detour and navigate the maze of second-floor cubi-cles to pop in on or observe the Sub-35 Billionaire David Filo, one of the company's cofounders. When I stopped by recently to have lunch with a friend who's worked there since June 1996 (a month after Yahoo! went public), I thought I'd better go ask David Filo if he still slept under his desk. My friend has escorted numerous visitors who wanted to make this little detour. He says that most people walk away saying, "I didn't really get any im-pression. I was so distracted. I just kept seeing a billion-dollar bill hovering in the air above him." Most people who look at David Filo—and most people who look at Silicon Valley—can't see past the dollar signs. It's the same as how some people have a hyper-sensitivity to cilantro—put a little twig of cilantro in a salad and they can't taste anything but the explosion of cilantro. Except that having a hypersensitivity to a billion dollars is the norm, which is to say that the few people who can see beyond the flash-ing neon dollar signs are the odd ones. It is normal to go weird around money, to be made uncomfortable by it, to get supremely excited by it. Money is exceptionally titillating.

I am one of the odd ones. I have an accountant's clinical calm around figures big and small; I don't go weird around money, and people get less weird around money when I'm there. It's like night vision, but rather than seeing in the dark I can see past the nine zeroes. It's made it easier for me to avoid snap judgments about what I've seen in Silicon Valley. I'm inexperienced as a journalist and I'm no good at asking tough questions, but I have green vision.

So I didn't want to ask David Filo what it's like to have a bil-lion dollars. I just wanted to ask him if he still slept under his desk. For some time, I looked for an icon of Silicon Valley—an image, thing, or place where one could go to take it all in. And in the course of my search, the photo editor for the *San Jose Mer-cury News* pointed me to a photograph taken by Meri Simon, titled "Sleepless in Silicon Valley." The photograph is of a programmer sleeping on the carpet in his cramped, cluttered office, head jammed under his desk, gray blanket draped over his fragile torso. The photograph became more meaningful when I learned that the programmer was none other than David Filo. However, the photo was shot when David was worth a mere $500 million, and I guess I had to find out for myself if life as a Sub-35 Billionaire was any different from being a Sub-30 Cinquentimillionaire.

David Filo doesn't even have an office. He shares a double-wide cubicle with another guy. It's a window cubicle, but located right on the thick support pillar, so there are only a couple feet of tinted window on either side. David was standing up, and he was awash in a trash heap of paper. I don't mean a metaphorical trash heap, I mean an actual one, forty inches deep of unread memos, promotional literature, office chatter. Enough paper to fill several refrigerators. An inopportune bump could trigger a landslide. This trash heap was not a political statement about tree-product waste. This trash heap was not David Filo's de facto overflowing garbage can (it contained no Diet Coke cans or Domino's boxes). It was his in box and filing system. How ironic that the guy who has engineered the most popular directory for organizing the morass of the World Wide Web is utterly unable to engineer an organizational system for his own paper flow. This trash heap was not to be thrown away. It was a plain old mess, the kind your mom hollers at you to clean up.

Another irony: David Filo, cofounder of Yahoo!, was wearing a fairly well-worn white company T-shirt from Excite, Yahoo!'s fierce competitor. Was this sarcasm? Was this humor? I have no idea. When his choice of T-shirt was pointed out to him, he glanced down at it and gave out a demure little acknowledgment but didn't really seem to register it at all. *He had other things on his mind.* If it had clearly been either sarcastic humor or a complete accident that he was wearing a T-shirt advertising his competitor, the moment would have sparkled. Instead it was a letdown.

So was our exchange of words, the entire transcript of which follows:

[Our friend casually introduces me.]

FILO: [mumble] [blank stare as if I am a television tuned to Home Shopping channel]

[Our friend mentions my novels.]

FILO: [mumble] Oh, uh-huh. [faint sign of recognition]

ME: [at a loss for words, trying to be friendly] You still sleep under your desk?

FILO: [Looks down; under his desk is trash heap.] Not much anymore. No room.

Okay, that wasn't the *entire* transcript, but things didn't really pick up from there. I did find it quite amusing that he no longer slept under his desk, not because he had doubled his money since then but because his trash heap doubled in size and squeezed him out. He did go on to say that he was moving to a new cubicle soon. He is not aloof, not somber, not antisocial, not particularly evasive. But he's something like all those things combined. He's blurry. I'm hard-pressed to put down a physical description, other than to say "medium." Medium in all respects. How *unbillionairish* of him! He defies being anything other than a fiercely hardworking engineer. He's certainly no icon. He emits none of the flash/dazzle/whiz-bang future-is-now excitement that we popularly associate with this burgeoning industry. And I can't say much more about him other than I think that, regarding his billion dollars, he too is one of the odd ones. It hasn't made him go weird.

However weird he may be, he already was.

I BEGAN MY search for an icon when a producer for the ABC television show *Nightline* called me up one day and asked for some help. They wanted to do a minidocumentary about Silicon Valley. Their objective was vague but open-minded: "We want to capture what's going on out there," said Lisa Koenig, the segment's producer. I liked their attitude. Something *was* going on out here, and I was heartened to hear they didn't pretend to already know what it was. Before getting on the plane west, they preinterviewed all of their subjects by telephone, and the correspondent, Robert Krulwich, decided to use the cable Internet company @Home as the documentary's protagonist. Being with a national television show, they didn't have trouble getting otherwise overcommitted CEOs to clear their schedules for two hours with Krulwich and his camera team.

At the end of the first day I asked Koenig how it was going. She said that the interviews were fine but there was a problem: neither she nor Krulwich nor anyone from the camera crew had been here before. Until they stepped off the plane that morning, they'd never seen "Silicon Valley, The Place." They had been hoping for an establishing shot that said "You're here!," the equivalent of New York City's skyline or the Hollywood lettering in the hills. They wanted visual anecdotes that captured the essence of life in the Valley: the high stakes risk taking, the long working hours, the area's congestion from rapid growth, the sudden wealth. More than anything, they needed to point the camera at something that captured the tremendous buzz.

So far all they found was an endless suburb, hushed and nonchalant, in terrain too flat to deserve the term "valley." Along the peninsula the setting seemed to repeat itself, a cartoon backdrop—every few miles another Blockbuster Video, another Chevy's, another Toyota lot. In between were office parks, quiet in the hot sun. The answer to "What is there, there?" was a cruel letdown.

Because I've been around the Valley since coming to college in 1982, I was so accustomed to the locale that I never noticed this obvious point. As I looked at it through this camera crew's eyes, though, the irony was acute: the industry that gave us the Macintosh smiley face and a screenful of icons that make computers touchy-feely familiar never coughed up an icon for the whole shebang. It lacks a place you can go to take it all in, to "get it."

When I worked at the investment banking firm First Boston in the mid-1980s, I would get requests from friends to tour our office "to see what it's all about." I would usher them out onto the sales and trading floor, and the iconicness of the place never failed to live up to expectations. Liquid crystal stock tickers rushed quotes along the walls. Suit jackets that cost thousands of dollars would be thrown over the backs of chairs like T-shirts. Men and women with prestigious pedigrees would be screaming into their telephones, standing up amid war-room-like computer monitors, their faces sweaty and their eyes jerky with the knowledge of having millions of dollars exposed in a moving market. It was an image with a sound track: trading activity in offices around the country was announced over a PA system, echoing in from an aural cyberspace. Fifty phones were ringing at the same time.

Silicon Valley has its places, and though these places whisper their own mantra, they never shout it. You've heard that Silicon Valley is glamorous and that it's a very exciting time to be here, but the glamour and excitement are rarely manifested in the moment. You can stand in the aisle at Fry's Electronics on a Friday night and see people's endless fascination with joysticks and *Dilbert* books. You can have breakfast at Il Fornaio in Palo Alto and know that probably half the people there are in the business, though there's no way to tell which half. You can attend speeches delivered by the industry's titans to faithful conventioneers at the Moscone Center, but the same scene in the same location is played out every week by every other convention that comes to town.

I've never found one place that said it all. One's understanding of Silicon Valley is built up over time, in many thin layers, by many small hints. Visually, what can be used is a montage, and that's what *Nightline* resorted to. I had pointed them to forty-foot-wide billboards beside Highway 101 that advertise job openings at Valley companies and to the campus of Silicon Graphics, which seemed, in its architecture, to embody the managerial principle of chaotic conflict: the raw materials of brick, glass, and unfinished steel butting up against one another in hectic polygons, interrupted by vibrant yellow and bold purple decahedrons. The camera crew also found the trailer home dentist who drives up to Netscape several days a week so employees don't have to leave work to get their teeth fixed and the washer-and-dryer facility at Excite where workers too busy to do laundry at home can do it at work.

I liked these visual anecdotes because they looked past the dollar signs to convey how the Silicon Valley lifestyle blurs the line between work and nonwork. This trend is going on all over the country and has been for two decades, but nowhere has it gone to the extremes it has in the Valley. What is an "office park" but an oxymoronic euphemism that blurs the distinction between indoors and outdoors, between building and forest, between work and rest—but always seems to result in more work and less rest? Silicon Valley is this concept taken to the level of a whole region: it's one big office park. In its uninspiring placidity, the Valley offers its workers a sustained level of nondistraction, ensuring that work remains the most interesting and compelling activity in one's view frame of enticements.

But neither a washing machine nor a trailer home nor an office park emits any buzz.

ONE PLACE that was getting some buzz for a while was called Mae West. In 1995 and 1996, as the Internet was being developed and people were openly wondering whether the system was stable, it was fashionable to sound informed at cocktail parties by blurting, "I heard Mae West was down today." Though the Internet was supposed to be a big spider web spanning the nation, it was really more like one big spider web on the East Coast and another on the West, connected by a fat hose of fiber-optic lines. The central hub in the east was Mae East and, out here, Mae West. People chatted a lot about Mae West without knowing that "Mae" stood for Metro Area Exchange and without knowing where Mae West was located, which was in San Jose. But it conjured something in our imaginations: half of the entire Internet, running through one room! The amount of equipment that must be there, the clicking and clacking and switching and routing, the loud roar of the Internet would put any Orwell/Kubrick vision of computer power to shame!

Then a few people were let inside, and in late 1997 it was a very cool thing to do if you were hosting a party anywhere near downtown San Jose: hop on a shuttle bus with your guests and take them over to walk through the Mae. Put that on your invitation, and the RSVP rate doubled. But nobody I knew who went to one of these parties seemed to talk about it afterward. It was as if they were sworn to secrecy.

In a way, they were. The Mae was a telecommunications co-op, managed by WorldCom but owned jointly by most of the big phone companies and Internet service providers. When I called WorldCom to ask to see it with my own eyes, I had to sign a nondisclosure agreement that they faxed to me. This NDA required me to agree not to write about those things anyone who belonged to this wire commune would consider trade secrets. I could, however, describe it in general. No photographs would be allowed.

Three gigabits of data flowed through the Mae every second. Surely here, in the secret center of the Internet, I would find the thrum and buzz of the industry. It's located in a fiery gold building in downtown San Jose that has so many internal backup systems that the engineer who escorted me upstairs liked to joke, "If the building had wheels, we could drive it to Arizona." I signed a couple more documents to satisfy the security guards in the lobby and took an elevator to the eleventh floor.

Outside the door the sound hit me first—a treble hum of fans and a bass thrum of thundering air conditioners that I could feel in my feet through the linoleum-covered floor. We entered into a vast labyrinth of gunmetal gray chain-link cages, their doors secured by Kryptonite horseshoe bicycle locks. Bolted to the floor inside the cages were ceiling-high racks of Cisco 7500 routers and FDDI concentrators and shelves of modems lined up like books in cases. The wiring of all this equipment twisted into vines and crept up to overhead trellises, then made its way along the ceiling and passed through a hole in the far wall, leading the way to Mae.

Exiting the maze, we circled the battery supply room. Each of these twenty or so batteries was the size of a refrigerator. They are so heavy that to prevent their crashing through the floor, the batteries sit on two reinforced steel I beams. I walked trepidly, close to the tinted windows. For whatever reason, this backup power system was given a corner office, with a view north up Silicon Valley that rivals anybody's, though, as I've said, that's not saying much. On this hot day, brown smog sat over the lowlands of the peninsula, and the only objects identifiable through the smog were the northern-running freeways. It reminded me again why I was here, and I turned around to finally enter Mae itself.

At last, the inner sanctum.

Two keys inserted into the door and a combination in the cyberlock get us in and . . . well, it's sort of like when Dorothy meets the Wizard of Oz. The same cruel letdown again. Mae West turned out to be three gigabit switches, each about the size of a minimicrowave. Each had fiber-optic lines jacked into its face, but—another letdown—fiber-optic cable looks exactly like ordinary phone cord, only it's colored bright orange so you can tell the difference. The room was perfectly quiet. Mae West, the great Internet hub of hubs in the heart of Silicon Valley, is composed of less high-tech equipment than most people have in their living rooms.

Now I understood why nobody who had been there had had much to talk about afterward.

THOSE ARE the two problems of portraying Silicon Valley:

1. There is very little there, there.
2. What is is shrouded in secrecy.

If you didn't know better, you might take a look at the tremendous amount of media coverage given to high technology and assume that this place runs like an open book, perfectly willing to be a media darling. It seems like a loose, freewheeling world. In fact, journalists are asked to sign an NDA at every workplace they enter: It's okay to write about this little gizmo we have coming out next week, but if you happen to overhear anything about this big gizmo we have coming out next year, we'll take action against you if it appears in print. You will have a PR representative with you at all times. You may not mention the names of our customers or clients without written permission. You may not interview employees unless we authorized them to speak with you. In other words, "Keep your hands inside the car at all times."

For example, I had a couple of acquaintances who sold their company to Microsoft and moved to Redmond; they invited me to fly up and go waterskiing on Lake Washington after work. Then they had to call back and cancel. They were quite embarrassed: Microsoft was insisting on putting a PR representative in the boat with us!

The machinery of work is as tightly kept a secret as our society has anymore. It's guarded by a legal firewall. There's just too much money at stake. And in the world of business, nowhere is there more money at stake than here. Everyone's lips are sewn up by severance contracts, nondisclosure agreements, employment contracts, term sheets, shareholder lawsuits in process, settlement papers, "hold harmless" agreements, formal complaints, ad infinitum. The recent past can't be talked about because of potential libel or violation of an NDA. The near future certainly can't be discussed because of the strict Securities and Exchange Commission laws forbidding forward-looking statements. When one company buys another, both parties are strictly forbidden to discuss the negotiations. Intellectual property and trade secrets are carefully guarded. Employees are briefed and debriefed.

That said, there really is a din of news coverage coming out of the Valley, and firms here are desperate to "rise above the noise." This created a perverted dilemma in which companies were desperate to talk to me but the things that I'd like to hear are exactly the things they're forbidden to discuss. They don't like it any more than I do; they are indeed, by nature, frolicsome, free-wheeling folks who find the nuances of what they do curiously compelling. They enjoy spilling the beans. They like to know that they have story-worthy lives, that their work really is as dramatic as they feel it is. They work away in relative isolation for months, and there's nothing more gratifying than a journalist showing up and saying, "You're important." Actually, there is something more gratifying than that. It's when a journalist shows up and says, "Your life would make a great movie."

But sometimes even that doesn't get the good stuff out of them. It's funny what rituals some sources want to go through before they're comfortable telling their story. Gina comes to mind. Gina recently resigned from working for Pixar after it had gone public, and she was now chilling out, decompressing, reevaluating her life. She was in that stage where the narrative of her life had broken down. Her head was full of so many stories that it was impossible to get them out one at a time. Getting a full story out of her was like catching a fish with your hands: I'd get really close, and then she'd sense my fascination and dart on to another topic. I had to spend long hours with her, and occasionally good stories would peep out.

A trust needed to develop between us. One day we walked the meditation labyrinth inside Grace Cathedral on Nob Hill. By demonstrating the necessary solemnity, I graduated to what I perceived to be the next test: stomach massage. We crossed the street to a busy park, where I stretched out in the sun on a warm concrete bench. The stomach muscles, according to my would-be masseuse, are the hardest ones to relax because they protect the organs. To let someone manhandle your liver is the ultimate test of trust. She would use my abdominal rectus as a lie detector test.

She began to poke at my thorax, and in the course of conversation, she started talking about the programmer nudist who worked the late shift at one of the animation companies that dealt with Pixar. Peep! My interest was piqued, my abdominal wall sprang tight, she sensed my fervor, and she was on to another topic. When I urged her to tell me more about the nudist, she dismissively remarked that everybody knew about the nudist, he was an urban legend. When I begged, she said that yes, she would tell me about him some time.

For the next year, I often wondered about the nudist. I didn't know if it was true, but it was sensational, buzz-worthy. Nobody can look at a nudist sitting there in his cubicle and see just dollar signs. Being a nudist on the late shift seemed to me to be the ultimate symbol of how people here want to assert their personal values on the job—a symbol of how tightly woven together work and play have become (a heck of a lot better symbol than a dentist trailer or an on-site washing machine). What some people see as a cold techno-Valley of ruthless corporate greed was nevertheless, to him, his Garden of Eden. And there was something innocent about nakedness, exposed and vulnerable. No money in the picture, no Ferraris, no lava lamps, no pocket protectors, no T-shirts—no distractions. Just a man, a computer, and a job.

I sent feelers out, asking friends who worked in animation and graphics. Occasionally I would get back "Oh, I've heard stories about that guy." But nobody I talked to had seen him or met him or could confirm that he wasn't just urban legend.

LATELY, I KEEP getting asked the same question: "Don't you want to join one of these start-ups you write about and make your bundle?" It's such an obvious question, but that's the downside of my green-vision oddness: I'm not very tempted by money. What I do see, when I consider the question, is access. I see a way to get beyond the legal firewall once and for all. I have done my share (but no more than my share) of mischievous trickery: posing as a sales assistant, sneaking into buildings, faking a résumé, getting into long conversations without identifying myself as a journalist, et cetera. I have a lot of fun chasing these stories around. Wouldn't taking a job give me the real inside story?

I didn't think so. Silicon Valley is a diverse free-for-all of experiences. The experience of being a freelance Java programmer is nothing like the experience of being a business development director for an Internet search engine. Java programmers practically don't even speak the same language as the business-deal makers—both have their own slang vocabulary. The experience of working in, say, the New Age human potential culture at Apple is vastly different from working for Intel, where employees go through what is called "confrontation training," in which they learn to call one another names and brutally speak their minds, believing that only through conflict will good ideas emerge. The experience of being a bootstrap start-up entrepreneur financed by serial credit cards is very different from being a fast-track start-up funded by Kleiner Perkins venture capital. The experience of going through an initial public offering is actually quite rare, and even those who have jobs at a company that does go public are excluded from seeing the nitty-gritty process, which is left to the three or four top people at the company who make up the IPO team. And none of the people just mentioned has the faintest clue what goes on in the sales side of the industry.

If the odds of making a million-plus dollars here in less than three years are one in seven, the odds of my getting a good story by taking a job are probably no better. In order to portray the broad panorama of Valley experience, I feel that my vantage point as a rogue journalist is better than having a job and probably second best only to being a venture capitalist.

So in the end, to capture this region, I fell upon the same device as the *Nightline* crew: a montage of the core experiences that define the work/life adventure. Because of the legal firewall, in a few places I have disguised sources, and these are noted in the text.

What's not in this book is a roundup of the Valley's Most Important People, its movers and shakers, its A-list. I'm just not drawn to those kinds of people, and that formula strikes me as a very East Coast paradigm being forced onto a West Coast phenomenon. The Valley is about the *opportunity to become* a mover or a shaker, not about *being* one. That opportunity is what gets young people to move here every day from Illinois and India and Canada.

Or, to restate, "movers and shakers" conveys the centralization of power, whereas the Valley's intrinsic paradigm is the decentralization of power. To create a "mover-and-shaker class" or an "A-list" would be to impose gods, to impose preordainedness, and to worship these gods.

In this day and age, some of us are lucky enough to be free to make what we can of the world. We have independent will at our disposal, and we have the urgent moral responsibility to exercise that will, not to follow in the steps of those held up as gods. There are no higher stakes in life, no higher ambition. That is the true spirit of entrepreneurism.

In Silicon Valley, a million-plus young people are lucky enough to wake up every morning to this opportunity. It is perversely amusing to watch us, a generation so afflicted with cynicism and irony, melt ever so slowly in the face of high-paying jobs. Usually it works the other way: the longer you've been around, the more hardened you get. But after having poked my nose into so many people's business, having watched horror stories unfold and successes play out, I am less jaded now than the day I began.

THAT WAS ABOUT four years ago.

Long ago we used to have a writers' group. Four guys. We'd meet one night a week at one or another of our low-rent apartments. We drank a lot of red table wine and discussed our stories with stubborn tenacity. The social component was high, we were bound together by a common interest, and it was impossible not to romanticize what we were doing. This definitely seemed to be *the* thing young men of Dionysian temperament *should* be doing in their early twenties, living in the bohemian city: stay up too late, rap, chant, smoke, drink, create.

Our writing got us into graduate programs, and one of us started to win awards, first locally, then nationally. I'm not really sure how to characterize what happened next, but I guess we got swept up in the fervor of the times. Or sucked in. One of us started writing newsletters for tech firms, then wrote a few nifty computer books, then became a columnist for a Ziff-Davis report, and soon was a full-fledged high-tech guru, the kind of guy who walks around tech conferences with a small entourage of devotees and PR flacks pitching him the latest buzzword.

Another of us switched his major to computer science and became a graphical user interface programmer, now in high demand. He rants on the theories of computer usability with the same headstrong passion he once devoted to Saul Bellow.

The third—the award winner—started working in the Valley, hoping to save enough money or score with options to take a year off and give his fiction another concerted push. Now he ghostwrites best-selling Web developer books.

I started to record the stories I was hearing from Silicon Valley. Our generation was taking on the label of having been born cynical/passive, and the Valley seemed to me to be the place where that was least true. It offered a chance to leave a mark on a world that already seemed terribly marked up. I started to visit workplaces, go see friends of friends, simply soak up the milieu. The domain of working life, particularly in corporate America, has the stereotype of being inhabited by working stiffs. But I kept meeting young people at the proving point of their lives who risked it all and would either succeed wildly or go down tragically. I wasn't as interested in their success as I was in this way of life: taking risks, forging the future, everything a maybe. For young people, it is very important not to be able to see one's fate, very important to have the sense that one's life is not preordained.

I know why these stories interested *me*. I know what nerves in me go "Quaannngg!" Some journalists have what they call a "bullshit detector." I have what I call a "Goose Bump Meter." If I don't get goose bumps hearing someone's story or experiencing it with him, I throw my notes in the trash. I was interested in one thing: people in pursuit of unusual lives.

A writer's job, in the romantic notion, is to document chaos and to remind us that chaos exists—that the pretense of forward progress is a lie. That life is crazy and a struggle and haunted. A writer's job, in the romantic sense, is to indulge one's Dionysian energy, to let it dominate our Apollonian energy, and to have a keen nose for adventure. (Dionysius was the God of wine and revelry; Apollo drove the chariot that carried the sun across the sky with such regularity, such order.) But it's also just so obvious that the phenomenon of Business has taken over the world, imposing its own form of order. Apollo's resurrected, and he's wearing a suit and has his money in index funds and is incredibly popular. As a writer, to ignore the sweeping transformation of what was culture into "the entertainment business," to ignore the obvious ways business elected itself the new culture, would be to turn a blind eye at what most needs to be seen clearly.

In Silicon Valley I found, for a few years, the vociferous expression of both those impulses. It is wildly chaotic. It tears itself down continuously. It teeters on the brink of self-destruction. But it is a chaos unlike any other chaos. It is a *smoothly working* chaos. It is a chaos that generates endless growth. It is the chaos of hard effort, rather than the chaos of need gratification.

And I would argue that this tapping of both impulses is exactly its appeal to our generation.

If I could say just one thing about Silicon Valley, this is it: every generation that came before us had to make a choice in life between pursuing a steady career and pursuing wild adventures.

In Silicon Valley, that trade-off has been recircuited.

By injecting mind-boggling amounts of risk into the once stodgy domain of gray-suited business, young people *no longer have to choose.* It's a two-for-one deal: the career path has become an adventure into the unknown. More happens here and so quickly, satisfying anybody's craving for newness. In six months you might get a job, be laid off, start a company, sell it, become a consultant, and then, who knows?

I JUST NEVER know when and where Silicon Valley's bizarre way of life is going to suddenly reveal itself.

On a wet Sunday morning in late March, I was at the West Sunset soccer fields in San Francisco, playing in a regular pickup game that has passed down to new generations for more than twenty years: same time every week, ever since the 1970s. Almost all the players are immigrants, and the game is theoretically open to all comers, but the players are verbally abusive to anyone who doesn't have the knack.

On this Sunday, we were kicked off our regular field by someone who held a city permit and waved it in our faces. We resumed our game on the open grass beside the field. Men in Smith & Hawken rubber raincoats came out to rechalk the field lines and hang brand-new nets. Bright orange corner flags were planted, and then the referee showed up with two linesmen—the latter a real luxury. I knew the ref from over the years.

"Hey, Hal, who's playing?"

Hal didn't know, but he said whoever it was was paying him big money.

Then the teams showed up. It was a coed game, and all the players were adults. Their game began, and when I bothered to look over I could see they were klutzes. I suspected, at that point, that it was some sort of gung ho corporate picnic, determined not to be defeated by the drizzle.

When our game ended, I walked over. I could see then that the uniforms of the team in blue said "Scopus" across the chest, and those of the team in white "Siebel." I knew from the business pages that these were two software companies and that Siebel recently bought Scopus.

I struck up a conversation with one of the players kneeling on the sideline. I asked if this was the way the two firms were getting to know each other. He said it was; then he took a good look at me for the first time—my question had implied that I might know a little about the software business—and asked, "Hey, what do you do?" Before I could even answer, he got to his point. He asked, "Do you want a job?"

I couldn't believe it. But it indeed happened. *Do you want a job?* His words rang in my ears. There I was, a complete stranger standing in a soaking wet T-shirt with mud splattered on my knees, and I was encouraged to apply for a job merely because I had recognized the name of his firm. How could this be? It wasn't enough to buy an entire company of people, the fire needed to be fed. More people! The oddity didn't seem to register on him. Maybe he did this all the time, asking people wherever he went: *"Do you want a job?"*

I said I was a writer. This disappointed him, but only slightly. He said, "We really need programmers. But we need technical writers too. Do you ever write about technology?"

I said that I did write a little about that, occasionally.

He pointed a blond woman out who he said worked in Human Resources and urged me to talk with her. Then he brought up the subject of programmers again. Did I know any?

Feeling a little mischievous, I pointed out a pack of my friends who were taking off their cleats and packing their bags seventy yards away: "See those guys? Most of them are programmers." This wasn't at all true, but the guy's eyes got big and he dispatched the blond lady to go talk to the group.

This was just the sort of occurrence that to most hair-trigger cultural forecasters indicates what is called a "market top"—the equivalent of when grandmothers take their savings out of the mattress to buy mutual funds. When jobs are being offered to soaking wet strangers, perhaps this is a sign that Silicon Valley has hit its market top.

But later, I was researching software salespeople, and I spent some time with a competitor of Siebel. I learned that Siebel Systems is one of the hardest-driving, most aggressive sales outfits in the industry. Around that time, I received e-mail from a man who identified himself as a Siebel salesperson. He'd read my books, and he was wondering what to do with his life because he could no longer take the relentless pressure of meeting the staggering quotas. It was ruining his life and his personality. Siebel wasn't a company that had a reputation for being fat or lazy, and its revenue results for that quarter far exceeded the financial analysts' predictions.

What kind of life is this, working for a company that will smile and shake your hand and offer you a job but if you take that job might cruelly drive you to exhaustion? *Sure, join the game, come on in! Doesn't matter if you speak the language. Everybody's welcome. But dammit, asshole, quicker! Pass me the goddamned ball! Shoot!*

CAN THE VALLEY'S high-tech pickup game keep growing forever? Isn't there some natural limit where the degree of chaos caused by the churning of start-ups and failures exceeds the degree of order established by standardized protocols and it starts to tear itself down faster than it builds up? Doesn't the fact that the business is running on vapor—without revenues, without offices, without physical products—mean that at a certain point it will lose its ability to float? Do the principles of economics work in space, beyond the reach of gravity? Is there any oxygen up there? One fad after another has been proven to be no more than that, but amazingly, everyone still has a job, plugging sixty-hour weeks into the next fad. Surely, surely, a crash is due. Not just a brisk correction that can be patched by repricing options, but a real crash.

Where are the fundamentals? It's a business based on nothing more than ideas and thus can't be stable. And aren't all the good ideas taken already?

Outside, that's what everyone is thinking. From a distance, the business seems unsustainable.

But here's what you see from the inside.

I was researching the process of what it's like to go public, and a firm invited me down to its office to meet its investment bankers, who would have to approve of letting me into their show. I arrived at the building, entered the lobby, and got into the elevator for the ride to the third floor. Stepping in behind me were two guys just a little younger than me, wearing blue jeans and striped polo shirts. They were also headed to the third floor, and they were in the midst of a conversation about the pros and cons of developing software on the Sun Microsystems Solaris 2.4 operating system versus Microsoft's Windows NT 3.51 system. I had my little reporter's notebook with me because I'm always looking for telling anecdotes, and I figured, this is good, these are the engineers, and later I'll meet the bankers.

On the third floor, these guys popped into the bathroom, and I went in to meet with the company. I met the CEO, the corporate counsel, and the venture capitalist, and we sat down in a conference room.

"Those bankers should be here by now," said the CEO. I was offered coffee.

And then in walked the bankers—the two guys in blue jeans and polo shirts.

The Valley has changed dramatically. I used to be an investment banker, and we used to do deals for Hewlett-Packard and Genentech. On a good day, in front of a customer, we might have pretended and faked a little knowledge about the technical stuff. On a good day, we might have been able to sketch a diagram on a napkin. But we hadn't really known anything. We'd been good at changing the subject. When we'd been on our own—in elevators, say—we'd talked about sports. If we'd ever been seen out of our suits, we wouldn't be recognizable.

It's extraordinary how savvy everyone is about everyone else's turf. Even the generalists have a high degree of specialty knowledge. Just a few years ago—around the time I was researching the Valley for my novel *The First $20 Million Is Always the Hardest*—there existed a tectonic divide between the bankers, the engineers, and the marketing whizzes. Engineers, in particular, held a deep scorn for the moneymen. Knowledge was strictly on a need-to-know basis. But under competitive pressure, you need to know everything.

After the meeting with those investment bankers in blue jeans (in which I was dinged, forbidden to observe the process further), I strolled through the engineering/programming cubicles with the public relations liaison. Several of the programmers were working with split monitor screens. On one screen they were programming; on the other, they were trading their own personal portfolios on E-Trade or some such on-line brokerage. They were trading put and call options to give their trades further leverage, and they didn't think anything of this. It wasn't unusual, they assured me. Even the public relations liaison held puts and calls on tech stocks. "Don't you?" she asked.

So here's what I think. I think if we have grown to this level despite the tectonic divide and scorn between the specialties—with so much lost in the translation every time and so much bumbling ineptitude as the result—now that the divide is gone, now that bankers can chat about workstation operating systems and programmers trade puts and calls and over dinner people debate stupid business ideas, we may be on the verge of the biggest growth explosion yet. We've survived the steep learning curve and the embarrassments of goofball concepts and Ponzi scheme financing. We know better. If this industry is driven by ideas, the fundamentals have never been better. The next five years will be the Valley's greatest boom of innovation to date.

I'm perfectly aware that such a statement will be misinterpreted as being a prediction for Internet stocks, which are a circus unto themselves. Though people are willing to make bets, nobody pretends that stock prices are rational. By now it's perfectly clear that the national fascination is riveted on people who are getting rich quickly and easily—and that it's hard for the country to see beyond the dollar signs. The Internet is the plot device for the '90s; it's the thing people are using to get rich, like oil and real estate in the '70s, or stocks and bonds in the '80s. Average people no more understand the importance of Java purification than they did prepayment rates on high-coupon Ginnie Mae mortgage bonds or tax rebates on drilling costs. People on a bus can tell you that TheGlobe.com was initially priced at $9 per share and finished its first day of trading at $63, but they can't tell you what you might see if you visited its site. Middle Americans missed their chance to buy Data General in 1975 and Microsoft in 1986, so when they hear there's a whole 'nother computer revolution going on, they don't want to buy the software so much as they want to buy the stock of the company that makes the software.

But that's fine with the people out here. They'll be happy to take your money.

I RECEIVED AN e-mail. "Looking for me?" it asked, attaching a phone number. An e-mail I sent out was forwarded through several rounds of recipients to reach him. My e-mail did not say I was looking for "the nudist on the late shift." Someone I'd encountered had thought she remembered the nudist's name, and I sent out e-mails with every spelling variation of this name, wondering if anyone knew how to get in touch with him.

So now I had the phone number of some guy. But I didn't know if he was the nudist. It took me two days to work up the nerve to call. How do you ask somebody such a question? If he weren't the nudist, he would probably be offended and hang up. If he *were* the nudist, it was probably a deeply personal matter and he would either deny it or be offended by my intrusion and hang up. I developed a strategy: the more apologetic I was up front, the less I might piss him off and the longer I might keep him on the phone. I dialed the number. Right then I realized that the best strategy might be not to apologize at all, to act as if it were no big deal—not give any indication that this might be sensational. I hung up the phone and wrote out a whole new script of questions in this tone.

Two hours later I called back. I had a lump in my throat, and I was growing dizzy with trepidation. His voice came on the line: casual, friendly, well-spoken. He called me by my first name, and we started to chat, in increasing earnest. Then I asked the dreaded question, and he laughed. "My gosh, it's grown to the size of urban legend."

"Is it true?" I asked.

"It's [click] true," he said. The "click" was the sound my phone emits for call waiting, which I forgot to turn off. Of all times! So what had he said? I'd heard the word "it's" and the word "true," but had they been separated by a pause or by the word "not"? "It's . . . true" or "It's not true!"? The damn click! What if he hangs up on me now? I'll have come this close and then lost it.

He began to talk about the urban legend and how people misconstrued the truth; how everyone misinterpreted what had happened. How because of this, his reputation preceded him wherever he went. I felt deflated. He wanted to know what version of the urban legend I heard, and I told him what little I heard, as sketchy as it was, and how I'd heard it.

"Typical," he muttered.

"So there's no truth to it, huh?" I asked, my last hope.

"Oh, no," he said. "It *is* true."

IN THE PROGRAMMER community, eccentricity is de rigueur, and when David Coons and his wife held skinny-dipping parties, he invited his friends from work. So nobody made much of it that he took his clothes off at the office after ten P.M. At that hour, there was nobody left in the building but programmers and animators working on deadline, and these were open-minded people who couldn't care less. Besides, David was no ordinary programmer; to get his work done, he invented tools that everyone else could use. He invented one of the first film-to-digital scanners and an award-winning digital ink and paint system.

David had been working slave hours for two weeks straight. The company was trying to get a feature film ready for release, and he would come in around four in the afternoon and stay until 2 or 3 A.M. Working that hard, focused, is like having blinders on. One night he looked at his clock, which said "20:06," and his tired brain misfigured. He thought, "Oh, good, it's after ten." Still inside his office, he took his clothes off.

About half an hour later, he went down the hall to the CGI department to discuss something with his friend Bijon. On the way back, there was a lady in the film printing room who wasn't supposed to be there that late—all union workers were reliably gone by ten. That was when David realized he misread his clock by two hours. She was a union employee, and that was the problem. What was perfectly acceptable in the programming culture wasn't at all acceptable in the film union employee manual. David already had one run-in with the union, which enforced its rule that nonunion workers can't touch celluloid, so he couldn't even use the film scanner he invented.

But he still didn't know anything was wrong. He went back to his office and continued working. A couple of hours later, two security guards knocked on his door. They didn't know what to do other than to tell him to put his clothes on. Then his boss called from home and told David he'd better go home for the night. For a while, David refused: "I'm working on the project!" He had to get it done.

He was put on "minihiatus," quarantined at home for a week. The film union pressured management to have him fired, but everyone who'd ever had their bugs fixed by him—and everyone he'd ever met a deadline for—stood up for him. He laughed through the whole thing.

Regardless, he got the project done on schedule. That's the important thing. Eventually the fiasco blew over.

"The whole thing was fun as hell. My little adventure into corporate squabble. If they didn't want me because I'm nude, then I didn't want to work there. They had no sense of humor. You've got to inject fun into the workplace, or else the force of order will win over creativity. The lieutenants who establish procedures and protocols will eat away at the imagination. Work today has to be half work, half play. We spend our whole lives at the workplace.

"You understand that, don't you?"

WHEN YOU GET right down to it, the real work of Silicon Valley occurs in the mind—the minds of workers sitting in their cubicles, staring at screens, pondering their challenges. That's where innovation occurs. That's where the buzz is. That's where you can go to take it all in. I keep thinking about this quote from Kafka:

You do not need to leave your room. Remain sitting at your table and listen. Do not even listen, simply wait. Do not even wait, be quite still and solitary. The world will freely offer itself to you to be unmasked, it has no choice, it will roll in ecstasy at your feet.

THE NUDIST ON THE LATE SHIFT

CHAPTER 1

THE
Newcomers

If the most torturous fate
was a mind, caged,
who would understand?

If you always found life's elixir
in striving rather than getting,
who would understand?

If you gambled rather than nest-egged
and hit jackpot once of seven,
who would understand?

BY CAR, BY PLANE, THEY COME. They just show up. They've given up their lives elsewhere to come *here*. They come for the tremendous opportunity, believing that in no other place in the world right now can one person accomplish so much with talent, initiative, and a good idea. It's a region where who you know and how much money you have have never been less relevant to success. They come because it does not matter that they are young or left college without a degree or have dark skin or speak with an accent. They come even if it is illegal to do so. They come because they feel that they will regret it the rest of their lives if they do not at least give it a try. They come to be a part of history, to build the technology that will reshape how people will live and work five or ten years from now. They come for the excitement, just to be a part of it. They come because they are competitive by instinct and can't stand to see others succeed more than they. They come to make enough money so they will never have to think about money again.

They are the new breed, Venture Trippers, who get off on the dizzying adventure of bloodwork. It is a mad, fertile time. Working has become nothing less than a sport here in Superachieverland: people are motivated by the thrill of the competition and the danger of losing, and every year the rules evolve to make it all happen more quickly, on higher margins, reaching ever more amazing sums.

They come from places wallowing in an X–Y-axis attitudinal coordinate, a slow-mo way of thinking about one's life that offers a plodding story line they can't manage to suspend their disbelief of. They try to live that story, but they keep popping out, keep finding themselves saying, "What the hell am I doing with my life?"

They come because what they see ahead of them, if they stay where they are, is a working life that seems fundamentally and unavoidably *boring*. Nothing seems worse than the fate of boringness. They feel they are being offered a neo-Faustian trade-off by society: all of life's sprawling dimensions will be funneled through the narrow pipe of the career path.

And rather than choosing not to work hard, the Venture Trippers are taking the opposite approach from the Slackers. They're saying, If I'm going to have to make that trade-off, then hell, why the fuck not? I'm young, let's raise the stakes. Let's up the bet. *Let's make it exciting.* Let's put it all on black. Let 'em roll.

And they come.

One

An e-mail I received in January:

> **My best friend moved there last summer, and though he lived 5 minutes from the beach, 4 months = 2 trips to beach. And I get excited by this! We are sick. Am now planning a trip to the Big Stew on High Heat to see if maybe I might like to spend some time simmering.**

ON A FRIDAY afternoon in January, Thierry Levy is standing in the aisle at Internet Showcase in San Diego, a smorgasbord of start-up concepts pirouetting and curtsying to a crowd of trigger-happy investors. He is one of only two foreigners to have been invited, but that morning he totally botched his presentation: his business model, not yet glued together; his pitch, unhoned. He had no idea what he was doing up there. He knows now that an edgy attitude is an insufficient substitute for professional expertise. His plane home to Paris is scheduled for a 6:20 P.M. departure.

His mind is seized. He can't stop thinking that this very moment his fate will be decided forever. *I can stay here and I may or may not make it, or I can go back and I surely will never make it, and I will regret it the rest of my life.* His gut boils with panic. Nobody likes having to choose on the spot, but in the land he comes from, the phrase "French entrepreneur" is considered an oxymoron. A couple years before, a Paris newspaper had run a poll: What is the best way to achieve wealth? Inheritance walloped entrepreneurship, 70 percent to 20 percent. Terry had grown up poor. He is thinking of what his father used to tell him, "In America, if you grew up poor, it's something to be proud of. It is a badge of honor. You say, 'Hey! I started from scratch!' " His father had been in the French Resistance during World War II and had been rescued by American soldiers. His father had always said of America, "It's the place where heroes are from."

Thierry borrows someone's cell phone to call the airline, trading his return ticket for one to SFO, where he arrives at Gate 22 of the South Terminal at 11:10 in the evening, one suitcase in hand. He's wearing blue jeans and a green polo shirt. He's done it. Now what? His first instinct: to see Silicon Valley. To feast his eyes on this golden land of opportunity. From Thrifty he rents a Geo subcompact and motors south on the 101. Burlingame. San Mateo. Redwood City. Atherton. Menlo Park. Palo Alto. Mountain View. Then the county line. It's raining. He is expecting something like the Great Wall of China, some demarcation line telling him that he is *here*. He gets off the freeway, finding only suburbs and low-slung office parks, an occasional fluorescent light still illuminating some worker's window, so he gets back onto the freeway, but at the next exit, same thing. No place to celebrate, nothing to toast to, no sense of arrival. No welcoming committee. It's dark and wet and too flat to offer a sense of place or direction. Hey, I'm *here*! I, Thierry Levy, am *here*!—but the Valley takes no notice. Eventually, he finds himself on a road called the Great America Parkway, excited to be on such a road but confused by the syntax—Great America*n* Parkway, yes? There is nothing particularly great or particularly American about the parkway. He doesn't know where it's taking him, maybe Sunnyvale, but he checks into a Days Inn, taking the last room for $58. He has two glasses of water before he climbs under the bedspread and attempts to sleep.

He has seventy more days before the tourist stamp on his passport expires.

ON A TIP from a friend, I call a number in the 413 area code, and a sly talker I'll call Michael Zilly tells me that yo, he'll be moving on out from Massachusetts next week. He says Silicon Valley is "phat" and "quite excellent," and he calls me "homeboy." He wants to *do* Silicon Valley and all of it. He wants to soak it up. This includes (along with snowboarding and meeting mall girls) being a kick-ass entrepreneur. He's hammered together a cardboard-thin featherlight "keyboard" that uses touch-screen technology rather than plastic keys; it's a superportable typing accessory designed to be plugged in to Palm Pilots and other PDAs. He calls it the SupraNova, a cryptic reference to *Naked Lunch*. His hobbies are running up hills and smoking dope. He listens to Ice-T, Body Count, and Parliament. He says we'll hang.

We'll check it out. "Where's the party? Where's the girls? Where's the fish?" We trade some e-mails, all of which he signs, "Keep on rockin' in the free world."

He needs to raise $80,000 in the next three months.

A HUB FOR the newly arrived, the Café Bean is on the respectable fringe of the Tenderloin district in San Francisco. Its clientele: primarily *internazionali* slacker-tourists staying at the nearby residential hotels, where $297 a week buys a bed, a shower, and a hot breakfast. If they show up at the Café Bean more than a couple of times, or if they have a particularly sweet smile or offer a bit of conversation in an English that is comprehensible, the counter girl will snap a Polaroid picture of them and staple it to the photo mosaic that climbs the walls, documenting the ever-revolving Café Bean family. The place is every bit as friendly as a communal hot tub and not much bigger. It spills onto the sidewalk, a river of youth and hope and anticipation.

Interspersed with the coffee mugs and ashtrays on the small round tabletops are the clues to their lives ahead: maps of the city, Amtrak passes, money belts, joint papers, Bic lighters, stash tins, language dictionaries. On the top of one table, at which sits a young man with men's-mag style and buzz-short hair dyed brassy blond, an Apple Newton with its snub-nosed antennae points to the sky.

He says his name is John Foster but I should call him David. There were too many Johns at his last job, he tells me, but in my mind it becomes another indication that he's starting a new life. John introduces me to Nora, Kiersten, Michele, and a few other nymphs whose names I didn't get. They call him David, so from here on, I will too. As he and I talk, the girls take their leave one by one, each one planting a parting kiss somewhere on David's face.

His face is pale, providing high contrast to his buggy blue eyes and deep red lips. He's swaddled in a heavy black wool overcoat and his shoes are silver-buckled with cap toes, the black leather well taken care of. He's a bit of a lounge lizard, a hip-hop fop. He's got a know-it-all tongue but an idealist's heart. "I trust anyone until they give me a reason not to," he says, as if in response to a question but not one I asked. He's in sales.

David jumped ship from a forty-person e-commerce software company in Salt Lake City when it wasn't fun to be a part of anymore. He got here four days ago. He came because it is the place to be. Already he has a job with another e-commerce software firm in the Valley with maybe fifteen employees. His starting salary is a mere $21,000, plus options and a highly leveraged incentive clause. A few minutes later, he admits that in order to make the company more profitable to attract investors, he is forgoing his salary entirely and the company will be paying just enough to cover his expenses. David's main expense is the $1,475 a month studio apartment across the street. He's eaten pancakes for dinner four nights straight.

I ask why he doesn't go get a job at Netscape that might pay better.

"Look, for programmers, okay, being a college dropout, that's a badge of honor. But not for sales, okay? A college degree is proxy variable number one, okay? So okay, if a firm is big enough to have a human resources department, they won't hire me, okay?"

Okay. He lasted only two weeks at college. He was so depressed over his mother having died from cancer that a psychiatrist prescribed drugs for him. The drugs, David says, that shot his pulse rate up to 240 and induced a mild heart attack. He would sit dumbly in class, looking conscious but mentally blacked out. He was rescued by computerized music—wav files and MIDI boards and mixing software. The only way to get the necessary high-end computers for cheap/free was to become an authorized reseller of high-end computers to others. His life as a wheeler-dealer had begun.

He cherishes being the battle-worn sales guy fronting undiscovered programming talents. David is only twenty-seven. His new boss is twenty-three. It's a romantic role. All his sales guy fast talk is an act; underneath, he's a sweetie. In my notebook, I give him the nickname "The Man Who Trusts Too Much."

Last year, before Utah, he moved to Australia to find adventure. And did. "This is my next great adventure," he says.

His incentive clause: If David brings his boss $500,000 or more of investment capital, he told me, he gets a $100,000 salary. Anything less, and he gets only his expenses paid.

*   *   *

THIS E-MAIL came at the end of the month:

> last fall, a friend from high school co[...]
> from silicon valley where he is apparer[...]
> his ass off and making huge bucks.
> to you is this: is everyone out there [...]
> constantly tells me what he owns, what he[...]
> he even recently mailed me some fine wine and
> INCLUDED the receipt to show how much money
> he spent. he is a great guy, but i just feel as though
> he isn't "real" anymore. something tells me that
> may have more to do with the industry than him.
> can you shed some light on what the hell happens
> to people out there?

I'm on my way out of a party on a Saturday night when I glance up and see a face that is vaguely familiar, plastered with a merry whiskey grin, perched on a high stool tipped back against the wall. I had met him three years before when he was in town for a convention. Back then he was based in Knoxville, Tennessee, and he had loudly trumpeted the notion that in the telecommuting age one could work anywhere.

"Another convention in town?" I ask.

"Nope. Moved. Been here a week already."

Already. His first week's experience has given him plenty of meat to satiate his hunger for broad social observations. He's flip-flopped on the telecommuting theory because there's no substitute for the cultural immersion that occurs off the job. He's torn between whether the appropriate *über*-metaphor for Silicon Valley is the Gold Rush or Florence during the Renaissance; that is, does the enthusiasm come from all the new money or all the new media? Money or art? And then, if it's the Gold Rush, he debates himself as to whether it's the Sierra Nevada rush of 1849 or the Alaskan Klondike rush fifty years later. In the midst of all this, I ask him if he happens to have a job.

He says sure, but he doesn't think he'll last there, it's just a gig, and he's looking for something that takes more brainpower. He started looking the morning of his second day on the job.

Sure, the money matters, but day in, day out there's nothing itchier than an unchallenged mind.

few days later he puts me in touch with a twenty-seven-
ear-old friend of his from Tennessee days named Scott Krause.
Scott and I go for some lunch at the Slanted Door in the Mission
District. Scott is a Human Resources' wet dream. He's a modern-
day Hardy Boy; he wears jungle pants cut off at the knees and a
yellow plaid Bermuda shirt, untucked. He is twenty-seven and
has an MBA from the University of Tennessee and wants to build
the technology that changes how the world lives and works. I
don't hear this kind of idealism very often anymore; it's like
Scott's time traveled here from 1994. It's a plain vanilla idealism,
perhaps the sort of unironical viewpoint that can only develop in
the heartland of the country—where they know absolutely nothing about what it's really like here. I give it three months, and
then, like an accent, it'll disappear.

"If I'm going to work seventy-hour weeks, I might as well
do something purposeful." He lives kitty-corner from here in a
second-floor studio apartment that he shares with a roommate
(bunk-bed-type interior design) for $1,200 a month. He's not
home enough for paying more rent to feel worth it, though six
hundred for a bunk bed hardly seems worth it to me. When he
first got here he had the impression a great job would fall into his
lap. After six weeks of looking the first time, he got impatient and
took a job with Intershop, supposedly to do "business development," but that turned out to mean cold-calling for the telesales
division. After a while, he couldn't convince himself anymore
that this had anything to do with changing the world.

He's been looking for two months now for work he can love.

AT TEN O'CLOCK Michael Zilly is supposed to hook up with a man
named Henry Silva, Jr., who might invest that eighty "G-large"
Zilly needs. They are supposed to meet at the Big Brother and the
Holding Company poster in the front lobby, which is where we're
standing.

"There's no turning back," he says.

It is another one of those many nights in Silicon Valley where
the late '90s wants to see itself through the Day-Glo Technicolor
prism of the late '60s. The party is at the legendary nightclub
the Fillmore; under framed billboard posters memorializing the
great performances here of Jimi Hendrix and Jim Morrison,

today's new media elite (and the men who fund them) have packed the joint elbow to elbow to see, well, one another. There goes Tony Perkins, oops, you missed him, now he's behind that pillar. And over by the bar, isn't that Jerry Kaplan?

Buzzed on Mary Jane's reverie, Michael Zilly thinks the '60s/'90s thing is fine. He hit town yesterday and is "happy-campered" on his homeboy Andy's couch in Fremont. Zilly's clothes make the statement "catalog shopper." Boat shoes with raw leather laces, a coarsely stitched button-down, and pleated wrinkle-free khakis. He's five feet ten with blunt milk chocolate hair, brown freckles, and stone gray eyes so deeply set that his eyebrows cast his eyes in shadow. Though he's only twenty-nine he has a white skunk stripe sprouting from his temple. He talks in an incomprehensible dialect, a chunky gumbo of snowboarder reggae mumble and high tech's pissing contest ".comming" jargon.

"New business is pop culture, is it not?" he says, soaking in the scene. I'm getting a floating-in-space sensation. This grab bag of cultural references has overloaded my palette. Nothing here seems to have made up its mind what it is.

We mingle. I pick up on a pattern with Zilly. He's shy around women, unless the woman is shy too, and then he's suddenly a fast talker. Zilly heads up to the balcony, where some Web sites are showcasing their latest features. One of the girls working the match.com dating service booth is plain-looking and particularly shy. She arrived only last weekend on a bus from New Hampshire.

She's twenty-two, just graduated from Plymouth State College, and she's here to see, "You know—"

Zilly: "Hey, it's the place to be, is it not?"

"Yeah . . ."

"Yeah, for me too."

She's been staying at her aunt's house in Santa Rosa, which is an hour north of San Francisco and still a long way from Silicon Valley, but she can't afford the deposit on an apartment. She got tonight's gig through a temp agency, for which she will net only $10 an hour, but she's hoping to meet someone who might hire her.

She hasn't.

Henry Silva, Jr., never shows, but Michael Zilly does meet a middle-aged woman who is so sucked into new media's whirl-pool that she doesn't know if *Rolling Stone* magazine still exists in print form. She invites Zilly to a "salon" in Berkeley that Saturday to discuss why new money doesn't give to charity. There will be nine new-money men sitting around her living room trying to tell her why they'd rather invest in start-ups than donate to modern art museums or UNICEF. Technology *is* modern art. Technology *will* save the world.

"And I'll be the tenth man, sitting there ready to accept their money," he says. "*Mission: Impossible* continues."

Mission: Impossible refers to the extreme nature of Zilly's venture. For the last two years, he funded his start-up by growing ganja in the swamps of western Massachusetts and selling it wholesale. He didn't deal. In ROTC at UConn he had learned about night-vision, camouflage, and concealing his tracks, all handy skills for this ambitious entrepreneur. On Memorial Day weekend, he would slush into the marsh at night hauling sixty-pound sacks of peat moss and a Baggie of highly evolved organic sensimilla seeds. The terrain's so wet that there's little foilage to block the sun. He'd build a little peat island, plant his seeds four inches under, and erect camouflage netting. Three months later, on Labor Day weekend, he'd harvest eighty pounds (at $1,000 a pound) of God's gift to man, the healer of all aches, the drowner out of voices, the key to living in the moment. All of that profit (except what he needed for mandatory twice daily "quality control") has been invested in two part-time engineers, who built the SupraNova prototype.

Giving up that life and coming out here is not a sellout. It is not like giving up one's noble ideals and deciding to make a killing in real estate. Here is the continuation of adventure, maybe even ratcheting up a notch. I guess having a BS, an MBA, and three quarters of an MS prepares a guy for an exotic career track, though I doubt his unique funding method will ever make it into a B-school case study.

Michael Zilly came here because he'd like to wipe that dark past from his résumé. But the experience may be invaluable. If the parameter of success in Silicon Valley is one's willingness to throw oneself into situations most people would feel are out of control—risk transforming the gray-suited commerce of our dads into the must-do modern adventure—then Michael Zilly should be a paper millionaire within twelve months. This is his strength: risk taking.

Two

"Are you lost?" asks the postman, seeing that I am unable to decide whether to get into the elevator or not.

"I'm looking for Quiz Studio," I say.

"Haven't heard of that one," he says, going up.

Backtracking, I believe, along the labyrinth of hallways, I find the suite number.

"Hello?" I try tentatively, opening the suite door.

The walls smell of new paint, white. The carpet, chemically refreshened. The six empty beige cubicles purchased from the previous tenant have been stripped of any decorations that made them personal, and the whiteboard in the conference room has yet to be inked. A jungle of unspliced white phone lines drapes cubicle to cubicle.

The only office occupied yet belongs to the founder, Thierry Levy. He moved in this morning. It's been four months since he arrived from San Diego that rainy night. On his desk here rests a laptop, beside it a cellular phone, and stored on the cubicle shelf are a tub of protein powder, a carton of Ultra SlimFast packets, and a half case of bottled water.

Silicon Valley today: Get lean, get stripped down, live on nothing. Bare bones. Focus. Be a fighter. Stamina. Ration yourself to one Snickers bar, one jacking off, and one *Dilbert* cartoon daily. Forget about love that nourishes. Forget about food that satiates. Forget about long conversations that get good only late in the middle of the night, when the third bottle of wine is uncorked. Forget about poetry: the whisper, the leaf, the tuck of hair. Forget about politics: the bilingual ed revolt, the dams diverting more water south.

Get ready for ultracapitalism.

"No, when I make my first twenty million, forget about it," says Thierry.

"Forget about it?" I ask.

"No, forget about it."

"You won't be here?"

"No, I'll go home. Maybe here in small doses only. Those people you write about—they make twenty million, and it is not enough for them. I am not greedy like them."

Thierry's applied for an LIA visa, under which he can stay for ten months as a "visiting executive" as long as he's officially employed back home in France. His official employer in France is also himself.

Without an American credit record, he had to pay three months' rent in advance for this meager office space. His software, Quiz Studio, turns plain Web pages into interactive quizzes. If he can get certified 100 percent Java by Sun Microsystems, he figures Sun will plug him in to the venture capitalists. Six months to prove himself, and either the change will happen or it won't. When Thierry was twenty-two, he spent a year in East Berlin managing the construction of a factory. There, six months was not long enough to get *anything* done. In East Berlin at the time, it took fourteen years of waiting to purchase a car. It took fifteen years *just to get a phone line.* That was the old adventure: go abroad, help the needy. This is the new adventure. This is his strength: perspective.

"Here is the opposite," says Thierry. "Ultracapitalism. The only value system is money." I hear a note of defensiveness. I hear fear in his bravado. It's daunting.

This is what particularly scares him: he recently went to a crash course on starting a business. They told him that perception is everything. They told him to hire a PR firm, that he won't win by just having the best product. They gave him three principles to live by: marketing, marketing, and marketing. Thierry can't afford a VP of marketing until he gets venture money, but he also hears that VCs will never give him money without a VP of marketing.

Thierry's paying a thousand dollars a month to rent a room in a woman's house in Menlo Park. Though he lived in motels until he found the room, it did not take him long to get his bearings here. He found the all-night gym, the 24 Hour Fitness in Mountain View. Thierry stays buff. His blue jeans can't disguise the muscles in his legs, and his forearms show a pulse. He's not just a pecs and quads guy, you can see the muscular balance in his physique. He's one of those guys who separately work out the anterior, medial, and posterior heads of their deltoids. He has less fat than an unflavored rice cake. He's ready for the ultra-capitalist fight. He is armed with an undergraduate degree in engineering and an MBA from the most prestigious business school in France. His most valuable possessions—really, his *only* possessions—are his RollerBlades and his road bike. He can't buy a car because his visa doesn't allow him to take a driver's test. He doesn't mention friends.

"I fit right in," he says, and I think he's right, but I don't know whether that's swell or sad.

At night, after another fourteen-hour day, Thierry hits the weights. The strong will survive.

The other thing open all night is the Safeway, great for his long-houred "lifestyle." They sell Barilla spaghetti, the same brand he would buy in Paris, in the same blue-and-red box, $1.59 for 16 ounces. He says that when he gets venture capital financing—when he gets rich—he's going to move up to the real stuff, De Cecco brand pasta, twice as expensive at a bank-account-draining $2.59 per box.

"Three months, come see me maybe," he says. "I'll be making spaghetti."

I'M HAVING A drink in the bar at the Stanford Park Hotel, and I strike up a conversation with a very sincere Taiwanese-American financial accountant who tells me about a friend of his. This friend started a karaoke gig in Taiwan, didn't want to do what he would have to do to succeed, and has come to the Valley to start an Internet business. I am instantly attracted to the question of which environment is a more ruthless place to do business. He promises to put us in touch.

I'M TRYING TO get Ben Chiu to tell me what he got into in Taiwan. The information's not going to come without a certain level of trust, so I ask a lot of questions about his background. Ben is wearing the same thing as his three employees: brown leather lace-up shoes, dark hard jeans with the ankles cuffed, black belt with silver buckle, and a short-sleeved black polo shirt. He's twenty-seven. He has the slightest of freckles along his broad cheekbones. His forearms are slashed with keloid marks from his wrists to the nook of his elbows. I never find out about those.

It takes a while for Ben to understand that I'm interested in him, not his technology. He's not used to anybody caring about his life story, and when he finally gets it, he goes, "Ohhh" and walks out of the room. We're on the second floor of a "tilt-up", so called because the cement walls were poured flat into frames laid on the ground, then tilted up when hardened. It is hidden amid a few monkey-tail pines in the marshlands of Fremont. The bay is two miles west of here, but at low tide you can smell the decomposing mud.

Ben comes back with an artist's sketchbook. I open the pages. "Anal, huh?" he asks, a little embarrassed.

He says "anal" because they're illustrations of wildlife—rams and bald eagles—done in painstaking detail, nearly photo quality, every feather and hair drawn in. They're stunning. Each one must have taken hours of work. This is his strength: attention to detail.

"You do these recently?"

"Not since I moved here."

"You go dancing?"

"I used to go every night. In Taiwan. But not here."

"How about karaoke?"

"Oh, sure. I still do that."

"When?"

He can't remember when.

Is he sapped, is he worn out? He'd prefer to think that his "creative energy is now channeled into his company," which is the sort of groupspeak turn of phrase people who read too many business magazines learn to use.

Ben was born in Taiwan but grew up in Toronto. When you graduate from college, you're supposed to spend a lot of time thinking about who you really are so that you can answer the question of what you want to be. Ben didn't know who he was, so he went back to Taiwan to find out. Taiwan is seedy, the buildings are not designed to last, the streets are a web, and it's one big party. He started some discos—one would be hot for a while, then he'd start a new one at the first sign that the old one wasn't the scene anymore. Always one step ahead of the hipness. It sounds a lot like the Internet business. But in Taiwan, all business is based on *guanxi*—relationships. Having great ability, a great club, great style wasn't enough to make it big. In the end the only way to get ahead was to know the right people.

In the nightclub business, there's a special dimension to knowing the "right people": the "right people" would instruct how to make the right payoffs at the right times to "the Black and the White"—the cops and the organized crime element. If you didn't know the right person, you didn't even know who you were supposed to pay off or when. Ben refused to do business that way.

He came here hoping to get away from that. He arrived without any friends or contacts, but has gone back to Taiwanese companies for investment capital; and he believes the Internet will be a level playing field.

He arrived without any personal connections. It never occurred to him to get a job. KillerApp.com is a price comparison shopping engine—if you want to buy a new computer, for example, you can go to his site and find out whose price is cheapest. He wrote the code himself, but at least he's hired a few people now. His days are eighteen hours long. He looks trim, but he says he doesn't work out. He says he gives 300 percent to his job to make sure he's in a position to reap the rewards of that kind of commitment. He still doesn't have any friends, not really—only business acquaintances.

He walks me out to my car. It's hot enough to melt the asphalt into that fresh-laid tar smell. We rehash what we've already said. I get the feeling he doesn't want me to leave.

JULIE BECAME OBSESSED with getting out here before it was too late. At one point back in Boston, her job was to sell attendance at medical conferences, and over the phone she met a doctor who eventually put her in touch with a friend at a start-up in Redwood City. She took its job offer sight unseen and moved out with her best friend, and they got an apartment in San Mateo. The next day she went into the dumpy office and quickly realized she would still just be selling over the phone. She wanted to get into field sales. After one day on the job she called back and said no thanks.

"My mom says, instead of going to Hollywood to become an actress, I've come to Silicon Valley to be a . . . a . . . well, whatever grandiose term we might call it."

"A salesperson," I respond.

"Yeah. I guess."

We are drinking in a microbrewery in Redwood City.

"Sales is the way to go for a nontechnical person," she adds.

If you want to get to know people, Julie is a shortcut on two or three degrees of separation all by herself. She doesn't just knock on doors, she knocks them down. Through the friend of a husband of a gal she worked with two years ago, she got an interview at Yahoo! with a guy who introduced her to some programmers who play ultimate Frisbee, and they got her interviews at Infoseek, Sun, and Ziff-Davis. In the meantime, as a temp, she's worked at Oracle, E-Trade, and Cisco. She has a great feel for the Valley after just four months. This is her strength: networking. "I'll interview for anything," she says, figuring it's good practice. Of all the places she's seen, where she'd really like to work is Yahoo!

But no job offers so far.

Headhunters look at her résumé and tell her she looks like a job-hopper. They ask if she lacks stick-to-itness. She says she's a prisoner of her ambition. She's thinking of creatively editing her résumé, but she knows she should really just sell herself for what she is and be proud of it.

"When I find a job that's right, I'll have plenty of stick-to-itness. I think."

Julie has a bombshell buxom figure and big auburn hair and high cheekbones and almond hooded eyes, but she is a sort of Cubist rendering of herself. One eye is higher than the other; one tooth is gray. She's not quite what you think she is when you first see her. It's her voice: Bostonian vowel sounds remixed and digitally remastered by an early '80s Valley girl. Lispy and sweet-toothed. She's a lot sharper than her accent conveys. In interviews, I'm sure it's a deal killer.

Silicon Valley is not quite what you think it is when you first look at it, either: you can have skin of any color and be from any country and have any disability or sexual orientation, et cetera, but if you're white and educated, all sorts of prejudices may be held against you.

Julie is at the bottom of the food chain, and she treats others in the same spot kindly. Several nights a week, she goes to the public library in Redwood City and teaches a young black boy to read. She's got I-can-do spirit. She dreams of moving to the city, of having a salary to afford those rents and the savings to cover the security deposit. Her dream is sung in a minor key, but she is pursuing it every bit as fiercely as an entrepreneur.

JOHN/DAVID WANTED ME to meet his twenty-three-year-old boss, Kevin North, who brought along his girlfriend. They're sitting on a couch in the lobby of the St. James Hotel and John/David is playing butler/host, making sure our beer glasses are full. Kevin left college after a year and a half to start an electronic commerce company, eFree. His father was also an inventor, and between them they have twenty-eight patents, including one for a motorized toilet paper dispenser. Kevin gets most of his "idears" squatting on the can. His girlfriend nods enthusiastically: "I'm always having to go off and get a pen and paper for him." The fact that he has a big brain hasn't kept Kevin from being a hick.

David interrupts. He's selling now. The audience for this pitch may be as much himself as me. He's watching his boss tell a journalist about his crapping routine, and David needs to remind himself why this isn't silly. "You know what's different about eFree? It's real. Real people and real money. So much of business here is vapor. You get a concept, you run some ads, you score easy money. It's all show. Our company isn't bleeding. We have three million dollars in revenues. We're profitable. How many twenty-employee companies in this industry can say that?"

Of the thousand-plus companies that run their Web sites using eFree's software, a large number of them are overseas. Overseas banks are extremely reluctant to set up merchant credit card accounts. So eFree has a spinoff company that handles their financing, eFree-Global, which takes a cut of the action. Global takes the on-line shopper's credit card, gives the 3 percent cut to Visa, takes a 5 to 15 percent cut for themselves, and wires the rest overseas. The profits from Global flow into eFree. That's how eFree is profitable.

This business model has a rock-solid base, since a lot of overseas companies are porn sites, and porn isn't going away.

I ask David how the $500,000 is coming. He's negotiating with a bank in Los Angeles.

He says adamantly, "It's going to happen," and again that may be more for himself than for me.

I'M WORRIED ABOUT Michael Zilly. He blew off the salon because that seemed so ephemeral. He didn't get what they were in it for.

Here's what he didn't understand: Valley money, particularly angel money, doesn't behave commonsensically. Money here is puppylike, untrained. And people haven't gotten used to their money yet. It's as if everyone's wearing an overly fashionable new five-button jacket and nobody's quite sure if his is a keeper. So he's prepared, at the slightest feeling of self-consciousness, to take the jacket off. Money is greedy here, sure, but it has all sorts of peripheral motives. People give money out here just to be part of the excitement of the deal. They're in because their friend is in. They're in because they think your product is important. They're in because it's spicy to have something at risk. They're in because you asked and they like you and they don't know how to say no. People will invest in your start-up simply because watching you struggle is far more entertaining than going to the symphony.

We confer by e-mail and phone, and one day I fly with him to Portland to watch him try to swing a deal. Since I last saw him he has hooked up with the Fillmore party no-show, Henry Silva, Jr., who turned out to be not an investor but an investment scout who takes a finder's fee. So began Michael Zilly's descent into Silicon Valley's version of the creepy underworld. The rest unfolded like dime-store noir. Silva put him on a plane to Washington, D.C., to meet a man named Mark Conegan, who turned out to be what is called a "Beltway bandit," lending money at short-term high (but legal) rates to government contractors low on cash who are awaiting congressional appropriation funding. Conegan proposes to give Zilly the up-front money Zilly needs to manufacture the SupraNova if—and only if—Conegan can manage to simultaneously arrange a bulk buy of SupraNovas on the back end. This is money Zilly trusts—when everyone's in for a cut.

Zilly and Conegan shake hands on a number: $500,000. But Conegan doesn't come through with the advance sale, and so his cash never shows.

Zilly had trouble on the manufacturing end too. The Supra-Nova's magnesium keypad created magnetic interference with the touch-screen overlay, and the microcontroller chip's customization was kept on hold for a long-delayed chip upgrade. The project is derailed. Zilly will not talk much about how this makes him feel. I just don't hear from him for a while.

A little later, when his mood has recovered, he can write, "What's up homey? I had a most excellent winter licking my psychic/financial wounds, chasing chicks, and snowboarding. I had a monumental season, 40 days, and picked up some decent moves." The catalyst for his recovery of mood was a job offer from a man named Paul Jain to join his new start-up.

Paul Jain, I happen to know, was under continuing investigation for violation of SEC securities laws with his last company, MediaVision. He is hated and feared in the Valley. The Media-Vision fiasco was the main reason that California's state Proposition 211, which made it easier for stockholders to sue, was written.

I can't help but warn Zilly that his old hobby of dope growing and his start-up flameout were, on the grand scale of things, merely cute adventures that he could put behind him, chalk up to youth. But to get in deep with Paul Jain was, in my opinion, to risk never being able to turn back.

All of this makes it just that much more edgy for Zilly.

He takes the job.

Three

In LA, everyone has a screenplay. It's on their desk at home, or in turnaround, or at their agent's, or in a drawer, or in the back of their minds, or on the back burner, or just *in them* waiting to come out, as in "I've got a screenplay in me." You can be a nobody, but as long as you've got the screenplay idea fermenting, you're always *this close* to being a somebody.

In Silicon Valley, everyone has a business idea. Or a business proposition. Or a "value proposition." It's their little secret. "Something with intelligent agents" is about all they'll say, which usually means they haven't thought it through, or they have the idea but don't know how to make money off it and don't need you to scoff at them. Or they'll be cryptic: "It's WebTV meets RealNetworks."

And they're always *this close* to a $20 million payday.

I've heard that in Silicon Valley what a best friend does when you tell him your idea is to return, "That's the stupidest idea I've ever heard." He doesn't pat you on the back or offer encouragement. He'll play the devil's advocate, and he won't hold back. The logic goes, if you can't get an idea past your own friends, you will never be able to get it past the market.

When I hear the ideas—when they start erupting out of someone's brain like popcorn out of sizzling oil—I don't think, "Oh, that's a good idea" or "That'll never work." Instead, I find myself reacting on a metalevel: I ask myself, "Why does this person so need to remind himself he's *this close* to a twenty-million-dollar payday?"

John/David has two ideas this week. They are X and Y. X is a ten-cent-per-lead shopping referral service. Y is a chat-based, live, on-line help service. Next week X and Y will be something else. X is neither greater than nor less than Y, even though John spouts things like "I figure the service can net ten million first year running." We are at the Café Bean, which is the only place I could find John because when I dialed his cellular telephone, the line was not in service. "Temporarily," John assures me, and I nod, careful to keep the flow from his mouth going.

"You've got to learn to roll with the punches," he says. "Yesterday, I had one day to rewrite my entire business model. But I did it. Hey, that's what it's like here."

What happened yesterday?

"iCentral got bought by OpenMarket for ten million."

iCentral is the e-commerce company in Utah that John left a few months ago when he stopped having fun. In leaving, he abandoned his stock options. He won't tell me how much money he would have had today if he'd stayed in Utah. I'm confident it's a smallish figure that wouldn't strike anyone down with envy, but

John is twenty-seven years old, forgoing all salary, and his new employer didn't even pay this month's phone bill.

He's psyching himself up again by using me as his audience. "The great thing about our e-commerce software is, it helps small companies feed their families. And it helps them hire people. Jobs and food, that's what this is really about. It's not about getting rich."

If he keeps talking, he won't feel the pain.

He sucks in a huge breath and lets fly with his finale. "You know," he says, drawing it out. "If iCentral was just valued at ten million, that's great for us; we're worth at least twice that."

This is his strength: optimism.

In the next few days, this wishful thinking proves to be a reasonable prediction. There are at least a dozen electronic commerce software firms out there. iCentral got bought and Intershop has listed to go public, and suddenly the crowd mentality sweeps the market. This is how *it* happens—*it* being that everyone and her best friend suddenly get rich. Suddenly the makers of *every* search engine think they need to incorporate electronic shopping into their site or at least to send a message to the stock market that this is what they intend to do, and the best way to send a crystal-clear message is to acquire an e-commerce software firm.

The other catalyst for the buying spree is that search engine stock prices have risen to stratospheric highs. All these acquisitions are stock swap deals. It's sort of like when the exchange rate of the U.S. dollar to the Mexican peso suddenly shifts from one to three to one to eight and San Diegans zip down to Tijuana to get drunk on mescal for next to nothing. Last month, it would have taken Yahoo! 800,000 shares to buy a company it thinks is worth $50 million. This month it can get the same company for only 550,000 shares, and it just can't afford not to save that kind of money.

John's voice mail messages are punchy with euphoria:

"Yahoo! just bought ViaWeb for fifty million! Excite will be the next to move."

"These are the wild times, the big lions are out hunting. They're buying up the gray area. I've got a meeting with Look-Smart tomorrow."

Now, confident, he'll tell me what he missed out on at iCentral. He had 300,000 options, which would have been worth about a hundred grand. "But I'm going to blow that figure away," he says. "That will be peanuts." He's on his way to Manhattan to meet with the vice president of Prudential Securities' investment arm. They are discussing a possible acquisition at a valuation of $25 million.

"Not just any old VP I'm talking to. This is *the guy,* the VP of the whole VP department." Being the vice president of the Department of Vice Presidency sounds a little like being Major Major Major Major in *Catch-22,* but I take it to mean that when he's talking to people that high in a bureaucracy, some real money is about to get shaken loose.

THE NEXT MONTH, when Intershop goes public riding this e-commerce craze, I have lunch again with modern-day Hardy Boy Scott Krause (from Tennessee). Intershop was the company he quit after a couple months because it wasn't challenging enough. (I had two other friends who went public with Intershop; one, who was only twenty-eight, had just retired and was going to endow an alternative high school.)

I ask him about this near brush with sudden wealth.

"I don't think about it," he says.

"As in 'I *avoid* thinking about it' or as in 'It's just not on my mind'?"

"I've got the best job now I've ever had."

He's been working at the search engine Infoseek for the past couple months. He loves the position, loves the people he works with. That's the added bonus: networking, people, friends. Everybody's so open to change. "They may never have been rock climbing, but they're willing to give it a try, and in the same vein they're willing to switch careers or change jobs, to try something new simply because they've never tried it before."

His project is "a side-bet venture with the potential to fundamentally change the way that search engines interact with people," and then, in case that's not emphatic enough, he adds, "I'm contributing to something that has historical implications."

He's the human press release. I suspect a psychological adjustment going on—nobody wants to admit they made a mistake, such as "historical implications." But Scott is so earnest, maybe I just don't want to admit I was wrong in predicting the demise of his idealism. Maybe my perspective is skewed.

I saw this phenomenon with people at Yahoo! in the spring. One week they talk about how they've got the greatest job in the world, defining the new medium, being the future's arbiter of which Web sites are deemed important and which are deemed crap, and what more could a young person want than to be on the cutting edge? And then on Friday the stock market suffers a 10 percent correction, and by Monday everyone's hangdog, suffering a wild mood swing: they're encountering the painful reality that 20,000 options under water is no compensation for the mere thirty-five grand salary draw they're getting, particularly when their job is the lowest of the low—reviewing stupid little unknown Web sites and trying to pretend they're not. They might as well be writing classified ads for a suburban weekly. They're thinking, "I went to business school for *this*!?"

It's normal for optimism to wane, and that Scott's doesn't leaves him a mystery. I ask him what his project is.

"I can't tell you. It's a secret even within Infoseek."

IT'S A GORGEOUS summer day in the Inner Sunset neighborhood of San Francisco, and we are eating lunch at P.J.'s Oyster Bed on Irving. Julie is telling me about a friend of hers who made it big in the radio business. In order to be a success, this friend had to network *so* hard—it was hard to get to know the right people—that she became very shallow.

Julie doesn't want that to happen to her when she succeeds.

In the meantime, Julie got a job selling Web sites for CitySearch. Her district is the Sunset, which means that Julie, who has big hair and that lispy voice, has to cold call all day long on Chinese Laundromats and Chinese construction material suppliers, trying to convince them that they need a "Web presence" or they will be left behind in the twentieth century. A previous rep has already worked the territory over and picked the low-hanging fruit. Every day she checks in at the CitySearch headquarters, and there is a freshly updated chart pinned to the corkboard showing each rep's results. Julie has made only three sales.

I'm getting the impression that it might be a while before Julie has to worry about success going to her head.

Julie has the same reaction to the psychological dissonance as John/David and Scott: "It's very important that all these small businesses not get left off-line. There's a heart to this business."

There's also a minor-key payoff. CitySearch has announced that it will be going public in midsummer. An on-line hodge-podge of Laundromat addresses and restaurant menus is not quite the same as electronic commerce, but it's close enough for Wall Street. "It'll be exciting just to go through the process," Julie says in the same way that famous baseball pitchers say, upon signing their new free-agency contract, "I'm just in it for the love of the game."

Okay, now I finally understand why she's talking about how she will handle success.

I'M HAVING DRINKS at the Stanford Park Hotel with a group of all-around earnest guys in the twenty-five-to-thirty-five demographic. This is an organization called "Round Zero," a nifty euphemism for the mill grist and sweat equity that goes on before the venture capitalists swoop in with rounds one, two, and three of financing. They're still young enough to regularly pull all-nighters. There's a drinking hour before the dinner, but most attendees are holding Diet Cokes, served in highball glasses and garnished with a maraschino cherry. Dinners are semistructured debates. The main point of the monthly salon is to retain an intellectual framework around one's job.

Over by the bar I see Ben Chiu.

"You're out making friends," I say.

He has a big, happy grin on his lightly freckled face. But there's more than that—a sparkle in his eye, a boldness in his posture. There's more to this than finally making friends.

"I can't talk about it," he says, which is a term of art, nondisclosure agreement code for "I'm in negotiations." In saying he can't talk about it, he gives me the hint I need.

I crunch on recent news and put it together. Last month there was a buying spree for e-commerce software companies. This month there is a buying spree for the next piece of the portal puzzle, comparison shopping engines, such as Ben Chiu's

KillerApp.com. Amazon bought Junglee for $180 million. Info-
seek bought Quando. Inktomi bought C2B, which won't even
have its beta ready until January, for $90 million. KillerApp is
easily in their league. *Internet World* magazine has ranked Killer-
App the most efficient Internet site for shopping.

I think of all those eighteen-hour days Ben put in.

Ben is sanguine. Tactfully, he brings out the words: "It's a
natural thing to be bought. It's not selling out, really. I've had this
vision for a few years, and slowly the rest of the market has begun
to value what I've done at the same level that I value it. When that
happens, when you get offered what you know you're worth,
then every entrepreneur knows it's the right time."

He's only twenty-seven years old. I ask him what might be
next. Next, meaning his next project—does he have an idea?

"A whole queue of them," he says.

Four

**"The Cellular One number you have called is no
longer in service. If you feel you have reached this
recording in error, please check the number and
dial again. Message number SF 22."**
   *—is what I hear when I dial the mobile
   telephone number for John/David Foster,
   just a few weeks after he was expecting to
   sell eFree.*

**"You have reached a number that has been dis-
connected or is no longer in service. If you feel
you have reached this recording in error, please
check the number and try your call again."**
   *—is what I hear when I dial what was the
   West Coast office of eFree International.*

Two days later I receive:

**I met you through John at Chalker's a few months
ago. You may know him as David. The reason I'm
writing is to inquire about John's well-being. The**

last message I got from him was redirected. I've tried reaching him by e-mail a couple of times since—to no avail. Is he okay? Has his e-mail address changed? Thanks,

—Mark

I'VE FOUND THAT proud people tend their wounds like dogs: they crawl off somewhere to die alone. I find that I like to keep them at that distance, as if they might be infectious. Michael Zilly sends me e-mail: "It seems premature to write about my adventures in California, because nothing has come to fruition." It is the first e-mail he has ever sent me that is not signed, "Keep on rockin' in the free world." We talk on the phone and make arrangements to go see the granddaddy of reggae, Bunny Wailer, at the landmark Maritime Hall.

This revisiting of the '60s trip feels even more forced than it did the night I first met Zilly at the Fillmore, mostly because I know Zilly's trip has been a bummer. He had the sense to leave Paul Jain's company after a couple of months, calling it "another house of cards, without technology or talent (except for me)." But now he's out of a job, and though he's plenty talented, he can't put down on his résumé either that his start-up fizzled out before round one or that he worked for the tainted Paul Jain. There's a big hole in his résumé. He doesn't know what he will say when recruiters ask him, "So what have you been doing the last year?"

Zilly's thinking of taking a class to be able to pass a Cobol certification exam, which will qualify him to be hired on as a thirty-five-dollar-an-hour "implementation consultant" with one of the many Y2K conversion firms.

He's down to his last month's rent.

ON A THURSDAY NIGHT in August, I bump into Julie reading *Business Week* at the bookstore on Van Ness. She's wearing a checked sport coat. Her voice is different, more sultry, she's ironed out the accent. Then she says it's just because of her sinus cold. I ask her how she's handling success, that is, what happened to her company's IPO. She tells me the market tanked recently, and CitySearch canceled its IPO and instead has merged with Ticketmaster. There's no jackpot, just more pressure to come through with revenue.

"What a rat race!" she says. She complains about cold calling and bad management. She says her job "isn't feeling like a good fit." She's looking for "a window out."

These are phrases she's learned from *Business Week*. What she means is, she's unhappy.

More specifically, she got a new sales manager. He used to be a knife salesman. Some of the tactics he used to light a fire under her included putting her on "probation" and threatening to fire her for not making his unrealistic quota, even though she had milked several $2,400 deals out of tiny shops in a poor neighborhood.

"Because of the job-hopper image," she reminds me when I ask why she doesn't take a new job. Headhunters and recruiters earn their fee only if a candidate hired stays on the job for a year. They won't even look at the résumés of job-hoppers. Julie's been at CitySearch for only three months. She has to give it another three.

Prisoner of ambition.

"I'm all confused now and really don't know anymore."

I DECIDE IT'S about time to go share a plate of pasta with Thierry Levy.

"But no pasta," he says. He's off food entirely. He's switched over to the Apex nutritional system, a powdered substance laced with amino-acid chains. He still has no friends, no social life. He's tried to bring a couple of friends from France over to work with him, but their visa paperwork has been held up by the debate over immigration in Congress. He's bored, bored out of his wits, so bored that he cannot even work hard anymore, too distracted. "It's a very lonely society here," he says. He calls America "the country of the clean cars," which is a far cry from what his father called America, "the place where heroes are from."

When he came here, he got the impression that everyone was successful. Now he quotes statistics: of every 1,000 business plans sent to venture capitalists, 6 are accepted. Of those 6 companies, 4 will go bankrupt. Only one will go public. Among the 9,994 rejected business plans is his. He made a strategic mistake: he sent it out asking for $2.5 million and was told by the venture capitalists that they want to fund projects only at the $5 million level. They won't look twice at a business plan his size. He's rewritten his now, but he's used up his "eyeball time." "I shopped the deal," he admits. "I sent out too many of the first business plan."

Venture capitalists say all the time, "the good ideas always come by referral," and therefore they hold the inverse to be true: if it didn't come by referral, it must not be a good idea.

Thierry is right on with his estimate of venture capital, which has been affected perversely by success. The average VC firm used to raise a fund of around $50 million and spread this out into about ten start-ups (giving each a first round at less than a million, followed by further rounds as each company grew, so each start-up used about five million over five years). Now investors are so willing to throw money at venture capitalists that a VC firm can raise $500 million in just a few hours, with just a few phone calls. But a VC can still only manage five to seven deals per partner. So now they're looking for start-ups that will use $25 to $50 million each ($5 million alone in the first round). And to get a return on investment, these start-ups have to project being a leader in a market of over $1 billion in sales. Thierry had estimated that the future market for interactive training software would hit a mere $300 million. Even if he became a leader in that market, it's too small for most VCs. Many VCs have privately bemoaned the economies of scale they're working in today. VCs used to be cool. They used to fund cool risky technology plays, but the only Internet companies that can predict $1 billion plus market sizes are pretty boring on-line commerce ventures: insurance on-line, auto parts on-line. What's cool about insurance? What's sexy about auto parts? Furthermore, VC firms used to syndicate their deals to other firms, which was a way to get market corroboration that they weren't fooling themselves about a start-up's potential. But now, under pressure to spend all that $500 million, VC firms are taking the entire deal. No syndication = no corroboration. And without the corroboration on wild ideas, VCs are looking for safer plays, such as auto parts. VCs have priced themselves right out of the domain of cool.

Thierry knows that there are angel investors who are willing to fund start-ups his size, but he has no idea how to find them. He's realizing he doesn't have the practicality of Americans, their marketing savvy. Americans go to college, take out a student loan; that's training for the Darwinian world. "As an entrepreneur, you experience a lot of rejection. Ninety-five percent of the time is rejection. You must be able to take a lot of beating. The French do not have that much guts. They give up too easy."

The other day Thierry was standing in the aisle at Fry's Electronics superstore in Palo Alto and heard French being spoken. Thierry introduced himself. Thierry was invited to a monthly meeting of French entrepreneurs, where he met Jean-Louis Gassée, one of the creators of the Macintosh. This is his only hope.

He has four more months of cash left before he is broke. "There's a knife at my throat. Sometimes I get really, really scared."

I NEED some good news, so I call Ben Chiu. He doesn't have any. He says, "The window is still open," but "we're missing windows too." Sometimes, when you're young and it's the first time some big company comes knocking on your door to talk about an acquisition, you can't tell if it's for real. Maybe they were just knocking on your door to get a good sense before making an offer on your competitor. Since then, Ben has corresponded with Broadview Associates and with a stock analyst at Morgan Stanley. But he says that in order to be acquired, you need "name-brand VCs." You need to have well-connected investors, Kleiner Perkins or Draper Fisher Jurvetson.

It's *guanxi* all over again: connections.

Ben's investors are Taiwanese. They don't play golf with the right crowd.

"We didn't know where to start in terms of talking to them," Ben says. *Them* being whoever was knocking on his door.

So much for the level playing field. So much for the meritocracy.

He says, "I've been through hell. I feel like one of those mice on the wheel with someone cranking up the speed, I have no control. No sleep. It never ceases. There's no lull."

Originally, I had convinced Ben to talk to me by arguing that his story would be inspirational for other young entrepreneurs.

Now he says, "Maybe I'll be the first founder to drop dead of exhaustion—that should make a great motivational piece, huh?"

JOHN/DAVID HAS turned up. He's living on a friend's couch. When he got back from New York from his meeting with Prudential, he found himself locked out of his apartment. David says his boss, Kevin North, the twenty-three-year-old kid who comes up with his "idears" on the toilet, hadn't paid the rent. (Kevin North says Daivd just disappeared on him.)

eFree had bit the bullet and stopped doing business with porn sites. Unfortunately, with the big sale of his company in sight, Kevin North was running out of money and couldn't make payroll. He urged his employees to hang in there, but they blew up when they discovered their health insurance had been canceled. He was fending off creditors and begging friends for money. If he had lasted another month, he might have sailed through the eye of the needle, selling out to Prudential and paying back his creditors. Instead, North was having to let go of most of his employees. Seeing where this was headed, David resigned.

John says several things:

"That little fucker."

"I'm not only unemployed, I'm out millions of dollars."

"I'm thinking of writing a book about how not to get screwed."

I take heart that John is still a big talker, still prone to sweeping generalizations. He hasn't lost his attitude. I think of one of the first things John ever told me: "I trust anyone until they give me a reason not to."

John doesn't have the two grand in back rent he needs to get his stuff out of his old apartment.

BEN CHIU'S attorneys recommended he get a personal financial adviser; and they referred him to a man who by chance was also the accountant for Jerry Yang (of Yahoo!) and Mark Andreessen (of Netscape/AOL). He was Ben's ticket to *guanxi*. He introduced Ben to the mergers and acquisition investment bankers at Alex, Brown, who were able to revive the interest in his company, KillerApp, when the stock market rebounded.

His life suddenly became very external. I was privileged to negotiations that followed, but under the condition that I not reveal the various parties until an outcome was finalized. But the negotiations he began felt as hectic as a sport tournament ladder with home and away matches. He received a soft offer from a television/Internet media company, which Alex, Brown parlayed into a second soft offer from that company's even larger competitor. Alex, Brown then parlayed this interest into informal negotiating sessions with three of the top ten Web portals, and Ben was flying off to Seattle and Boston. Within a month, Ben had five major companies poking him with a stick, conducting technical due diligence sessions. Another spate of high-level mergers took the industry by storm, which continued to alter the playing field. He'd learned his lesson in the summer to be careful. He stayed his course, adding consumer electronics and music to KillerApp. His company doubled in size in one month. He talked about how "going public might still be the best option," and "look for me on NASDAQ in eighteen months." Either way, a major deal seemed imminent.

SUCCESS IS SO seductive! As Ben neared a deal, I lost touch with the other newcomers. It was so much easier to hear about how he was on the verge of millions than to hear about the struggle of others. I had set out on this journalistic expedition to remind the world of the other six pilgrims you never hear about, to record the cold truth of fate. But I was swept along, needing good news, wanting to believe that it was possible to come here and make good. In falling out of contact with the others, I almost missed it. Nobody gave up. Nobody went home. Their appetite had been only whet. There is no true failure in Silicon Valley, just an expectation that one will pick oneself up and try again. In the fall, Julie Blaustein was thinking of getting out of sales, saying "I don't function by number." Then she was called in for an interview by one of CitySearch's competitors, GeoCities. She suspected the interview was just a ruse to glean information about how CitySearch's sales effort was organized, so she gave very hesitant answers to the questions about territories and quotas. Her distrust was unfounded; their interest was real. Someone finally recognized her go-get-it*ness*. After three interviews she was given a job at a much higher salary than she'd earned at CitySearch. They held a sales conference in Vegas. She'd always wanted to work at Yahoo!, and while she was in Vegas she got her wish: Yahoo! announced it was buying GeoCities. She began talking about buying something in the city, maybe in Hayes Valley. Perhaps I've just gotten used to her intonation, but when she calls, I take in what she says without noticing how her voice sounds. For me, the accent is gone.

JOHN/DAVID FOSTER was so low he called me to say he had sold his Newton, his last prized possession. "I can't even buy groceries," he told me. "For once in my life I have no answers." But John didn't know how to be a quitter. He didn't know how to be pessimistic. He couldn't help himself. Two days later he called back. He'd formed a new consulting business called Empatheia, offering business development to small start-ups. Rather than charging hourly fees, he would take a retainer and a cut of the deal. "It comes from my distaste for what I saw. I'm tired of the guys who make it on the backs of other people. Everybody deserves a shot, and that's what I want to make possible. I don't want other entrepreneurs to go through what I've been through. I want them to have an advocate they can trust."

He showed me the business plan, and when I wondered if he could survive long enough to sign up clients, it turned out he'd already signed four—interclient, Brooklyn North, Something Now, and Deskgate. The latter was going in the next day for a meeting with Excite that John had arranged. All this in two days! When you hit a big creative vein, it happens remarkably fast. I think he'd found his purpose. Within a week, he had ramped his staff up to eight. He was his old self, gung ho. "Since I take a cut of the revenue, all it would take is one deal and I could be at retirement level."

I BUMPED INTO Scott on the street outside my gym, and he invited me upstairs to Infoseek's San Francisco satellite office, located on the third floor of the old Hamm's Brewery. We sat down in the conference room, so encased in concrete that even at a whisper his words echoed at me from all sides, driving home the point: he is doing well. After a whole year here, his plain vanilla idealism hasn't melted. He could tell me at last what his secret project had been, except that it had been killed at beta phase, just before launch. Here was my chance to hear about his defeat and aggravation, but no. He was unshakable. I probed for signs of defeat and glumness, but Scott was still frustratingly buoyant. He'd been reassigned to a new community product that won't go on-line for another six months to a year. I'm confused by how he can suffer a failed launch without a scar. I probed, and then it suddenly became clear: Scott's father was a steamfitter, repairing boilers for a public school district. Coming from that kind of background, just to be in Silicon Valley working in the Internet space was insanely heady stuff. "I tell my dad how much money I'm making and it's just unbelievable to him." During Scott's employment, Infoseek stock had climbed from 16 to a high of 90. "I remember when I was back in Tennessee, just over a year ago. I was so ready to come out here. I dreamed of it, but I never thought that dream would actually come true. I got to work at one of the most prominent companies, on one of the most cutting-edge products."

THIERRY LEVY WENT to the Software Development Center in San Jose and met two business brokers, who advised him to sell his Quiz Studio technology to a company that has the market muscle to introduce a new product. It would be easier to sell the business than to grow it himself.

I had to ask: he used to say he would leave the Valley once he'd made his twenty million; if he sold his company, would he stay? It was a philosophical question, but he answered it literally: "If I sell the company, it is customary for me to be asked to stay on for two years."

During this time Thierry shared with me his diary. In his impressionistic prose poems, the sky is gray, bridges are gaunt silhouettes, office buildings are marble bunkers. His eye notices earthquake ruts and derelict gas stations. He longs for a road on which he can drive that is at a high-enough elevation to give him the perspective he fears he has lost. He does not understand how Americans retain such unshaken confidence in the face of the chaos. To him, we are slightly robotic in our relentlessness.

"Californian secretaries drive their spotless Hondas to work with the utmost application. Their business letters are as flawless and predictable as an IRS form."

Thierry told me he had thirty days before he would be selling his clothes, but thirty days later he was still answering his phone—to tell me he had three days left. He could not make that Friday's payroll, and office rent was due Saturday. French accounting law is much more strict than in the United States; the following Monday he would have to file as insolvent under the French bankruptcy code, he told me, even though he didn't have any creditors hounding his company.

But in the meantime, he had released a new version of Quiz Studio, which had solved the incompatibility problems between Sun's Java and Microsoft's Java. The new product was featured in several trade magazines, which helped one of the brokers arrange meetings with Macromedia, Isometrix, Oracle, and Knowledge Universe. Then he was introduced to Maria Rosatti of the law firm Wilson, Soncini, Goodrich & Rosatti, which is the preeminent law firm in the Valley. Rosatti was in a position to play a role similar to that played by Ben Chiu's financial adviser.

These prospects for a sale were bright enough that one of his original French funders invested another $150,000 in expectation he'd make it back in the sale.

He had another six months to pull it off.

MICHAEL ZILLY INVITES me to meet him on a certain bench beside a certain fountain on the peninsula at four on a Friday afternoon. The fountain is a water-driven sculpture, a twenty-five-foot-tall bronze man slowly hammering the air.

When he arrives, he has a much hipper look about him. His hair is brush cut, his jeans jet black, his shoes boxy black leather loafers with chunky heels. His face sports a chinburn ear to ear. He still has a bit of a stoner's hush to his voice, but his eyes are clear.

Zilly passed the Cobol certification exam. Properly credentialed, he became a contract worker, a full-time temp, on call for a Y2K service firm. After two months on one location, he was moved to another contract at another location—one of the most respectable and professional firms in the entire Valley. The company's campus is where we are meeting today. The fountain feeds a man-made lake big enough to froth up in whitecaps on windy days. The campus's twelve glass-and-brick greenhouse buildings that surround the hammering man fountain are beautiful monuments, particularly so in a valley of ugly tilt-ups.

A couple weeks ago, this company decided to end the service firm's contract and handle the Y2K conversion internally. They asked the five implementation consultants for their résumés. Zilly had a moment of panic. Then he fudged it. Lied. It worked. The company hired him as employee number umpteen thousand, with full bennies. The badge he shows Security as he enters each building is now laminated plastic rather than flimsy card stock.

He's found that he really likes working here, in the warm corporate bosom of a treacherous industry. "The people here are whip smart. They get the job done. The company really has its act together." As a Y2K implementer, he gets to wander around rather than be stuck on one floor in one building. Even here at a computer firm, everyone has computer problems, and he says, "I've met maybe half the people who work in Buildings 1 through 8."

He is still taking risks where he can. Last week he took his accumulated life savings, $4,000, and bought stock in a company whose share price was $2, meaning it was on the verge of being delisted. He believes it will go up, but in the meantime it's somewhere less than $2.

Despite the apparent bedrock stability of this company, management still creates an atmosphere of transience. Zilly introduces me to a guy who's had twelve different offices in three years. To have lasted here three years is a long time; the company stays the same, but the people come and go. If you last five years, you're awarded a six-month sabbatical. Few come back after that. Workers come here to get the seal of approval on their résumé, to be properly trained in sales or in management.

That's what Zilly wants. The way the Mafia launders money, Zilly will use this company to launder his résumé. Once he's worked here, it doesn't matter where he worked before, sort of like getting an MBA at Stanford after doing your undergrad at Foothill Community College. "After a year or two here, I can get hired anywhere. Anywhere in the world."

He's dreaming of moving to Gibraltar, the tiny British colony at the southern tip of Spain. "I'm still young, still single, now is the time for adventure."

In the meantime, it is the bennies that he seems so thrilled with now. Though Zilly jokes about recent college grads who can't get over their "free food!" euphoria—who often walk out at night carrying bunches of bananas under their coats—in the three hours he and I roamed the campus buildings, Zilly fixed himself no less than four gourmet espressos, steamed perfectly until the *crema* foamed from the nozzle. He was becoming a connoisseur, able to discern small qualitative differences among the espresso machines on every floor in every building. There is a dark-bottomed outdoor pool overlooking the Dunbarton Bridge. Zilly has swum in it every single evening. Zilly riffs on the quality of the water: not too much chlorine, not too bracing when he first jumps in.

The grand mystery for cubicle dwellers here is what life is like in the new buildings, 11 and 12. Though 11 and 12 look exactly the same to me as 1 through 10, there is this grass-is-greener envy sustained by the security badges: you can't get in without the correct badge. Employees project onto 11 and 12 as if it's some kind of Oz, assuming that since it's new, it must be better. A friend of his just had her office moved up to the third floor of 12. She's been brushing him off ever since.

We go see her. She brushes us off.

"Let's check out their refrigerator," Zilly says. We go to the third-floor kitchen and rifle through the cabinets. "Look at all that Diet Coke," Zilly says. "It's not even cold." He opens the refrigerator. "Look, no Dannon yogurt. Not even any malted milk balls. They're hosed here."

It's time to get going, but Zilly wants to try out their espresso machine, which he can't find. He spends several minutes searching but then concludes that it just hasn't arrived yet. "That's inhumane to make people work without an espresso machine on their floor."

Five

In mid-March, I went to see Ben Chiu one last time. I caught him at a moment when the negotiations were complete and the merger documents halfway signed. He had sold KillerApp.com to C/NET for "somewhere north of fifty." As in $50 million. And the portion of the company he owned prior to the sale—that is, how much of the payday was his? Also somewhere north of fifty. As in 50 percent. (Five days later, when the official announcement was made, the exact amount was $46.6 million.)

"I didn't know what hit me," Ben explained. He was walking on air. Yet the day he found out about the merger, he didn't do anything special to celebrate. He didn't have anybody to celebrate with. "There was nobody waiting in the wings to congratulate me," he told me. His parents were really just relieved more than overjoyed.

But Ben, he was overjoyed. He was stressed and giddy at the same time, goofy, apologetic, sweet—buying me a Pepsi from the vending machine. "When I got here," he told me, "I didn't know a soul. Every venture capitalist on Sand Hill Road turned me down when I went for money." He was trying to get used to his new situation.

CHAPTER 2

THE IPO

THIS IS A STORY I definitely wasn't supposed to witness, and I certainly wasn't supposed to write, and—most of all—you really aren't supposed to be reading.

Actuate Software of San Mateo was originally scheduled to go public in the first week of August 1998. On July 21, with the market at an all-time high, Federal Reserve Chairman Alan Greenspan spoke to Congress, stating that a market correction was "inevitable," and in so doing set off just such a correction—over four hundred points, the largest ever one-week loss. Every IPO in the pipeline was delayed.

This is the story of Actuate's battle to get out while the getting was still good.

IN THE SPRING of 1998 I probed my sources in the investment banking community for which high-tech IPO deals the banks were really jockeying to get in on. I kept hearing about Actuate, an enterprise-reporting firm. They weren't a particularly sexy play, but it was *the* solid hit in a season of iffy gambles. Actuate was run by Nico Nierenberg, *the* guy in enterprise reporting (software that companies use to distribute information to employees, partners, and customers), and it was backed by one of the top venture capitalists, Jim Breyer at Accel Partners—a real A-team package that, inevitably, chose the top-ranked underwriter, Goldman Sachs.

"They're not supposed to talk to the press right now," said Actuate's public relations firm, when I asked to be let in on the nitty-gritty of their IPO the day their S-1 filing showed up on EDGAR, the SEC's electronic data gathering and analysis system. "They're in the Quiet Period." But the public relations firm, always keen on building friendships between their client companies and reporters, encouraged me to head down to San Mateo to have the rules explained firsthand why I couldn't do the story.

Theirs is a standard-issue office building shared with several other firms, 16,400 square feet jammed with standard-issue cubicles from which the employees, 114 of them, emerge on Friday afternoons for standard-issue Friday lunches, tacos or hoagies. They are perched on the outer lip of anonymity, within sight of neither the mountains nor the water but a stone's throw from a Target and an Office Max. This could be any office development in America this spring, overlooking any mid-construction housing development, just a block from any freeway. But this happens to be San Mateo, California, east of the 101 and north of the 92— smack-dab in the middle of Silicon Valley, during the longest boom time on record.

Actuate's in-house counsel, Bill Garvey, flashed his frosted pale blue eyes and calmly delivered the long list of no-no's with just the right hint of ominous legalese. To start, there's Rule 174 of the Securities Act, governing the Quiet Period, which extends from due diligence until twenty-five days after the IPO. The firm has to be careful of gun jumping, or what is known as hyping the stock. The easiest way to prevent this is just not talk to the press. And Rule 135, which states the specific limited nature of what can and can't be said to the press. Then there's Section 2 (3) to think about, as well as Section 11, regarding liabilities for making false statements or omissions from the prospectus. Actuate is allowed to talk to investors very carefully on the road show, but the only document they can leave behind during this period is the

S-1 prospectus, and anything else that gets left behind could violate Section 5.

In addition to marshaling Actuate through its IPO, Garvey's wife just had a baby and he's going to run the San Diego marathon next week in under four hours. He makes it all seem effortless. "What you are proposing to do is to write another document about this period. You would be watching meetings in which the valuation of the company is discussed, in which accounting write-downs are debated, in which various pitches will be tried out. You will be watching us edit the prospectus itself. And all it would take is for one line of what you write to contradict the finished prospectus, and it could trigger a slap on the wrist from the SEC."

A week later, the company's venture capitalist, Jim Breyer, fleshed out the background. "As far as we know, this story has only been done twice before in journalism history: in 1991, Mike Malone followed MIPS through its dramatic IPO in his book *Going Public.* And in 1986 *Fortune* tracked the Microsoft IPO for a cover story, but Microsoft's investment bankers were Goldman Sachs—and Goldman (also Actuate's lead underwriter) vowed never to let such a story ever be written again."

Indeed, Actuate relayed that Goldman Sachs was adamantly opposed to my presence on principle. For many weeks the Goldman guys wouldn't even look me in the eye, as if they were under edict to pretend I didn't exist. Goldman had every logical, risk-averse reason to oppose my presence, including a biggie not mentioned above: Goldman Sachs announced shortly into this process that after 129 years as a limited partnership, it was filing to go public. So my presence might tread upon Quiet Period regulations for not just Actuate's IPO but Goldman's too.

Throughout the entire IPO process, these securities laws handcuffed Actuate from coming out and honestly saying what was going on. Confidential information must be leaked in circumlocutory ways in order to get the message across, via a relay link of stock analysts and independent research firms, utilizing code phrases while piggybacking the credibility of the investment bank and the venture capitalists. Investors are brought along to a state that one Goldman syndicate manager called, "They know but they don't know," which is to say that investors haven't officially been *told* anything outright (other than what's in the prospectus), but through an ancient ritual of winks, nudges, passive verbs, rhetorical questions, and comparisons have been brought up to speed.

For instance, though the prospectus says outright "As of March 31, 1998 the Company had an accumulated deficit of $18.9 million," and shortly thereafter adds "Given the Company's history of net losses, there can be no assurance of revenue growth or profitability on a quarterly or annual basis in the future," investors manage to develop the expectation that in just a few years Actuate will control a double-slice share of a billion-dollar market. This estimate is something they know, but, *officially*, they don't know (wink).

I have come to call this manner of communicating the great Hall of Prisms. The grand story of what it really feels like to go public—to wake up one morning worth $28 million—has been protected by the Hall of Prisms.

I got this story for one reason. Nico Nierenberg, the CEO of Actuate, is willing to defy convention. That is the hallmark of all entrepreneurs, the defining characteristic that sets them apart from those who merely scheme, tinker, work extra hard, and are generalists. Rules do not intimidate Nico Nierenberg. He is forty-one years old, son of a Manhattan Project physicist who became the director of the Scripps Institute of Oceanography. Raised in laid-back San Diego, when Nico was young he nevertheless had that alpha thing, jettisoning college before graduation for its lack of true challenge, then always having trouble with bosses or working in large companies. He's been programming for pay since he was sixteen, founded his first company when he was twenty-three, and had the resolve to stick with that firm until 1993, when he left to form Actuate. Five years ago, he got a vision that there was an opportunity for enterprise-reporting software, and then he set out to single-handedly build that market.

The other trait that I kept hearing about Nico Nierenberg is that he can make crucial strategic decisions very quickly, working with only imprecise information. I didn't really know what that meant, and in my prescreening research I kept asking for an anecdote that elucidated this. Usually, I got back only anecdotes in the negative, stories of other CEOs or venture capitalists who could not come to a decision without better information. They'd rather pass than pull the trigger based on imperfect information. It's one thing to decide; it's a harder thing to *decide to decide.*

Then, on the day I met Nico, we sat down in the Actuate conference room with a team of legal advisers who exposed the damning vagueness of my stated intentions. No, I couldn't tell them what angle I wanted to take, because I hadn't seen the story unfold yet. No, I couldn't tell them which publication I would write the story for, since the nature of the story would determine to which it was best suited. No, I couldn't point to any other stories I'd written in which I'd massaged such legally treacherous material.

We had the conference room reserved for an hour. Nico heard me out for about ten minutes, took in the texture and trustworthiness of our rapport, and then somewhere in our interchange I could see it happen. He'd *decided to decide.* He was wearing the determination of a decision on his face, delivering those little head nods and "uh-huhs" of impatience. After some time, everyone else sensed this, too, and I was asked to leave so they could confer.

While being escorted to the door an official message was beamed to me through the Hall of Prisms, "There's just no way to know yet what we'll want to do. We'll get back to you."

Yet I was sure I'd get the story.

I didn't know, but I *knew.*

"UMM."

We are in the Sequoia conference room at the Hyatt Regency in San Mateo to rehearse Nico Nierenberg's road-show pitch. We will be here all day today, and then two more additional days, each a week apart, to get Nico comfortable with being a public person. In the back of this small room is a video camera, trained on the front of the room. In the middle of the room is Jerry Weisman, the sixty-two-year-old former novelist and TV producer who is the founder and president of Power Presentations, which specializes in preparing executives for their road show. Weisman is far more than an image consultant, far more than an acting coach; Jerry Weisman is a holistic practitioner of communication. He teaches people to connect with their audience. In the front of the room is Nico Nierenberg, a slender six feet three inches tall with a vibrantly pink, round, happy-clam face, and the first public utterance from his mouth: "Umm."

He is pacing. His face is getting red. His body lists. His gestures are small. His arms cross his body and his shoulders hunch. It is the posture of someone defensive. He is doing what Jerry Weisman calls the "body wrap." Nico Nierenberg has an athletic grace, but when we replay the videotape his carriage gives the impression of a much mousier man.

This is not the Nico Nierenberg I have been seeing. The Nico I've seen is boisterous, jocular, and keen as a hunter. His gestures are normally huge—he'll thrust his arms out with indignation or slap his forehead and then spout some off-the-cuff cynical remark to let out steam. The most striking characteristic of Nico Nierenberg is his laugh, which in normal meetings finds something funny to release it every thirty seconds. His laugh is an enchanting laugh, because it doesn't shock—it begins as if he is being tickled and then in a couple seconds escalates into a full guffaw. It is a full, mouth-wide-open, head-tipped-back horse-laugh with a little calming chuckle behind it, and then he is back to business. Nico is not a casual person—in fact he is a very intense, competitive person—and his laugh is his release of tension. The more intense things get, the more he laughs.

But he is not laughing now. All that tension is bottling him up.

Jerry Weisman nods knowingly. "When that little red light on the camera goes on, the adrenaline bolt shoots down into the veins and freezes you." Much of what Jerry Weisman is going to teach Nico Nierenberg today is about managing that adrenaline bolt.

Nico tries to get started. "Okay, I'll do that part about thanking everyone in the room for coming," he says. But he doesn't actually *do* that part.

Weisman prompts him. "Go ahead and say it. Say 'Thank you George, thank you everyone for having me, thanks for coming.' Burn off that first jolt of adrenaline with the amenities. Give your eyes time to find the room."

Nico says, "I'll be fine for the real thing. I'm fine once I get on a roll."

Of course *everyone* is fine once he gets on a roll. This is about how to get on that roll, how to manage the very first public seconds, how to manage that very first bolt of adrenal hormones, and get your first words out.

In eleven days Nico Nierenberg will be standing in front of the entire 341-person salesforce of Goldman Sachs at their 1 New York Plaza offices, and he will be asking for thirty million dollars. And on that morning of June 30, those Goldman salespeople will give their best effort to be attentive, but they are jacked into the market, and their ears will be ringing with that morning's shotgun of market indicators. The market down 200 yesterday, up 200 today, what's for lunch? If Nico cannot handle one little red light on a video camera, then how will he handle this army of Goldman salespeople, and how will he handle the videoprompter that beams his speech live to Goldman conference rooms in Houston, Chicago, and San Francisco?

"I've got a question," says Nico.

"Shoot," says Weisman.

"I know I come out and take a deep breath and pick one person to look in the eye for a moment. But *how long* do I look that person in the eye? How long before I move on to another person?"

Jerry Weisman grins. Good question, Nico. Even better answer coming. "You look at him *until you feel him looking back.*"

Until you feel him looking back. One by one you make your way through the audience, until it is not an audience at all, but just a string of one-on-one conversations.

So Nico backs up, then reenters the camera sight. He takes a deep breath, and then his eyes pick me out.

These will be the first public words spoken by Nico Nierenberg. These are the first words out of the mouth of a man who six years ago had an idea, five years ago formed a company, three years ago sold his first software, two years ago hired the CFO, one year ago started looking at revenue forecasts and the timing of profitability and began to realize that he'd be ready to go public this summer. The first public words of a man who a year from now, if the company and the market grow as they are expected to grow, will be very well known among the investment bankers who have made so much money off his successful IPO, and two years from now famous among institutional investors who have sat pretty with the gradual incline of the company's stock, and three years from now known by all tech investors as the pioneer, the leader, in the billion-dollar market for "enterprise reporting." The tectonics of all those years culminate in this movement right here: from five years of past crashing into three years of future. The past, private; the future, public. The past, judged by nobody but himself; the future, judged by every mutual fund and research analyst and Joe Q Cyber Trader who handicaps the market.

His eyes lock. "In 1993 . . ." Nico starts, "back when I was with another company, I was in a meeting with AT&T pitching them on our products, and I bothered to ask for their feedback, 'What was it that we *weren't* doing?' " He stops at the end of this sentence. He is thinking how this will look on video. Jerry Weisman will play back the tape without the sound, so all we will see is the gestures, the embarrassing slow-motion hip slides, the excruciating frame-by-frame analysis of lack of eyebrow motion, and— oh-my-gahd—the *eye dance,* nineteen eye shifts in the first ten seconds alone. Then Jerry Weisman will turn off the video and just play the sound, and Nico will hear his own voice, every "um," "ah," and "so" tidbit of connective drawl . . . ugh. It will be ugly. Nico's voice is trying to follow his script but his mind is racing ahead, racing ahead to the videotape playback, racing ahead to eleven days from now in Manhattan; and suddenly the voice coming from his mouth just stops. It can't find the next sentence. Stops right there, and an adrenaline bolt pumps up his heart and his eyes constrict and the signals cross and nervousness and, boom, dead air, right before he gets to tell you about the start of his company.

"It just feels so fake," he says. Nico is a genuine person, and he hates the forced quality of rehearsing. He believes that when it's the real thing, he'll be fine.

"Get off your script," says Weisman. "Speak from concepts. Don't recite. Talk."

Another deep breath. Eyes lock again. Then another thought hits his mind, and he steps back.

"Here's what I'm thinking . . ." Nico says.

"Tell me," says Weisman.

"I'm thinking ahead to all those road-show meetings, all those investors. . . ."

"And?"

"My fear is, 'Why do they care?' Will they care?"

Another tremendously pleased grin comes across Weisman's face. Good question again, Nico. And an even better answer coming. "Connect with that, then. So tell them why they should care."

"What do you mean?"

"Say it aloud. Say, 'Let me tell *you* why *you* should care about my company.' Every time you say the word 'you,' reach out with your hand to that person. Let go of the body wrap. Open up your body. Reach out and close the gap between you and that audience member you're speaking to." Jerry Weisman demonstrates, reaching out and forward with his arms.

Nico tries this gesture, his arm reaching what seems to him like ten feet away from his body. Comically big. "That feels weird."

"But it looks great." It does look great. In reality, his arm only moved about eighteen inches.

"Okay," he says. Deep breath. Survey the room while the adrenaline passes. Eyes lock on me. This time he is not reciting. This time he is just talking, him and me. "Let me tell *you* why you should care about enterprise reporting," he starts, and just like that he is on a roll. The redness in his face passes, his eyes glimmer. Rock-solid balance. In the video replay of this one, we count the eye dance, and his eyes shift only four times in twenty seconds. Lock on. He speaks in complete sentences. Not a single "umm." This is a man who can lead. This is a man with a story and a vision. This is a man you would give $30 million.

Jerry Weisman pauses the replay on one single video frame for Nico Nierenberg, one frame where it all goes right. His arms go out, his eyebrows go up, his smile breaks, and there is the guy I've seen in meetings for the last three weeks—the scientist, the leader, the joker, the guy who's been having fun all this time.

There. That moment. Freeze on that.

"HOW'S THE IPO, AL?"

"It'd be fine if those Indonesian students just stopped rioting."

Cratering is when the market goes spongy. Cratering is when for no explainable reason there are more sellers than buyers out there. Cratering is not a statistical event, such as a "down blip" or a "profit taking" or a "correction" or a "sell-off." Cratering is a broad market event. Cratering is an emotional state, a great unease, an anxiety that boils in the gut. When the market craters, the first region of the stock market to feel it is the appetite for initial public offerings, fledgling companies with untested business models and dressed-up income statements.

On April 22, 1998, around the time that Actuate had its first organizational meeting and due diligence session with its underwriters Goldman Sachs and the Deutsche Morgan Grenfell Technology Group, the NASDAQ Index set an all-time high at 1,917. Actuate's IPO was confidently penciled in for the first week of August. But by the first week of June, when its S-1 filing put Actuate's IPO on the market's radar screen, something had gone awry. Only 13 percent of the IPOs filed since the beginning of the year were trading above their offering price. The scariest thing was not just that this softening of interest had happened, but that nobody really knew *why* it had happened.

So in the late spring of 1998, every start-up firm that had been thinking of going public sometime in the next year held a meeting to debate what the hell they were waiting for. A whole lot of them jumped into the IPO pipeline right behind Actuate just hoping to raise a wad before the great bull run of the '90s ran its course.

"There's a fear out there," said Jim Breyer, speaking of the interchanges between VCs as they perch over urinals or get in and out of limousines. "There's an underlying urgency to take advantage of these best of times."

I asked Breyer whether this fear of the bull market ending was a *later-this-year* fear, an *any-month-now* fear, or an *any-day-now* fear.

"It's an *any-day-now* fear."

In response, Goldman Sachs accelerated Actuate's schedule by three weeks. There was a meeting held in which the decision was made, yet even on this action the unknowing seemed to pervade. Everyone at Actuate knew the IPO had been accelerated three weeks, but everyone had a different impression as to why. Helena Winkler, the director of strategic marketing, had heard it was because investors take their summer vacations in August. Dan Gaudreau, the CFO, believed it was entirely an internal-to-Goldman scheduling matter—they'd committed to three IPOs for one week, and Actuate's was the most ready to jump-start.

Someone else had heard it was to make sure that Actuate went public before its competitors, who had also filed with the SEC. Melissa Centrella, who would have to plan the big blowout party if this thing ever came off, had heard it from her boss, Al Campa, and his opinion was blunt: "Why wait? We got to get this thing out before the market craters."

It remained a question whether the market was already cratering or not. There was no question that guts were boiling. "Tough market," said one Goldman banker, arriving for a meeting. "Jittery," was what one person at Actuate said of the market. "Skittish," said another, punching his browser's refresh button on Dun&Bradstreet.com to check the latest prices. Just about everyone at Actuate had watched the market for years, invested some, read the papers, et cetera—but that hadn't prepared them to get in bed with the market, to tie the fate of their company to this roller coaster. Those rational fundamentals—the CPI, the unemployment figure, and the Fed funds rate—disguise the reality of how damned *emotional* she is. The market is a tyrant; it's a crack-high speed-whacked monster; it's a moody morass. It's the market of Joe Q Cyber Trader, quick to snatch and quicker to panic.

"But the fundamentals are still great," chirped Helena Winkler, trying to keep her spirits up.

"Sure, they're great," retorted Al Campa, who tried to maintain a levelheaded attitude. "They're so great that they can't possibly get better. They can only get worse. The market can only go down."

"No news is good news," said Helena Winkler, but of course every day there was news. Every day the newspapers were filled with news, and the market was just looking for a reason to let out a little fart of irrational exuberance.

Everyone has his disaster story. For Helena Winkler, it was her last company, which also went public, quite anticlimactically. Broadvision was all set to go out at 12 in the spring of 1996 when suddenly the IPO market went soft, and it eventually cratered later that summer. Broadvision managed to get out in June, but at a price of 7, where the stock stayed for almost a year. The employee options weren't worth nearly so much. What had been plans for a house became plans for a condo. Thoughts of retiring at thirty-five turned into thoughts of a Caribbean vacation.

"It's so difficult for entrepreneurs," explained Jim Breyer.

"They're used to having a great deal of *control*. This is one of the first times they can't control the situation at all. External forces shape the market, and there's nothing they can do about it."

Entrepreneurs are incredibly hands-on managers; they like to understand just about everything in their purview. Suddenly, when the entrepreneur's company goes public, he's letting these new investors, who've only just met his company, who only collectively own about 20 percent of his firm, decide the valuation and direction of his company. And more often than not, the valuation has nothing to do with him and everything to do with the crazy events driving the broad market up and down—riots in Indonesia, the collapse of the Russian exchanges, nuclear tests in Pakistan, and Prime Ministerial elections in Japan.

Suddenly every Actuate employee is opening his morning *Chronicle* to read about how the market is reacting to the possibility that Iraq will respond to one of its warplanes having been shot down over the no-fly zone. They want to understand! Hey, if their IPO hangs on whether some Iraqi MiG-15 really did or did not lock its radar on a British transport plane, then these guys will become instant experts on radar locking. They will be calling their old college buddies at NASA or Lockheed; they will learn. Because what an entrepreneur hates more than anything, hates worse than bad news, is no news at all—he hates not knowing.

But that's exactly what the emotional market will do to the rational-minded entrepreneur—it will demand that he bow down to its unknowingness. It will humiliate his attempts to rationalize. It will make him accept its complete fallibility and unpredictability. And the market seems intent on proving this lesson to every young entrepreneur whose company goes public. It is sort of the price of being made so suddenly wealthy: before the market makes him so big, it will make him confront his utter puniness.

For Nico Nierenberg, it hadn't happened yet. With six weeks to go, there was still a long checklist of action items for him to deliver on. He had to rehearse his road-show presentation to perfection; he had to deliver that speech seventy-five times in twelve days on two continents; he had to convince the big institutional investors one by one. Nico was just one factor; he recognized that the market would have to hold steady through six weeks of Federal Reserve committee meetings, two unemployment numbers, four inflation indicators, and the washboard of Q2 earnings reports. But the sense that he still had an influence on the outcome was very much alive.

That *would* vanish. The market always exacts its price.

BILL GARVEY HEARD something about it the day before, from "a well-placed source," meaning a buddy at his old law firm. Jim Breyer had heard strong rumors a week earlier, and on the morning it was happening heard "substantive information to its effect," which was the Hall of Prisms manner of saying he'd got it from someone who was there. Al Campa heard about it from Bill Garvey before the newspapers picked it up, and Helena Winkler heard about it from Al Campa when he came back from lunch. Melissa Centrella hadn't heard anything at all, but once I asked her if she'd heard anything she was suspicious and soon found out.

Dan Gaudreau heard about it from a message left on his voice mail by Bill Garvey. At the time, Dan was seated in first class row 2, seat B, in a 747 sitting on the tarmac at Kennedy International Airport. The Boeing jet was about to turn on its flight computer and the flight attendant purred over the intercom, "Ladies and gentlemen, please turn off all cellular phones for the duration of the flight until we land at Heathrow." The last one of all to hear about it was Nico Nierenberg, who heard it when Dan handed him his cell phone and replayed the voice mail. And then he had to turn the phone off, unable to respond, to react, to move.

It wasn't the riots in Indonesia.

It wasn't Alan Greenspan predicting inflation, though that was coming.

It wasn't Intel's low earnings announcement, though that was coming too.

This uncontrollable tornado was touching down far closer to home.

At 8:30 that morning, wearing an olive-green suit, Nico Nierenberg had kicked off the road show at the midtown offices of the deal's comanager, Deutschebank Securities/DMG. In their multimedia room equipped with videoconference technology to beam Nico to the DMG salesforce across the country, Nico stood up in front of a few dozen equities salespeople, thanked George for inviting him to speak and thanked everyone for attending, let his eyes find the exits, took a deep breath, reminded himself not to rush, and locked eyes with one of the bankers that he'd met previously. That he knew a few people in the room calmed Nico. He was aware that the adrenaline bolt was coming, knew it would charge his veins and fry his nerves, but it hadn't hit yet.

The words came fine, full sentences, balance steady—hey, I'm on a roll!—and then that little bit of self-awareness seemed to trigger it—woah!—welling up behind his eyes, tingling in his fingers, lifting the hair on his neck, crunching the arches in his feet, flushing his face red—I am here, I am presenting my company to the world, I am actually doing it!—so high-voltage electric that the intensity of the adrenaline bolt amazed him, wow, and a huge teeth-beaming smile broke his face open as his arms crawled with goose bumps and all he could do was pause to let it pass.

"That was it!" he yelped, chuckling and sputtering to let himself recover. "Whooooo!"

And then he locked on again, and got on another roll.

Meanwhile, about that very same time but across the continent in DMG's offices in Menlo Park, the CEO of DMG, Frank Quattrone, was reviewing an e-mail to send to all 160 DMG employees, notifying them that he was leaving for competitor Credit Suisse First Boston along with fellow bankers Bill Brady and George Boutros. This e-mail, which they would receive around midday, further said that his contract with DMG prevented him from offering any of them jobs with his new employer. It was a bombshell. DMG, the fourth-ranked underwriter of high-technology IPOs, was effectively gutted of leadership.

"It could not be worse timing," said Al Campa anxiously, letting out a long breath at his desk. "There's no way to react. It's something we just have no control over."

Not only could they not react, they couldn't even get good information. Nico's cell phone wasn't roaming in London or Amsterdam, where he'd moved on with the road show under Goldman's leadership. They were trading messages with Nico at his hotel rooms. They'd all heard about it secondhand, but so far nobody had heard from Frank Quattrone or Bill Brady directly, and that hurt because about eight other investment banking firms had managed to leave messages on Nico's voice mail, suggesting he give them DMG's spot on the lower right-hand side of the prospectus.

"We had anticipated that maybe Frank Quattrone would leave DMG," Jim Breyer said remarkably calmly, considering that he had about $120 million hanging in this wind. "But not until after this summer. We're just grateful that Goldman's on the left."

What did all this mean? Nobody at Actuate had any idea what it meant. What did they know about investment banking? At the very least, it seemed that it would lead to some sort of delay. In this tricky market, a delay could sink a deal. The terrible thing about waiting out a delay is that the firm is in the Quiet Period, so it can't comment. It can't even put out a press release saying, "Hey, it's not our fault." It didn't seem possible to go forward with a handicapped DMG, but to switch bankers probably would mean having to go back to the SEC and refiling, et cetera, wouldn't it? To reallocate the syndicate, to print new prospectuses, to line up new investors—that would take weeks, wouldn't it? Weeks of waiting out the market, weeks of watching every firm in the pipeline but them go out at 11 and jump to 18, weeks of announcements on the Producer Price Index, the trade deficit.

This shows how little they knew about investment banking. In fact, swapping bankers in the middle of the road show is just another Business as Usual power shift in this well-oiled system of going public, where the bumps in the road are seen but not felt.

On Friday morning, Amsterdam time, Actuate's banker at DMG, Cameron Lester, got Nico on the phone between presentations. Lester had already moved over to Credit Suisse First Boston. The whole DMG team was moving, eighty people, from the top on down, *immediately*—that day. Lester proposed that Actuate stay with the group, letting Credit Suisse have DMG's role as comanager. Credit Suisse would pay to reprint the red herrings that weekend. DMG's name appeared in the prospectus only three times, so it would be no trouble to swap it out. It appeared that DMG was going to let First Boston take over the lease on the Menlo Park offices, so the team could just go back to work with a new nameplate on the door.

Nico decided quickly. "You're hired," he said. Then Nico called

Frank Quattrone, who was still at DMG officially, locked up under contract for a few more days. "So you still officially represent DMG right now?" Nico asked for clarification. Quattrone said that he did. "Well," Nico said, "then you're fired." The two laughed, knowing that soon enough Quattrone would be over at Credit Suisse.

And that was it. Business as Usual. No delay. Some weary bankers had to put in a few extra hours over the weekend, sure, but by Monday Al Campa was even tired of talking about it. "It's behind us already, to tell you the truth."

On Tuesday, Nico was sanguine, speaking with the retrospective tone as if this had all happened last year. "I always had a sense that we'd be okay," he added, which I took to be a bad sign. If Nico had always had the sense that he'd be okay, then the market hadn't exacted its price yet.

"**DO YOU THINK** everyone will wear Armani around here?"

"Do you think the parking lot will be filled with Ferraris?"

"Do you think our stock will split ten times over, like Oracle's did?"

These are the whisperings in the hallways at Actuate, the musings at the refrigerator where cookies and Diet Cokes are resupplied daily. They can't help getting excited.

"Friends and family call us," explained Melissa Centrella, who'd decided on a '70s theme for the celebration if the offering succeeded. "*They* think we're going to be millionaires. They put that idea in our heads."

As we drive to lunch one day, Al Campa says, "The two biggest misconceptions about going public are that, one, we all get rich, and two, there's tons of cash around to spend. We may get rich, but not on the IPO. We'll get rich over time if the company grows and the stock splits. And as for cash to spend, we have more pressure to be on budget now than ever. As a public company, we absolutely have to meet our estimates."

Campa remembers when Silicon Valley was just olive orchards. He was born in 1961 and grew up in San Jose, on the border of Campbell and Saratoga. His dad worked for Lockheed. They used to go up on the roof of their house and see orchards for miles. The nearest school was five miles away. He considers what this industry has done both an economic marvel and an ecological disaster.

"Keeping the spending on budget is the easy side of the income statement," Campa says. "The real pressure is to make Wall Street's revenue projections."

Campa was working at Sybase in April 1995 when the company announced first-quarter sales were $250 million, a figure 8 percent off Wall Street analysts' projections. With revenues off by $20 million, the quarterly profit was wiped out. "Any private company could weather that situation. An eight percent miss is just not that substantial. The revenues were still up significantly from the year before. It wasn't like the company wasn't growing, it just wasn't growing quite as fast as the Street wanted." The morning after the announcement, Sybase's stock, which had been trading in the mid-40s, dropped to 21.

"The next three months were the worst time of my career. Suddenly all the employee options were under water. The reorganizations were endless. We had to tear down, to fire people, to consolidate groups. Nobody wanted to work in that environment. I'm a builder, not a slasher."

Wall Street's seemingly enormous valuations of technology companies are predicated entirely on those companies' ability to keep growing at a rate of *at least* 50 percent, year after year. Once you're on Wall Street's radar screen, it's a treadmill. There is very little forgiveness. "If the growth slows down, analysts stop talking up the stock. Researchers stop writing reports. Investors can't get any information about the company, so there's no buyers. The stock drops like a plane running out of gas," says Campa.

A similar story haunts Nico Nierenberg. The company he founded at age twenty-three evolved into a database firm called Unify. As Unify grew, Nico went from being its founder/CEO to its chief engineer. The company had lasted through many incarnations, weathering the market transitions from mainframes to desktops and back to networks. Though Nico left in 1993, the company continued to grow and in 1997 went public. "He was so proud that Unify went public, and that he was known as its founder," says Campa. "But then Unify missed its first-quarter estimates."

Its stock sank from 12 to 3. Now Unify is known as one of the

IPOs that shouldn't have been done. Nico hadn't had anything to do with Unify for five years, so he wasn't responsible. But his reputation was at stake. "He can't forget about that. He carries that cross every day."

The burden of meeting sales estimates falls on Actuate's COO, Pete Cittadini. Pete is a recent transplant from Boston, where his roots ran deep. He says "idear" rather than "idea." He says he has lots of scar tissue from his years in the business at Oracle where he went through just this kind of transition. Pete was the first Oracle salesperson in New England, pre-IPO, and when he left in '91 Oracle had over a billion in sales. Then he became the number two executive at Interleaf. He's learned to be a systematic planner. At Actuate, he wanted to "architect it right." "I started with a clean sheet of paper, bricked and mortared it by hand. I brought in people I know. All of them pros. They know what they're capable of, they tell me, they go out and do it. *No surprises.*" Of Nico, he says, "He designs, I implement. He's cerebral. I'm the heavy."

I popped in on Pete Cittadini on the last afternoon of the quarter, June 30, a day that finds most VPs of sales in Silicon Valley in a cold sweat. The industry is notorious for a sales pattern nicknamed the "hockey stick," in which up to half of a company's quarterly sales close on the very last day. I found Cittadini hopping mad, and he was letting someone have it over the phone. "I don't care if you have to do it all over again," he was saying, "you get it done right."

An underperforming salesperson? Nope. On the last day of the quarter, Pete Cittadini was, of all things, moving into a new home in Hillsborough. "The contractor cut the marble countertops wrong. I told him to do it again."

Wait a minute. Moving, on the last day of the quarter? Didn't he have deals to close? Didn't he have salespeople to motivate? "I had a garage sale yesterday to clean out my house. Couldn't seem to move the queen mattresses."

Besides, he explained, it wouldn't make any difference if he rushed to close deals. In order to prevent the last-minute desperate price-cuttings that only undermine a company's revenue structure, Actuate doesn't pay sales commissions when contracts are signed, only when the cash is collected. Dan Gaudreau, the CFO, refuses to play hockey.

"I'm not focused on the end of the quarter," Pete says, which I take to be a good sign: Hall of Prisms code for *got it in the bag.* "I'm already planning for '99."

THE ROAD SHOW is a time-blurred blitz, a montage of hand-shakes and faces and well-rehearsed spontaneity. It is a series of todays, seven presentations per today, and it gets so *now*-focused that Nico has stopped even looking at the schedule to see who he'd be speaking to. They would be there, he would be there, he would lock on.

"Who are we calling on now?" I ask, flipping up the armrest of the limo to make sure it is stocked with unmelted ice.

"I don't even know," he responds, as on the other side of the world a U.S. F-16 fighter jet fires a missile at an antiaircraft site in southern Iraq and the Dow nervously drops 10 points.

Today is Denver. No, today is Kansas City, tomorrow is Denver, where Dan's luggage—lost somewhere in Reno—will finally catch up with him. Sorry about the blue jeans. Set your watch an hour back. Or three hours ahead, if you didn't make yesterday's adjustment. Is this the same Learjet we took this morning to Chicago? No, that one had a brown leather couch. Or was that the one we took to Philly? In Washington, a Department of Commerce official steps up to a microphone to announce that construction spending in May recorded its steepest drop in more than four years, and the Dow, giddy, leaps 96 points.

Oh, this pillow is just so comfortable. Hey—there's a woman in the bed beside him! Oh, wait—he's at home. His wife. Last night, five minutes with the kids. The sun is not up. The limo is already parked in the driveway. It is going well. Everywhere, Nico and Dan are well received. Nobody is going, "Okay, so what is it that you *do* exactly?"

"What about 'The Book'?" I ask. "Aren't the orders supposed to be filling up some black book?"

"The book is a myth," says Nico.

"The orders come in late in the cycle," says Dan.

I ask, "So you don't hear anything?"

"Jundt Associates put in an order for a hundred thousand."

Inktomi is up 20. Yahoo!, up 25. The jet has four seats and twin engines and gets from Milwaukee to SFO in four hours. It lands at AMR Combs, a half mile north of the big airport, where the signage on the automatic glass doors reads THROUGH THESE DOORS PASS THE MOST IMPORTANT PEOPLE IN THE WORLD. Every night, Nico thinks he's shot, he's fried, tomorrow he will surely suck. Two hours' sleep, three. Every morning there is the little hit of adrenaline and he is roaring to go. A hand, a face, a pair of eyes. A buffet of quiche and sandwich meats off to the side. In June, the Producer Price Index fell 0.1 percent. "Let me tell you why reporting has such huge growth prospects . . ."

"Can we talk about Q2 results yet?"

"The accountants haven't signed off."

At the Actuate offices, the employees are maxxing out their ESOP plans, 10 percent of their salary. Getting out the check-books. They are becoming experts in valuing the alternative minimum tax versus the short-term capital gains penalty if they wait to exercise their options in a same-day transaction. The SEC sends Bill Garvey a fax with its comments—all Business as Usual stuff.

It is not visceral. It is not exciting. Some investors just listen. Some don't listen at all, just ask questions. Some say, "Give me your forty-minute presentation in twenty-five minutes." The questions are straightforward, all sales calculations and making sure Microsoft isn't about to enter this market. Business as Usual. Nobody asks about the soundness of Nico's heartbeat. Nobody asks how his life coach has helped him be a better person. Nobody asks why he dropped out of school. The setting takes care of that. The setting sends the metamessage "he would not be here if he was not top-notch." Except for Fidelity. Fidelity asks about Unify, the stock that dropped. Wanted to make sure he had nothing to do with it, which he didn't. The *now* approaches, banging itself like a drum.

"Okay, can we talk about the Q2 numbers yet?"

Up comes the Hall of Prisms. In Japan, Prime Minister Ryutaro Hashimoto is getting killed at the polls, winning only 44 of 126 seats in the Parliament's upper house, and in San Mateo, California, Actuate announces that second-quarter sales growth is a stunning 127 percent.

Alliance Capital is in. Amerindo is in. Both put in orders for 300,000 shares, which is 10 percent of the deal. They don't actually *want* that many shares, it's just a Hall of Prisms term of the art, to signify they want the top allocation. The book is filling up, filled, oversubscribed. When it is over, Nico will miss having everything planned for him like this. Wellington Capital is in. Palantir. JW Seligman. Everyone is in. It is Tuesday, July 14. One week away. The offering is oversubscribed twenty-seven times over, which is meaningless—the orders are all terms of the art. The real question is how many of those buyers just intend to flip the stock versus how many intend to accumulate in the secondary market. Nico wonders how much time he will get with his kids when he is CEO of a public company. That afternoon, Intel announces second-quarter earnings below analysts' expectations, and the market manages to shrug it off, but everyone involved in Actuate's IPO is wondering, "What the heck are we waiting for?" How many more scares can the market shrug off?

Indeed. The next day, when the NASDAQ sets an all-time record, it seems silly to wait until next Tuesday, when Fed Chairman Greenspan is scheduled to give his semiannual Humphrey-Hawkins testimony to a congressional banking committee. In New York, Nico Nierenberg enters his room at the Essex House hotel on Central Park South, parts the three layers of curtains to give himself a view of the columnar forest stretching out below, and takes a deep breath. It is a sweltering oven out there. It is a killer 107 degrees, the cement buildings radiating absorbed heat like sauna rocks. It is the hottest day on record and the hottest market on record and there seems no way it can get any hotter.

The time is now.

I BEGAN to wonder, if it's such a hassle, why is there such a relentless march to go public? If going public means completely forgetting about your long-term objectives for three months to entirely focus three of the top four executives on threading the legal and financial needles, then why bother? If going public means you can't suffer perfectly normal growth spurts and plateaus in revenue without destroying employee morale, then is it really worth it?

What's really driving this?

"It's the path to liquidity," said Dan Gaudreau. "For the owners, primarily the VCs and Nico, it's the only way to make their asset liquid." Dan interviewed at twenty firms before choosing Actuate over them all.

"Customers view us as more stable," said Pete Cittadini.

"We want to be the first ones out," said Al Campa. There was a rumor that one of their competitors, Sqribe Technologies, had been meeting with Robertson Stephens.

"There's a sense that when the bull market is over, there will be Haves and Have-nots," said Jim Breyer, when I caught up with him one morning during a break in a software conference. "You want to have the currency for acquisitions, to be a consolidator rather than a consolidatee."

Sure, sure, sure—I knew all that. Those were all perfectly valid reasons lifted right out of some business school textbook, summarized into a talking-points memo prepared by those $600-an-hour attorneys. I wanted to know what burns in the heart. I wanted to know what wakes them up in the middle of the night. I wanted to know what fills their daydreams as they drive along the 280 every evening. Nobody daydreams about "liquidity." These guys don't even really daydream about money, since they already have nice houses in one of the most beautiful places on earth.

Prestige. That's what this is about. It's about getting the respect of one's peers. It's about a valley full of superachievers trying to climb up that highest rung on the ladder. They say that only one out of ten companies makes it public, but that figure is actually way too high—it's one out of ten firms *funded by venture capitalists*—and for every firm given a $10 million first round by VCs, there are another X dozen getting off the ground with "friends and family" money, $100 grand at $10K a unit.

Going public is ingrained into this industry. For the last few years, every Friday afternoon at 12:30 a delivery driver has shown up with pizza or taquitos or crispy fried chicken, and everyone at Actuate—whether the 20 people two years ago or the 44 people last year or the 114 today—attacks the free food until the boxes are empty. As long as he was in town, Nico Nierenberg would show up and let anyone ask him any question they wanted. And every single Friday for three years, one of the questions has been some variation of, "When is it *our turn* to go public?"

"Hey, Nico, what's the IPO market doing?"

"Hey, Nico, are we filing this quarter?"

"Hey, Nico, did you hear Sqribe had a meeting with Robertson Stephens?"

"Hey, Nico, I saw Arbor registered its S-1."

"Hey, Nico, you see Brio nearly doubled on its first day?"

What about us? If there is anything the superachievers cannot stand, it's seeing success fall upon others who don't deserve it any more than they do. *We're just as good as they are. I'm just as smart. My product is engineered just as well as theirs.* Those rational minds are tortured by this illogical market allocation of riches and fame. So many voices, all whispering—*Hey, Nico.* Every employee, every customer, every friend, every family member—*Hey, Nico.*

To take a company public is *the* badge of honor in this business. The peer pressure from other CEOs overrides all other motivations. The sense that you are not an industry leader unless you are running a public company. The sense that you have not proven your independence unless your company has an unaffiliated, stand-alone public presence.

"I remember taking Nico to a 49ers game last fall," said Jim Breyer. "He was riding in the back of the car with Bryan Stolle, the CEO of Agile Software. It didn't take long, two CEOs talking. Pretty quickly the conversation cut to the chase. 'So how about the offering—when do you think?' 'Oh, sometime in '98,' said Nico. 'How about you?' 'Oh, sometime early '99,' said Bryan. And I could just see it. Among their peers, taking a company public is *the* thing to do.

"What you have to know about Nico is underneath that sense of humor there's a tremendous underlying intensity," said Jim Breyer, who's known Nico for more than ten years. "Even watching a football game, or a basketball game, he's very analytical, very involved. Will call out plays, will point out who screwed up their blocking patterns."

"We used to go golfing a lot," said Al Campa. "Nico just has to win. If he's losing, he's so intense that it's just no fun to be around him. He really kicks himself if he's down. He doesn't take it out on anyone else, but he's so hard on himself.

"So same thing on the IPO. This is a guy who has to prove himself. This is his home run."

* * *

IF YOU ARE listing on the New York Stock Exchange, the ritual on the first day of trading is to have a grand breakfast with the NYSE officials and then to return to the floor to observe the first trade, which is a scripted event, much like the ceremonial first pitch at the World Series.

For NASDAQ offerings, there is no grand ceremony, no traditional ritual to mark the passage, but a rather undramatic custom has filled the gap. The CEO shows up at the offices of his investment banker, hoping to "see" some trading, even though he knows perfectly well that NASDAQ trades are executed over networks. For most of the morning, the CEO generally gets in his banker's hair, preventing him from getting any work done. At this point, there's nothing for the CEO to do. He borrows the phone a lot, calls his wife, his VCs, says stupid things like, "Hey— guess where I am? Nope, still waiting." When he's cleared to trade, he strolls over to the computer screens of the market maker, who demonstrates how the Buy and Sell orders fall into two columns on the monitor. The salesforce whistles and cheers for about five seconds. Shortly after the first trade, his company's stock symbol appears on the large lot NASDAQ ticker which hangs from the ceiling. It's not much of a ritual, but it serves the key purpose just fine: as a vehicle for the great adrenaline bolt.

On the day he is primed to make $28 million, Nico Nierenberg is deprived of being able to say with any confidence, "This is the day." As he slips into his blue button-down, knots his red party tie, shrugs into his olive sport coat, there is no sense that "that was the last night I went to bed ever having to worry about money again." Last night he learned that the SEC examiner on their case had gone home at 4:30 without clearing Actuate's application to become effective. The SEC still had two "gating items," as Bill Garvey called them.

We meet at 8:15 in the lobby of the Essex House. Dan Gaudreau is wearing blue jeans, sneakers, and a white Actuate T-shirt. "I've had it with the suit," he says. He was up late adjusting write-downs to the financial statements on the two gating items. He's disappointed, since the additional write-down will push Q4 of '98 from slightly profitable to negligibly unprofitable.

He's worried that this change will need to be relayed through the Hall of Prisms to investors, which could take another day to enact, delaying the IPO until Monday.

So even on *the* day, there's tons to worry about.

"Pins and needles." Nico explains, "Before he left work yesterday, the SEC examiner agreed to a nine A.M. conference call. So if all goes well, we'll be cleared to trade shortly thereafter. There won't be much to see." *If all goes well.*

Riding the limo down to Wall Street, Dan and Nico are blowing off steam. This involves cracking a series of inside jokes with embedded references to road-show misadventures. D&N are like junior high girls at the water fountain, giggling over details only they find funny. Any reference to a credit card, for instance, causes them to burst out screaming with laughter; apparently Nico can't use his credit card because he maxxed out the credit limit. Why that's so hilarious I don't know. Another inside joke is whenever they say aloud the number "three," they hold up four fingers on one hand. For some reason, this slays them as if Robin Williams were giving a private performance in the backseat of the limo. I take all this to mean that they are fairly jangled and punchy. They are also getting their sense of humor real warmed up, in order to tolerate events today that are truly beyond their control, such as—by my wristwatch—when our limo turns off Park Street for FDR Drive, in Washington, D.C., a Department of Commerce official steps to a microphone and announces that the United States trade deficit reached an all-time record in June, higher even than the worst months of the eighties, and the bond market, always open for trading, takes a huge collective frightened "oh, shit" breath. The sucking sound is felt around the world, felt certainly by all the beautiful grade-AAA eggs who work at Goldman Sachs as they skip out of the subway stations and dance off the buses and leap from taxis on this grand Friday summer morning at the tip of Manhattan. "Oh, shit," they say, as they take their seats on the fiftieth floor of 1 New York Plaza and glance at the Bloomberg.

"Oh, shit!" the whole market says, and it seems as if what everyone has been waiting for has finally happened, *that was it,* hope you enjoyed it while it lasted. It doesn't get any better than yesterday. Do they know that next week the Dow Industrial Average will set an all-time record weekly drop of 401 points? Do they know that on Tuesday, Federal Reserve deity Alan Greenspan will tell the congressional banking committee that "a correction is inevitable," and that on Wednesday he will add that congressional forecasts of a zero-inflationary economy understate likely inflation by as much as 2 whole percent? Do they know that if Actuate does *not* get its IPO into the market today— if it so much as waits until its *regularly scheduled programming* of next week—then all bets are off?

Meanwhile, in our limo, which is slaloming less-decisive cars on the FDR, Dan Gaudreau is holding up four fingers, chuckling, and says, "I'm glad it's over."

The car's phone rings. Nico picks it up. It's one of the bankers talking, to whom Nico makes the following responses:

"What do you mean we're not making any progress? [*Pause to listen*] What about the nine A.M. conference call he agreed to? [*Pause to listen*] I thought he agreed to a nine A.M. conference call? Yes, I thought he agreed to it. [*Pause to listen*] Well, is the guy even there? Is he answering his phone? Is he even at work today?"

Oh, shit.

So began the game of misinformation, a form of psychological torture. In Washington, D.C., an Actuate attorney was sitting in the lobby of the SEC. In Palo Alto, California, there were any number of attorneys gathered at the conference room of R. R. Donnelley Financial. At Mellon Bank there was another attorney, ready at the window to give wire instructions for the registration filing fee. Then there were bankers in San Francisco, in Manhattan, in D.C., and in Dallas. Connected by a series of conference calls that cut in and out, at any one time about half of these players were up to speed on the latest update—and the other half weren't. Any one of them might call Nico and give a report, so half the time that report was inaccurate, and there was no way for us to know which half was speaking. As we patched in to these calls intermittently, I began to attach the voices to the faces I'd met over the past six weeks, but very often nobody on our end could even tell who had just spoken, or whether they were in D.C., Dallas, or San Fran.

The phone rings again. Nico listens, hangs up. "Okay, the nine A.M. meeting is back on." He chuckles, nervously, collapsing into leather. "Who was it that said, 'No plan survives contact with the enemy'?"

The grade-AAA eggs at Goldman are radiant people, confident without being arrogant, good-looking in a rainbow-America way, and equally divided between men and women. It is casual Friday, so the suits have been traded in for a far more eclectic regalia than is seen in Silicon Valley—bell-bottom dungaree overalls, ribbed muscle-Ts, black leather boots with buckled ornaments, velvet skirts, aqua-tinted sunglasses. If the lights dimmed and a disco ball flashed from the ceiling, this crowd would hip-grind right on beat. It's good to see that the '90s have most definitely made it all the way up to the fiftieth floor of 1 New York Plaza.

The Goldman sales and trading floor is entirely without walls across its middle, an expanse broad enough for a professional hockey game, and this space is jammed with a couple hundred bivouacs of monitors and chairs and reports stacked chest-high. Nothing clearly distinguishes the equity capital markets syndicate from the institutional salesforce from the traders, though in the latter zone it is quieter before the market opens at 9:30, and afterward, a dozen decibels noisier. This hive of economic pitter-patter is ringed by glass-walled offices that don't block the views, north to Wall Street, south to the Statue of Liberty standing tall on Liberty Island. It is to one of these southern-vista offices we are escorted by a young goateed analyst from the San Francisco office, John Zdrodowski, who goes by the nickname "ZD." A childlike impulse takes over—we all press up against the floor-to-ceiling glass to check out Miss Liberty, but this morning she's shrouded in a white mist, not quite a fog but denser than just opaque haze. ZD, who does this escort bit four or five times a year, says, "We're lucky for this mist."

"What does the mist have to do with anything?"

"As soon as the mist burns off, all the investors on Wall Street start obsessing about getting on an early train to the Hamptons."

Nico finishes the thought—"So if we don't get out soon, there may not be any investors in town to buy our stock." This slays him, and he breaks into a fit of giggles.

ZD tips his head, lifts his eyebrows, the subtlest nod of confirmation.

We all turn back to the Upper Bay, just in time to see Miss Liberty's torch and crown emerge from the translucent curtains of weather.

Oh, shit.

"That conference call should be over by now," Nico says, worriedly.

THE SYNDICATE director at Goldman is a woman named Lawton Fitt. The ten-foot-long shelf along one side wall of her office is so loaded with prize tombstones that the shelf's braces have reinforced rivets securing them to the wall studs. She is a slender five feet five, with barley-colored short hair and a boxy jaw. On this morning she wears a short-sleeved blue silk sweater, navy slacks, and a medium-weight gold necklace. She exudes matter-of-fact competence. She's seen it all, but when the conditions are pressing she can still get animated, such as at 9:38 A.M., when she hustled into our office and excitably pointed to the Polycom starfish on the table—"George Lee calling from Dallas with *big news.*"

George Lee was in on the call, but the voice that spoke from the Polycom was that of Don Keller, one of the attorneys. His voice was tentative, like he knew what he had to say was going to make some people in the room *very, very* angry, and he didn't want the messenger to be blamed.

"The chief accountant at the SEC is still giving us a hard time. He's got two issues. The sticky one seems to be compensation charges for cheap stock. Specifically, the 200,000 options granted in April and May."

"But we already took additional compensation charges to meet his concerns just last night," argues Dan Gaudreau.

"That was for a price of 11," explains Keller. Goldman was preparing to sell Actuate's stock at 12.

If you didn't fully understand the references and implications of the above interchange, you were not alone. For the next sixty seconds, what erupted was a volley of random questions and rogue responses from the various parties in various places around the country, as everyone tried to get up to speed. People were pulling out calculators and trying to do the math and trying to keep straight yesterday's comp charges versus today's, and all the while the mist outside the window was looking more and more like haze.

Lawton Fitt glanced at her watch. "If we don't get out in the next half hour, it's probably too late. Then we're in to Monday."

The subtext of what was going on here was nothing less than a critical debate over how high-tech start-ups are geared to perform. High-tech firms award options with low strike prices to their employees in order to motivate them into all-out dedication. The greater the potential payoff, the fiercer the dedication. "Options are really a West Coast thing," said Dan Gaudreau, who spent eighteen years in management at General Electric. "On the East Coast, they don't consider options as having any real skin in the game. Only if employees really buy the stock does it count as skin." If options collapse in value, the employee doesn't lose anything, since the options were a gift. To paraphrase: the East Coasters prefer to see some Fear as well as Greed. But West Coasters know that having upside without downside is what stimulates entrepreneurs to take the wild risks on new ventures. Without options, there wouldn't be a Silicon Valley.

It's a fundamental accounting principle that when the strike price of these options is granted below fair market value, the difference is a form of monetary compensation, resulting in a compensation expense to the income statement.

Recently, the SEC has taken an aggressive stance in calculating "fair market value." The old way of doing it was to use the venture capitalists' last round as the benchmark for fair market value, and just slide up the scale a nudge from there. Now the SEC uses the IPO price as the benchmark, and slides down the scale a nudge. Firms used to grant options in the 60 cent range without hurting the income statement, but now it's more like the $6 to $10 range.

The agony is, the SEC has the benefit of hindsight. They can say, "Well, you're going public tomorrow at $18, so those options you granted four months ago were really worth at least $12." But when the firm granted the options, it never knew if it would be able to go public at all. At the time, it might have been perfectly justifiable to grant them at a low price. From the point of view of the average Silicon Valley CEO, the system seems to punish them for doing a good thing—giving employees a piece of the action up front.

Actuate had been taking appropriate charges for cheap stock all along. But the uptick from an offering price of 11 to 12 was seen by the SEC as necessitating another charge. This time there was a complication. The additional write-down requested by the

SEC was substantial enough that it would push analysts' estimates of Actuate's projected fourth quarter of 1998 from a slight profit to a slight loss. Though Actuate hadn't made any predictions publicly, the message that had been bounced down the Hall of Prisms from the stock analysts to the salesforce to the institutional investors was that Actuate would hit profitability in Q4 '98. If Nico Nierenberg took the additional loss as requested by the SEC, he also had a responsibility to get the message out through the Hall of Prisms that it would be Q1 '99, not Q4 '98, when the firm's ink turned black.

That would take a day. At least.

At this very point in time, 9:41 on Friday morning, the hundred or so big institutional investors that were expecting allocations of Actuate shares from the syndicate were expecting them *any second now,* and a delay of a day might start them second-guessing their commitment.

Nico didn't want to take a day. He'd been building up to this for five years, and he didn't want it to slip from his grasp. Just about anybody in this position would have taken a deep breath and remembered what they teach you in business school—think it through, check for flaws in the logic, make a list of pros and cons, run your decision past your board of directors, sleep on it. But Nico Nierenberg knew another five minutes might as well be Monday. His mind went down every path, and then I saw that *click* in his mind that I'd seen the day we met: he'd *decided to decide.* Everyone was still volleying scenarios around, and it took a while for his voice to drown the others' out.

"If the SEC will take 11, then we'll do it," Nico was saying.

"What?"

"If the SEC will take 11, then we'll do it!" Nico repeated.

This was the other option. Restore the offering price to 11 and the issue would go away. Nico instructed his attorneys to call the SEC and secure their authorization.

Actuate was offering 3 million shares. Dropping a buck a share cost them $3 million in capital reserves, or to put the trade-off in perspective, Nico judged that avoiding the risk of going public Monday was worth $3 million. Nico let out a long sighing harrumph. "Three million, gone, poof! Right there."

"I live by the motto 'you get stuff done,'" said Nico. "You get it done because you never know what's going to happen next.

The uncertainty is too great here." As we took a few minutes to decompress, Nico revealed a few other factors that had entered his wise mind. First, dropping from 12 to 11 was putting another buck per share in the Santa stocking of every employee who was buying shares through the ESOP. Second, institutional investors in on the allocation think in terms of average price, so if they got sixty thousand shares in the allocation, leaving an extra buck per share on the table for them would leave them that much more room in their budget to keep buying the stock as it rose from 15 to 16 to 17.

Still, it hurt. Decompression jokes bounced around the country, and the sound of Nico's horselaugh was heard in Palo Alto, Dallas, D.C.

Lawton Fitt returned and asked Nico how he manages to retain his sense of humor.

"I've seen a lot worse," Nico said.

"Worse than giving up three million?" asked Dan Gaudreau.

"You develop an instinct," said Nico.

Dan said, "It's not been a good couple of days."

Lawton gave the report on the market. "The traders are getting nervous. At least the weather's not too beautiful yet."

Dan Gaudreau's cell phone rang. It was Bill Garvey with urgent news. Then the line cut out. Nico's and Dan's digital PCS phones weren't working inside the office tower. Finally Dan was handed an analog phone and he got Bill back on the line.

"Okay, we've got it," he announced.

Another set of attorneys rang on the conference room line. "At a price of 11, the SEC has dropped the cheap stock issue. The SEC just says now they need to receive our filing fee, and we'll be deemed effective."

Filing fee? Confused glances shot around the room. Hadn't the filing fee already been paid? Was the money wire lost? No, it'd been paid, but someone along the way had paid it based on an offering price of $10. The extra buck's worth had to be tacked on.

Here began the bowing down to irrationality. Here began the utter frustration and hopelessness of having no control over one of the most important transactions in Actuate's history. The raising of $30 million was being held up by an incremental money wire amounting to two hundredths of a single basis point, or $1,017.75. And every step of this money wire became the next twist in a noir titillation. "Okay, the wire was sent!" barked a voice over the Polycom.

"So we're good, right?"

"No, it was sent, but the SEC hasn't *received* it yet."

Theoretically, in this era of high-tech networks, a money wire should take seconds. But time now has the consistency of thick mud. 10:05 A.M. Across the sales floor, we can see the head of President Clinton on the television, with the word "Live" overlaid on his image, but there's no sound so we don't know what he is saying. We're just hoping we haven't gone back to war with Iraq. 10:10. Lawton Fitt retires to her office to "keep my hand on everyone's head." The market hits that midmorning sugar low and starts making plans for lunch. 10:20. "It's not fun anymore," Nico says. Nico can't understand why someone at Goldman didn't have the leverage with the SEC to promise "we're good for the lousy wire." He didn't understand why the filing fee hadn't just been paid for a price of $20, and get the refund later. The agony of it is getting to him—he'd made the decision to forgo $3 million in cash in order to avoid waiting until Monday, and now it seemed like they'd get bumped until Monday anyway. He starts rehashing his decision, and concludes that it was probably a dangerous mistake earlier this week to think they could deal with the SEC's concerns by Friday. They never should have accelerated the offering. 10:25 A.M. "We're dead," says Nico. "Dead."

He takes a stroll. The long walk around the sales floor. His face hangs with gloom, he tries to give a pursed smile but it just shows hurt. He paces back and forth, his hands on his hips. His steps are ponderous, searching. He looks like he has been stretched like a Gumby. He is worried about Dan Gaudreau, who has just heard from his brother about his mother's condition, which hasn't improved. Have you accepted that you have no control over your fate, Nico Nierenberg? Have you accepted that being a public company means having a crack-addled manic tyrant as a business partner? Have you accepted, Nico Nierenberg, your utter puniness?

And Miss Liberty has just broken into the clear.

WHILE WE are waiting, Lawton Fitt tells Nico the story of the first public offering she ever managed. After the market had closed, the price was communicated to the investors for sale the next morning. Minutes later IBM announced its first quarterly loss ever. The next morning, trying to proceed with the offering "was like standing in the middle of the freeway just waiting for cars to hit you."

Lawton Fitt hangs in there. She still believes Actuate's offering can make it, but warns "every minute we wait, we're making a judgment that we're still okay."

It is not until 11:24 that the conference line crackles with hubbub.

"Okay, we're accepted," an attorney says.

"Accepted? Does that mean effective?"

"No, it means the SEC accepted the document."

False alarm? Maybe. Another attorney on the Polycom: "We're effective."

Lawton Fitt takes charge. "Effective as of what time?"

"As of right now."

"I show 11:24," she says. "We'll call it that." She wheels on her heel and grabs the receiver of her telephone and punches a button to address the entire syndicate over the squawk box. In offices all across the country, her voice rings out over the sales floor. "CAN I HAVE EVERYONE'S ATTENTION ON ACTUATE? BOSTON, ARE YOU THERE? CHICAGO? SAN FRANCISCO? HAVE I GOT HOUSTON? THANK YOU FOR YOUR PATIENCE. THREE MILLION SHARES TO GO AT ELEVEN DOLLARS A SHARE."

The Goldman syndicate machine, suspended in a state of readiness for the last two hours, does its work.

The rush that Nico gets from hearing Lawton Fitt make her announcement of going effective blows his mind. "What a rush," he says. "Like a drug. But at three million a pop, the most expensive drug in the world."

Nico then says, "Now the whole world's watching us." A moment later he adds, "I just went from being the poorest guy in Hillsborough to the bottom tenth." He cracks a laugh.

We have at least another hour to kill before trading in Actuate stock will open. During that time, we learn that Broadcast.com—a pure Internet play from Dallas—has also just gone public at an offering price of $18, but the retail demand is so great that trading will probably open at $35.

"I should have named the company Actuate.com," Nico jokes.

A half hour later we learn that every Joe Q Cyber Trader who was watching CNBC last night learned about Broadcast.com's offering today, and they've camped out hoping to get some shares. The stock opens at a whopping $72 and sets a record for the greatest first-day percentage gain of any sizable offering this decade. Nico Nierenberg is not the talk of the street today. Tomorrow morning he will wake up in his bed $28 million richer, but everyone will be talking about the two founders from Dallas, one worth six Nicos, the other ten.

I ask Nico what that feels like.

"It's a psychological game that I just don't play," he says. "You just can't think about it. I think it's a test of adulthood—to have accepted that there is always going to be someone smarter than you, always someone who writes better software, always someone who manages better. Always someone richer. It's a fundamental thing that one has to get over, and certainly in the Valley not everyone has."

At 1:00, we stroll over to the trading desks to watch Actuate stock open. The trader, Bob Shea, discusses the supply and demand with Lawton Fitt. His screen shows buy orders at the price of 15, 15^1/$_2$, 16 in lot sizes of 10,000 to 20,000 shares. These are mostly from institutional investors who got some at the $11 offering and want to accumulate their position. On the other side of the screen are sell orders, willing to sell at any price. These are flippers. The flippers—many of whom just bought the stock from Goldman—sell through the back door in order to hide their identities. There are a few dealers who specialize in these orders.

"They're short-term investors," says Lawton Fitt. "Short-term is measured in seconds."

Most flippers hold off their sell orders until trading begins, hoping the price will be high. So Bob Shea has to look at the few actual sell orders and make an informed guesstimate on how many sellers are out there.

Before he officially fills any of the buy orders, some dealers trade Actuate between themselves at 15^7/$_8$. At 1:06 P.M., Shea opens the market at 15^1/$_2$ to 15^7/$_8$. He fills all the sell orders, but that volume only fills one third of the buys.

"My pulse just stopped," says Nico. At this point, always the entrepreneur, Nico's desire is to understand the mechanics of the business. He asks a dozen technical questions, getting answers from any trader who has a moment.

Bob Shea needs more stock to fill his buy orders. He yells out over the floor, "We're a big buyer of Actuate at 15$^7/_8$."

At 1:11 P.M., the stock symbol ACTU rolls across the NASDAQ ticker, which records trades in large lot sizes, 10,000 shares and up. "ACTU 15$^7/_8$ 200s," 20,000 shares. A moment later the ticker is dominated by ACTU trades, interspersed with trades for Sun, 3Com, Dell, and Microsoft.

"There's usually more turnover," says Lawton Fitt, which means that not as many investors are flipping as had been expected. "It's terrific. Very stable." The stock shows a little pop. It will close the day at 18$^3/_4$.

"I have to go back to real life after this," Nico says.

"It's a good book," Bob Shea says.

Nico says, "Oh, man, what do I do now?"

"You go back to work," Dan Gaudreau jokes.

"This is great," Nico says. He sighs happily, checks his watch. It's taken him eighteen years to be an overnight success, and we've got a plane to catch in an hour. "Okay, we're done."

THE DAY YOU go public, it's sort of like a birthday. It's your special day, but you wake up and you still look like you and talk like you and act like you, and if people don't know it's your birthday they can't tell. Your day isn't really any different from any other day, but *you* know it's special, and you feel special, and for most of the day it *is* special, even though absolutely nothing has really changed except your liquid net worth is close to $28 million.

Nico Nierenberg didn't change anything else. On Saturday he drove his two kids to the Oakland A's game—and took advantage of a special deal, three tickets for $15. That night he went to his wife's grandmother's ninetieth birthday party.

On Monday, he watched his stock trade to 22, double the offering, before some institutions took a profit and pushed it back down. Of the IPO on Friday, he said, "I think the metaphor is childbirth. It was painful as hell but when it's over you say, 'Ahh, that wasn't too bad.' "

A Note on the Process

On the evening before the 31,000 red herrings were to be printed, I went over to the offices of R. R. Donnelley Financial on California Avenue in Palo Alto. I'd heard that the attorneys for Actuate would likely be up until 3 A.M. fighting with the attorneys for Goldman Sachs and the attorneys for Ernst & Young, revising the language of the prospectus before it was wired off to Donnelley's presses. This was the customary boil-down session, when every loose end has to get tied up and the prospectus has to be deemed "jury proof." The problem is, getting eight attorneys to agree on language is sort of like getting eight children to agree on pizza toppings—no matter what topping is suggested, mushrooms/pepperoni/pineapple, there's always at least one kid who goes "yuck!" and vetoes it.

I got there at 5:30, just in time to see this scene acted out. One of the Donnelley assistants popped her head into the conference room to ask the half dozen attorneys whether they wanted her to order Thai, Indian, or sushi.

"Hey, what do you feel like, guys?" said Jeff Higgins, Actuate's counsel at Brobeck, Phleger & Harrison.

There were some mumblings and checking of watches.

"Well, I'm really just about all done here," said Goldman's counsel.

"Yup, I was hoping to get a run in before the sun goes down," said another Brobeck attorney.

"I just told my wife I'd pick something up on the way home."

"I've got a volleyball game."

And so it went around the room. Nobody had any intention of putting in mere face time this evening.

I had to ask. "Aren't there any last-minute changes you guys are going to fight over?"

A laugh went around.

Apparently, Actuate wasn't that kind of IPO. Actuate was so clean Howard Hughes could have eaten off the prospectus. There weren't any last-minute changes. Jeff Higgins said, "At our very first meeting, Bill Garvey showed up with an entire draft of the book [prospectus]. We didn't even have to write it." Garvey used to work at Brobeck, where he managed several IPOs. He knew the drill.

Going public used to be like shifting from first gear to third, but the process is far more Business as Usual these days. Enough firms have gone public that it's easy to learn from others' mistakes. You still have to shift gears, but it's more like power shifting— you can jump gears without even using the clutch.

Actuate had done its homework, and the company had denied Goldman's due-diligence team the chance to look really smart with common recommendations. Actuate was already in full compliance with FASB SOP 97-2, recognizing revenues rateably, over the life of the sales contracts. Actuate had already taken a compensation charge for cheap stock issues, related to options awarded to employees with strike prices below fair market value. The company didn't need to reverse split its stock. The employees had already been briefed about Quiet Period regulations and the prohibition against gun-jumping. They'd already signed their six-month lock-up agreements.

From Actuate's point of view, going public was just the natural, next step in a normal course of a growing company. So much did they try to downplay the event (and avoid euphoria) that they encouraged everyone to take their regular summer vacations, so at key times in the last six weeks Al Campa was in France at the World Cup, Nico Nierenberg was at Disneyland with his kids, and Bill Garvey was in San Diego resting his legs post-marathon.

For me, more than any other sign of how smooth the IPO transaction has become is the culture clash that *didn't happen* between high tech and high finance. It used to be that these scruffy-bearded, sandal-wearing engineers would ride in their VW vans up to San Francisco, where they would take the elevator up into the world of summer-worsted pinstripes and gel-slicked hair.

Now the engineers follow the stock market closely, and half of them hold puts and calls on tech indexes. Every third sentence out of an engineer's mouth these days uses the phrase "value proposition." The investment bankers rarely wear anything fancier than polo shirts over khakis, and they can talk for hours about developing object-oriented software on the Solaris 2.4 platform versus Windows NT 3.51. The subcultures are gone.

I walk into a conference room and I cannot tell which are the bankers, which are the lawyers, and which are the entrepreneurs. High tech and high finance haven't met halfway, it's more that they've both gone all the way. It's not a culture clash, it's a culture mash.

CHAPTER 3

THE Entrepreneur

FROM THE MOMENT I met him, Sabeer Bhatia has given credit to the power of the idea. The idea was so powerful that when his friend and coworker Jack Smith, who was driving home to Livermore across the Dunbarton Bridge, called Sabeer on his car phone to brainstorm the pregnant thought that had just occurred to him, Sabeer heard one sentence of it and said, "Oh, my! Hang up that cellular and call me back on a secure line when you get to your house! We don't want anyone to overhear!"

It was so powerful an idea that when Jack did call Sabeer back fifteen minutes later, their minds melded as they talked, completely in sync, leaping from one ramification to the next as simultaneously as the steps of two soldiers marching side by side. It was so powerful that sleep that night was impossible for Sabeer, with the idea now in his head, exploding, autocatalytic, a bonfire of the mind. He stayed up all night, sitting at the glass-topped dining table in his small Bayside Village apartment, writing the business plan, which he took to his day job the next morning, looking so haggard that his boss stopped

him and said, "You've got to cut out the partying, Sabeer."
Sabeer—afraid the idea might pop out of his mouth if he opened
it at all—just nodded. He was afraid even to make a single photocopy of the plan he had printed out, lest a stray page find its way
into the recycling bin and then under someone else's gaze.

The idea came about this way: Sabeer and Jack had wanted to
start a company, and they had been brainstorming possible business ideas for a few months. They wanted to e-mail each other
notes, but they had been afraid that their bosses might glean
their e-mail and accuse them of spending their working hours
on personal projects (an accurate accusation). The budding entrepreneurs had personal America Online accounts, but these
couldn't be accessed through the office network. On the evening
he was driving home across the Dunbarton Bridge, Jack Smith
had been frustrated all day by this problem. Then it occurred to
him:

Free e-mail accounts that can be accessed anonymously, over
the Web.

In getting over their own obstacle to coming up with a business idea, they came up with just that idea.

It was an idea that had been lurking under the nose of every
budding entrepreneur in the world. Any disgruntled employee
who had ever worried about an employer reading his e-mail
could have had the idea before Jack and Sabeer. *Anyone* could
have had the idea. *You* could have had the idea. *I* could have had
the idea.

It was the kind of idea that inspires legions of entrepreneurs.
It was the kind of idea that spurs thousands of young people
to give up their lives elsewhere and crash the Valley party. It
sent the message and cc'd the entire world: to make it in Silicon
Valley, you just have to come up with the right idea. You don't
have to know the right people. You don't have to demonstrate
experience. Most importantly, in this new era of the Internet, to
come up with a good idea you don't have to be an *über*-geek who
understands fiber-optic switching and site mirroring and massively parallel processing. It was as if a great wave had broken. For
two decades, the science of technology had grown exponentially
more sophisticated, and the cutting edge of technology was being shaped by those with Ph.D.s from MIT and a dozen patents
to their name, the kind of deep brainiacs who scare the me-

dia elite into thinking that the future will be dominated by Birkenstock-wearing coders with poor sartorial taste. High tech was becoming harder to understand for the casual observer; it was all about 32-bit versus 64-bit chipsets and low-earth-orbit satellite routing and 3-D vector-based graphics. The East Coast establishment was getting very uneasy, in the mid-1990s, as they woke up in the morning to the fear that having a law degree from Yale or an MBA from Wharton was no longer a guarantee that their status in life was secure.

What Sabeer did, as had been done by Jerry Yang and David Filo of Yahoo! or Jeff Bezos at Amazon, was to return the cutting edge of ideas to the reasonably intelligent, superachieving everyman. What was Yahoo! to start, but a yellow pages? What was Amazon, but a bookstore?

You don't have to be a genius.

You don't have to be superhuman.

You don't even have to be a techie.

Just have an idea.

And the best ideas are right under your nose.

Nowadays, meet Sabeer at a party and ask what he does, and he will tell you only that he works in high tech, just like hundreds of thousands of other young people in the Valley. Sabeer is just twenty-nine years old, and he has a very regal air; he is a deep listener, a gentle giant. He wears chambray shirts over a stocky frame and metal-rimmed eyeglasses. Push him for more detail about his job, and he'll say he works at Hotmail. Ask if he's an engineer and he'll say no, he's the president. He's not being reclusive or coy, it just hasn't sunk in that he might be special.

What is Hotmail but e-mail on the Web?

In just under two and a half years, Sabeer has built Hotmail's user base faster than any media company's in history—faster than CNN's, faster than America Online's, faster even than the audience grew for *Seinfeld*. Truly mind-boggling. By the summer of 1998, with 25 million active e-mail accounts, the company was signing up new users at a rate of 125,000 *a day*. Most Internet companies experience a summer slowdown as the country spends more time outdoors and less time on-line, but in June and July of that summer Hotmail's sign-up rate *increased*.

One night I met Sabeer for a glass of sweet Indian rum at his apartment in Bayside Village, South of Market. Bayside Village is a five-story, three-dimensional crossword puzzle of boxy apartments. His humble apartment has a bachelor pad decor with unadorned white-Spackled walls, a framed print leaned up against the living room wall, a rug rolled up off to the side. His living room has a 180-degree panoramic view of other apartment units, but if you stand in one particular place and stretch your neck, you can get an actual view of the shallow end of the communal pool. It's the same apartment he had the night he wrote the Hotmail business plan. It's definitely not the place I expected from a man who's worth a couple hundred million dollars.

Sabeer believes in the philosophy of Hinduism, which he describes as a belief system different from any other—yet one that, I observed, distinctly parallels entrepreneurial philosophy. "With Hinduism, there is nothing to recite, no rituals to practice. There is no church, no temple. Hinduism is just a way of life. You define for yourself how to live your life. Aided and abetted by your conscience, you define for yourself what are the rules. And if you follow those rules, you are a Hindu." The rules Sabeer has defined for himself are to be kind to fellow humans, to respect their individuality, and to have the discipline to do everything in moderation.

Still, though, why hasn't he bought a house—even a moderate one? Is it that he hasn't had time to look? No, he's looked plenty. "They're just all so overpriced," he remarks. "I think I'll save a little money if I wait until they come down."

Beside the couch is a stack of industry trade magazines. At night he sits here, reading these magazines, trying to digest the chaotic splendor of the Internet. That's his pipeline of strategic info; he doesn't hire spies or pay for special insider research. Just magazines, the same ones you can buy. Available on any newsstand.

The big story of Silicon Valley is continuously being told and retold, skewed this way and that. It's the story of rags-to-riches success, and Sabeer Bhatia's story is one of its prime examples. The variable that differs is whether the success is due to the individual or the environment—to personal greatness or circumstance. The story that gets told most often—ten thousand times a day, this story gets retold—is the story of Bill Gates. For every time it is told as the story of an ordinary smart guy who could never have accomplished very much without the advantage of an operating system monopoly, it is retold as one of an amazing genius for strategy who has outwitted his competitors' every end run.

I hear it all the time about Sabeer—with any Silicon Valley success, there's an analytical community constantly debating the verdict of history, a chattering class fuming with jealousy. It's the Valley's restatement of the nature-versus-nurture question. One side argues, "Hey, if the big thing he did is just get first-mover advantage on an idea that anyone could have, then he's just a right-place/right-time lucky Joe." The other side argues, "Hey, any big company could have copied his idea and spent millions on advertising and walloped him, but he made all the right moves to avoid that fate, and that takes great talent. It must be something innate."

So is he great or is he lucky?

JUST OVER ten years ago, on September 23, 1988, Sabeer Bhatia arrived at Los Angeles International Airport at 6:00 in the evening. His flights from Bangalore, India, had taken twenty-two hours, and he was starving. Cal Tech, which had offered him a very rare transfer scholarship, had sent him directions that said merely, "Take a shuttle to campus," but Sabeer didn't know what a "shuttle" was. He was nineteen. In his pocket he had $250, the limit Indian customs allowed a student to take out of the country. He didn't know a single person in all of America. He had won the transfer scholarship to Cal Tech by being the only applicant in the entire world (there are usually about 150 who give it a try) in 1988 to get a passing score on the notorious Cal Tech Transfer Exam, a test full of brain stumpers so challenging that the Cal Tech undergraduate admissions officer told me, "Even most students with a math SAT score of eight hundred will do abysmally." Sabeer had scored a 62. Out of 100. The next highest score was a 42.

Sabeer intended to get his degrees and then to go home to work, probably as an engineer for some very large Indian company. He was following the modest path of life as set by his parents. His mom was an accountant at the Central Bank of India for her entire career, and his father spent ten years as a captain in the Indian Army, then became a manager in several public sector hierarchies. That was what life offered him. India is a very bureaucratic country, so kids like Sabeer grow up presuming that starting a company is impossible unless you are a superhuman.

But as a graduate student at Stanford, when most of his classmates would toss a Frisbee during lunch on nearby Roble Field, Sabeer was drawn to the basement of Terman Auditorium. There were being held brown-bag luncheons, and the speakers were entrepreneurs like Scott McNealy, Steve Wozniak, and Marc Andreessen. Their fundamental message was always the same: *You can do it too.* Sabeer knew that famous people always say such things. They want to be inspirational. But Sabeer's impression of these successful entrepreneurs was that they really were fairly ordinary smart guys, no different from him and his classmates. Sabeer was catching the bug.

When he graduated, Sabeer did not want to go home. So, along with Jack Smith, he took a job at Apple Computer. His parents were pleased—at such a big and important company, Sabeer could work for twenty or thirty years. But Sabeer had started attending cocktail parties of TIE, The IndUS Entrepreneurs, where he met many other older men who had come from India and succeeded here. And again, they seemed like such ordinary guys! Sabeer got swept up in the decade's fever: you haven't lived until you've gone solo. Every morning Sabeer would come in to work at Apple, stop by Jack Smith's cubicle, and tell him yet another story of some guy who'd sold his company for millions. "Jack! What are we doing here, wasting our lives?" But Jack was a shy person and had a wife and two kids to think about. Starting their own business was daunting; they were just two cubicle dwellers buried in the Apple bureaucracy, what did they know about running a business? They were not even managers. Finally, though, Sabeer wore him down: "Jack, given the enormous opportunities here, if we can't make it here, then we are complete failures."

At an IndUS Entrepreneurs dinner, Sabeer sat down one night beside a man named Farouk Arjani. Arjani had been a pioneer in the word processing business in the 1970s, and had since become a special limited partner of Sequoia Ventures. The two hit it off extremely well, and Arjani became Sabeer's mentor. Arjani says, "At first I was amused by him. What really set Sabeer apart from the hundreds of entrepreneurs I've met is the gargantuan size of his dream. Even before he had a product, before he had any money behind him, he had become completely convinced that he was going to build a major company that would be worth hundreds of millions of dollars. He had an unrelenting conviction that he was not just going to build a run-of-the-mill Silicon Valley company. But over time I realized, by golly, he was probably going to pull it off."

In mid-1995, Sabeer began shopping around a two-page executive summary business plan for a Net-based personal database called JavaSoft. The venture capitalists were skeptical of the software market, though—too hard to get good distribution and rise above the fray. When Jack and Sabeer came up with the Hotmail idea in December, JavaSoft became, in effect, the front for Hotmail. Sabeer knew that Hotmail was such an explosive concept, he didn't want a less-than-ethical venture capitalist to reject him, then turn around and copy his idea. He kept showing Java-Soft and showed Hotmail only to those VCs he had gained respect for. "It was fine that they were rejecting JavaSoft. But in so doing, I got to see how their mind worked. If they rejected Java-Soft for stupid reasons, then I said thank you and left. If they rejected it for the right reasons, then I showed them Hotmail."

"It's almost embarrassing to admit," says Jack Smith. "We hoped we'd make a little money on the JavaSoft product while we evolved this new thing."

At Sabeer's first presentation to Steve Jurvetson of Draper Fisher Jurvetson, things weren't going well—Jurvetson was having the same problems with the database idea every other VC was. But he was rejecting it for the right reasons. So, late in the hour, Sabeer played the Hotmail card. He mentioned it ever so subtly, characterizing it as a marketing tool. ("Everyone who used Hotmail would wonder how we built it and come buy our JavaSoft tools," he said.) Jurvey wasn't fooled—he saw the pot of gold.

It's fair to say that many investors found Sabeer's headstrong determination as arrogance. Jurvetson remembers, "Sabeer brought in these revenue estimates showing that he was going to grow the company faster than any in history. Sure, most entrepreneurs have that trait, but they also are concerned with looking like the fool. We dismissed Sabeer's projections outright, but he insisted, 'You don't believe we're going to do that?' He had hallucinogenic optimism. He had an unquenchable sense of destiny. But he was right. He grew the subscriber base faster than any company in the history of the world."

One might have presumed that since Sabeer had been rejected by twenty previous VCs and was virtually a nobody, he would be grateful to accept Draper, Fisher, Jurvetson's $300,000 on their terms. "He's the most interesting negotiator I've ever met," Jurvetson says. Tim Draper made the perfectly reasonable offer of retaining 30 percent ownership on a $1 million valuation. Sabeer held out for double that valuation—their cut, 15 percent. Their negotiations got nowhere, so Sabeer shrugged, stood up, and walked out the door. His only other available option was a $100,000 "friends and family" round that Jack Smith had arranged as a backup—not nearly enough money. "If we'd gone that route, Hotmail wouldn't exist today," says Jack. "I still sometimes can't believe he had the guts to walk out of that room."

Draper and Jurvetson relented; they called back the next day to accept their 15 percent.

It took an off-the-charts degree of confidence to do what Sabeer did: first, to hide his real idea, and second, to hold out for the valuation he thought the company deserved. Both are extremely rare. But Sabeer refuses to give the credit to anything other than the culture of the Valley itself: "Only in Silicon Valley could two twenty-seven-year-old guys get three hundred thousand dollars from men they had just met. Two twenty-seven-year-old guys who had no experience with consumer products, who had never started a company, who had never managed anybody, who had no experience even in software—Jack and I were hardware engineers. All we had was the idea. We didn't demo proof-of-concept software or a prototype or even a graphic printed on a piece of paper. I just sketched on Steve Jurvetson's whiteboard. Nowhere in the world could this happen but here."

Sure, but don't famous people always say such things?

THIS IS HOW the entrepreneur mind-set works: Did being turned down by twenty different venture capital firms undermine Sabeer and Jack's confidence? Nope. It just made them burn, it just made them work even harder to prove everyone else wrong. The very impossibility of what they were doing created its own motivation.

In order to keep the idea under wraps, Sabeer and Jack put the JavaSoft name on the front door of their first tiny office in Fremont, California. From February to July 1996, every morning Jack would come to work, log on to the Internet, and search around to see if someone had beat them to it. It always astounded him that he didn't find competition. He was sure Hotmail was too good an idea for them to be the only ones working on it.

The $300,000 was intended for the proof-of-concept version, usually a software system that works on a small scale only and without all the bells and whistles. But Sabeer was so adamant about not giving up more of the company than he had to that he stretched $300,000 farther than it had ever been stretched. Still obsessive about secrecy, they needed a paper-shredding machine, so Sabeer bought the cheapest one he could possibly find, for fifteen dollars. Without any collateral to offer, Sabeer convinced Imperial Bank to loan him $100,000 unsecured. Then he convinced McLean Public Relations to represent Hotmail in exchange for stock, even though he didn't have a product and he was insistent that they couldn't get started on the PR because he had to keep it secret. Montrese Etienne of McLean remembers, "In casual conversation he was always so nice and friendly, and then we sat down to negotiate on the stock, and this riveting fierce aura swept over him, it was almost scary. He became tremendously passionate, almost like another person."

In June, Sabeer was running out of money, but the product would be ready to launch in a month. This is exactly how venture capitalists love to play it—they love to get an entrepreneur into a desperate situation, so they can exact greater ownership for their next round of financing. Sabeer had been in contact with Doug Carlisle at Menlo Ventures, and Carlisle had expressed interest. Sabeer called Farouk Arjani, who told him only to do what he believed. This conversation reenergized Sabeer, though Arjani would later say that he had worried for Sabeer and felt bad for him, and admitted that if he'd been in Sabeer's shoes he never could have cut it so close. "The moment was prophetic of Sabeer's confidence," Arjani said. Sabeer knew that if he launched the service first, he would keep all the leverage over investors. Sabeer convinced all of his first fifteen employees to work only for stock options, not a very common occurrence in a place where the unemployment rate is nil and most jobs come with both pay *and* stock.

"My greatest accomplishment," Sabeer says again and again, "was not to build the company but to convince people that this is their company. I showed people how this would ultimately benefit themselves. My role is as an enabler. No individual made this happen. I didn't do the work. We initiated the avalanche."

They launched on July 4, 1996—Independence Day. It was a fitting date, because Sabeer and Jack believed that free e-mail was a great populist tool. By then, everyone who owned a computer had e-mail, but with Web mail you no longer even had to own a computer—you could log on from a McDonald's in Czechoslovakia or a café in Taiwan. That morning, Sabeer and Jack wore hip beepers, which they had programmed to flash every hour with the number of new subscribers. The first users found Hotmail all by themselves, but those who found it told their friends: a hundred in the first hour; 200 in the next hour; 250 in the third. The idea was so intuitively powerful that 80 percent of those who sign up for Hotmail say that they learned about it from a friend. It introduced the concept of "viral marketing," in which each e-mail message sent from a Hotmail account was, in effect, an advertisement for the service to its recipient. The service did not need the marketing budget that had originally been anticipated. Sabeer spent a few thousand dollars on some advertisements in college newspapers but then never spent another advertising dollar for the next two years.

By the time Sabeer went back to Doug Carlisle at Menlo Ventures to say in effect *okay, now I need your money,* Hotmail had 100,000 subscribers. His ploy of walking out of the room on Steve Jurvetson had increased the company's valuation by a million dollars, from one million to two. This ploy of stretching the money an extra two months increased the valuation by *$18 million.* So is he really so lucky? "Sabeer may come from a rather ordinary background," says Carlisle, "but he is a very extraordinary individual."

Hotmail began to deliver news and other content right into the e-mail boxes of its subscribers. This was nothing new, but the way the money flowed was. The content sites took the position "Hey, if you want our news for free, then you'd better pay us."

Sabeer refused and wanted it the other way around. He figured that a site's appearing on Hotmail was, in effect, a great teaser advertisement. His users would read the bulletin and go visit that site. He wanted the sites not only to give him free content but to pay Hotmail for the privilege of having it run. Sabeer instructed his director of business development, Scott Weiss, to make sure money flowed into Hotmail, not out of it.

"He would present partnership deals to the board of directors," says Steve Jurvetson, "and we would be amazed. 'How did you possibly get the partner to agree to these terms?' we would ask." The answer was always the same: partners had bought into his vision. He convinced them.

And again, Sabeer was right. Hotmail was growing so fast that some content providers couldn't handle the traffic that came in from Hotmail.

Sabeer was not a micromanager. He gave his people all the opportunities they could handle. "You can tell a lot about an entrepreneur by the quality of people he attracts to work with him," says Doug Carlisle. "If he is attracting strong, smart people, that's a good sign of true leadership quality."

What Sabeer did was get everyone in the company totally focused: telling the same story, harmonizing. That's the essence of what a leader in this business does. It may not sound particularly showstopping, but if you've ever been in a company where the engineers refuse to sign on to delivery dates because they fear they're being set up to fail by the marketing department, which doesn't want to take its share of the blame if the product is late—when harmony breaks down into cacophony, all minds grind to a halt. Nobody's productive. Mental energy is diverted to infighting. Getting everyone harmonized can make all the difference.

Sabeer also spent a great deal of time networking with people. When Sabeer and Jack started approaching VCs, one of their problems was that nobody could vouch for them. There wasn't that "friend of a friend" referral that puts moneybags at ease. If it's true that in the Valley you need Rolodex Power to pull strings and cut deals fast, how do we reconcile that with Sabeer's notion that any twenty-seven-year-old kid with a good idea can make it big here?

The answer is, any kid with a good idea can make it big—as

long as he networks like crazy. The only kinds of people the network discriminates against are those who turn their noses up at networking. So it's a meritocracy but a perverted one, based more on the merit of how well you knock on doors than the merit of your Java code. "Every morning Sabeer would come to work," says Jack Smith, "straight from a breakfast meeting. Then lunch with someone else, and after work put on a suit to have dinner with a third person. He likes that kind of thing. He's good at it."

Every morning, Jack Smith still scoured the Internet for signs of competition, and it continually amazed him that there was none. It was six months before the first tiny competition appeared, a one-man company out there in cyberspace. It was almost a full year before Four11's Rocketmail was launched.

In December 1997, Sabeer and Scott Weiss went to Ming's restaurant to watch a presentation by Jerry Yang, the cofounder of Yahoo!. Yang talked mostly about what has come to be called, in Internet strategy, "first-mover advantage," referring to the priceless benefits of being the center of attention for a while. Yang said that Yahoo! had had a three-month jump out of the gate before he had seen his first competitor, and it was that lead that was responsible for Yahoo! being the number one Internet search directory to this day. Sabeer was listening, and his eyes got really big as it dawned on him what that meant.

He'd always been concerned that Hotmail could be copied. He still had only twenty-five employees, a tiny operation. When they were shopping Hotmail to VCs, the objection Sabeer kept getting was "What's to keep Microsoft from copying the concept and eating you for lunch?" And as they were engineering the system, friends shook their heads and smirked for the same reason: "Like riding a tricycle in the headlights of an eighteen-wheeler." After Sabeer and Jack launched Hotmail on July 4, 1996, industry handicappers predicted, "Another bug about to be squashed on the Microsoft windshield." The gossip rose to a level of outright scorn for Sabeer's foolishness.

Listening to Jerry Yang, Sabeer gained confidence. He leaned over to Scott Weiss and said, "We have a six-month lead in our market. We're going to cream these guys."

"By the time Microsoft figured it out," Sabeer says, "we had six million users."

* * *

WHEN MICROSOFT CAME bidding in the fall of 1997, it came as a small army. Six at a time, they flew down from Redmond and sat in Hotmail's small conference room across the table from Sabeer. They offered a figure that would have put tens of millions of dollars into Sabeer's pocket. Sabeer rejected it, and they stormed out. A week later they were back, and every week thereafter for two months. At that point, it's easy to see it all as funny money—when you've got a week to think about it, it's hard to really see the difference between $50 million and $60 million. Are you really going to risk losing the deal for another $10 million?

They asked Sabeer to fly up to Redmond. He took Jack Smith and another manager, Steve Dowdy. They were escorted around campus, had lunch with a senior vice president, were shown the building devoted to e-mail and the building devoted to the NT operating system. Their meeting with Bill Gates was scheduled for 2 P.M. in a building that is mazelike, notorious for causing visitors to get lost. Sabeer got lost. He arrived just in time. Gates had just gotten back from Russia and was wearing a brown sweater and very-thin-soled Italian shoes. Gates also had with him two senior managers. They all shook hands. There were no ten minutes of get-relaxed time chatting about the flight, the lunch—one of the managers, Laura Jennings, just dropped the ball right on Sabeer. She said, "Sabeer, why don't you tell us about your company?" Sabeer wasn't quite prepared. He began nervously. He couldn't believe it, here he was talking to Bill Gates.

After about fifteen minutes, Gates began to ask questions. Gates is legendary for his Socratic method of picking on the weaknesses of business ideas. "But his questions were very normal strategy questions," Sabeer says, "the same things I had been asked by investors all along, from day one. And it suddenly occurred to me that Bill Gates is not superhuman either. He's human. He's flesh and blood, same as me. He's very smart, yes. But not superhumanly so."

With this understanding, Sabeer became very relaxed. He was completely reoriented, and the meeting lasted until 3:30.

Two stories floated around Hotmail as the talks went on. The first story had run in *The Wall Street Journal,* reporting that in the early days of America Online, Steve Case had spurned an offer from Bill Gates to buy the company. Case had gone on to grow AOL into a company with a multi-billion-dollar valuation. This story was photocopied and passed around. It inspired Sabeer. It reminded Jack Smith that Hotmail would be fine even if the deal with Microsoft never came to fruition.

The second story floating around was of what had happened to Pointcast, the push technology innovator, since it had rejected News Corporation's $400 million acquisition offer. Push technology had its fifteen minutes of fame, and then Pointcast fell back into the cacophony. Pointcast was struggling, its plans for an IPO put on hold.

Sabeer took a straw poll among his investors to see what price they might be able to anticipate. Doug Carlisle's figure, $200 million, was the lowest. Privately, Sabeer had half jokingly been saying he wanted a billion dollars, so he challenged Carlisle's figure: "You don't think we can get more than that?" Carlisle laughed, rolled his eyes, and said, "Sabeer, if you ever reach even my figure, then I'm going to build a life-sized bronze sculpture of you and put it in my front lobby."

Sabeer went back to Microsoft with the price of half a billion. "You're crazy!" his adversaries shouted, following it with expletives. "You're out of your mind! You've blown it!" But Sabeer knew those were only tactical outbursts.

As a kid in Bangalore, Sabeer had watched family servants haggling over groceries at the bazaar. He knew every trick. At the bazaar, the vendors would counter a low offer by saying, "Oh, I'm sorry, is that all you can pay? You must be very poor. I feel sorry for you. I want to give you a few rupees out of my own pocket so you have enough money to pay." Tensions were rising as Microsoft piled cash on the table. $200 million. $250 million. Carlisle took to saying, "It's Statue Time!" $300 million. This negotiating squad seemed to have a lot of "deep knowledge" about Rocketmail, Hotmail's competitor, and it was possible that Microsoft was negotiating to buy Rocketmail as an alternative. Or maybe it just wanted to scare Sabeer, to make him think it had another option. Sabeer, who had the go-ahead from his board and management team to negotiate the deal himself, stood firm: no sale. Several times, Microsoft's negotiator pounded the table and stormed out. Although the negotiations were secret, Hotmail's employees twice pressured Sabeer to accept Microsoft's most recent offer and guarantee their security. Sabeer's venture capitalists, who stood to realize gigantic returns on their investments, urged him to be careful.

Negotiating alone allowed Sabeer to present a unified front; it prevented Microsoft from taking Jack Smith to dinner and saying, "Jack, you've got a wife and two kids—c'mon, they'll be set for life." But Sabeer wasn't psychologically alone; his backers and colleagues kept the faith. VC Steve Jurvetson joked with Sabeer, "You don't have to sell now. Why don't you wait until you're big enough to buy Microsoft, rather than them buying you?" All the while, Hotmail kept signing up subscribers. Its lead over its imitators was increasing.

Sabeer would barely budge from his internal sense of what Hotmail was worth. When the negotiation team offered a figure of around $350 million, though, Hotmail's management team took a straw poll in favor of accepting, and then Sabeer was really alone. He cannot give the credit for this one to his talented employees or to Silicon Valley's culture.

"Saying no to that offer was the scariest thing I ever did," Sabeer says. "Everybody had told me, 'This is on your head if you screw it up.'"

On New Year's Eve 1997, a deal was announced. Sabeer is forbidden to state the price, but the S3 registration papers filed a month later stated that ownership of Hotmail had been exchanged for 2,769,148 shares of Microsoft. At the time of the deal, those shares were worth a walloping $400 million. Throughout the Valley, the gut reaction was shock: no way was the company worth so much—$400 million—for *e-mail*? The figure seemed out of proportion, and on its face undeserved, no matter how smart Sabeer may have been, no matter how hard he and Smith had worked, no way was two years' worth of work worth $400 million. There was a sense that Microsoft had gone wacko. Who was this kid, Sabeer Bhatia, and how had he done it?

This "He didn't deserve it" hubbub was particularly loud in the somewhat insular community of Apple and ex-Apple employees, which is where I heard a lot of it. "We weren't doing any great things at Apple," says Jack Smith. "We bummed, we drank, we brought up factories. And that's how people there remember us. With our success we blew away everyone we knew. They still can't believe it. 'What's the deal here? What the hell happened?'"

Farouk Arjani turns that logic on its head: "Sabeer had never had an opportunity to raise money, never had the opportunity to run a company or even a division. But when all was said and done, he did an outstanding job. Certainly, nothing in his background prepared him for it, so it must be something innate in him."

There's no doubt that Sabeer's success has provoked furious jealousy. People here need to believe in a meritocracy, they need to believe success is possible for themselves, and so they will insist that Sabeer is no better than anyone else around town—ordinary, in fact—even though they've never met him and don't know his story. When the Valley gradually learns how Sabeer stood up to his venture capitalists and then stood up to Microsoft, the verdict of history will be kind.

The other unsolicited comment I used to hear all the time is that Hotmail is nothing special, engineering-wise. I believe this comment is similarly superficial. Sure, if you go to Hotmail on the Web, it doesn't appear particularly special. The service offers fewer features than the e-mail software that comes free with an Internet account. But in the Internet era, features are not the test. What Jack Smith had to engineer was a system that continued to *scale*, meaning not to crash as it grew in number of users. And it was growing faster than any other media company in history.

DOUG CARLISLE IS holding true to his word about the bronze statue; he has commissioned a bust by an artist in Los Angeles. It's such an odd thing. It seems to me out of character, celebratory of the individual rather than the company or the Internet or the Valley culture. But Carlisle commonly offers his entrepreneurs such gifts when they reach milestones—a Porsche Carrera, say, or "If you make that, I'm going to kiss your shoes."

If anyone deserves it, I guess Sabeer does. But doesn't it make him uncomfortable? No. "It is an honor. My hope is that, just as I was given inspiration at those brown-bag lunches in Terman Auditorium, when entrepreneurs come into this most prestigious address on Sand Hill Road, it will give them inspiration."

Sabeer has always told his investors that, be it venture capitalists or Microsoft, "If you can find someone better than me to run this company, I will happily step down." As much as Sabeer makes out that he is just ordinary flesh and blood, no one has ever questioned his leadership. He is one of the few Valley entrepreneurs to remain his company's top executive beyond the 100-plus employee level rather than being moved off to some nether position as research guru or poster-boy spokesperson.

As of this writing, Hotmail has 144 employees, and it is a subdivision of a Microsoft superdivision called Web Essentials. Hotmail will move from its low-slung, anonymous offices in Sunnyvale to a new Microsoft campus in Mountain View, where it will be joined by WebTV. Sabeer now reports to someone who reports to Bill G., and he flies to Redmond in the middle of most every week.

With Microsoft's financial muscle now behind the company, Hotmail's juggernaut appears unstoppable. In the summer of 1998, Sabeer Bhatia invited me to sit in on his Tuesday-afternoon strategy session with his senior managers. He doesn't interrupt, and he doesn't interrogate or flex his power in the meetings—if he wants to raise a contrary opinion, he will ask benevolently, "Does anyone question that the search box should be on every page?" He let the company unfold for me like a play, each manager playing his part. I learned about a new search engine and an e-commerce plan, instant messaging and a universal Web site sign-on system, which could potentially be leveraged on-line much as DOS and Windows are leveraged on the computer desktop. The room was aglow with the anticipatory thrill of riding this bullet train up the exponential revenue curve.

At breakfast one morning I asked Sabeer if he felt at all powerful, considering he runs the world's fastest-growing media company. "That is such an odd, foreign concept to me," he said slowly, trying to think in that old paradigm. "When you say 'power,' that conjures to me control, such as having people do what I want them to do. It is just absurd. It is the nature of this medium that if something is a success, it is wildly successful. If you can come up with something that is of great value for just two people, then it is very likely it will also be of value for ninety million people."

Only eight months after the New Year's Eve announcement, Microsoft's $400 million price tag looked to be a bargain, particularly considering that Hotmail's subscriber base had more than tripled in size since the company was purchased. Everyone's buying into the story now. Nobody thinks the price was unjust anymore. Sabeer's internal sense of what Hotmail was worth was absolutely right.

"We often wonder what would have been," says Jack Smith.

"In retrospect, I'm not sure that a billion dollars wasn't the right figure," says Steve Jurvetson.

Meanwhile, Sabeer Bhatia has a three-year commitment to Microsoft, but there is no doubt he relishes entrepreneurism more than management. His passion for the big risk, the gargantuan mission, is unmistakable.

ON THE lucky-or-great question, I believe that you don't get to $400 million without a lot of both, and I have every confidence that if he were not here, Sabeer would be leading people somewhere else. But he believes he's lucky to live in this place and time.

Sabeer knows he never could have accomplished this anywhere other than here—certainly not in India, where corruption and political risk undermine investors' confidence in new ventures. "In America, you have a three-year moratorium on Internet taxes for electronic commerce. In India, e-commerce is actually illegal, because of the 1888 Telegraph Act, which forbids using telecommunications for profit. An 1888 law—can you believe it?"

Of Hotmail's 26 million users today, only 558,000 are from India. That it even has that many users is amazing, since there are only 150,000 Internet connections in the entire country. This in a country with one fifth of the world's population. India's telecommunications monopolies are so corrupt that an Internet connection costs around a thousand dollars to set up, compared to the $19.95 here. Even at that price, more than 2 million people have signed up on the waiting list—they're so hungry to get on-line—but only a portion of those orders has been serviced. The problem seems intractable.

The last time I saw Sabeer Bhatia, it was 1:50 A.M. on a Monday morning, and he was boarding a Korean Air 747 to start a twenty-four-hour flight halfway around the world—first to Seoul, then on to Bombay. He would meet with business leaders in Delhi and later deliver a speech at Internet World there.

Sabeer had thought hard about what he wanted to say to the

country he had left ten years before. He had started to get a vision of how India might be transformed. He had gotten his green card only a few months before he started Hotmail. The level playing field of the Internet has convinced him that in the future, young, ambitious people won't have to leave home.

"India is ready for the Internet revolution. You don't have to get a permit to start a business on the Internet. In India, just to open a little restaurant, you have to get eighteen permits."

Sabeer's vision involves TV, which in India is much more common than phone service. First, install a fiber-optic cable from London to Bombay. Second, use TV cable networks to provide local access points. Third, make available a sub-$50 Net device, somewhat like WebTV's. He estimates the project would take about $200 million to pull off.

It is a gargantuan vision, and it is based on the premise that his own greatness does not exist—Sabeer has convinced himself that he is just a product of the Silicon Valley environment—even though the very fact that he is dreaming such an unordinary-sized dream hasn't triggered the realization that maybe he really is exponentially more visionary than others.

"It's a herculean task," he admitted, "but the prospect of changing the destiny of a country motivates me."

I was witnessing what everyone had said of the early days of Hotmail—Sabeer's unquenchable sense of destiny, his nearly hallucinogenic optimism. As a story, it amused me. It was easy to interpret his enthusiasm as a self-induced late-night fancy that would downgrade from quest to cocktail-party conversation in a few days. It was easy to look at it through the Freudian lens: man returns home for his thirtieth birthday intent on saving other young men from the quandary of having to choose between family and self.

But he was right that India is still a sleeping giant. Sabeer seemed tenacious about it; he'd set up numerous meetings with various officials. After he boarded the plane, it occurred to me that, really, what did I know? Was it not possible that I was watching history at its inception? And I thought, by golly, he might just pull it off.

* * *

THE NEXT DAY, I was down in San Bruno interviewing an immigrant entrepreneur from Switzerland who had arrived here on a tourist visa with just a few thousand dollars in his bank account. On the day he had arrived, he hadn't known a single person in America. But he had started a company and was in the process of negotiating for venture capital financing. He'd been rejected by a dozen VC firms already, but he still had the faith. I asked him how he managed not to get dismayed. "I heard a story," he said. "I heard that the founder of Hotmail"—and here he mispronounced Sabeer's name—"was rejected by twenty venture capitalists before he got funded." Then he paused, stirred in his chair, and made a leap of faith masquerading as logic: "So if it can happen to him, it can happen to me, no?" Which was almost, but not quite, the same as *if he did it, I can too.*

EPILOGUE: Caging Sabeer up in the corporate lifestyle couldn't last. He bought a tenth-story apartment in Pacific Heights, then a Ferrari F1355 Spider, and then in March 1999, he quietly left Microsoft to begin a new venture, Arzoo! Inc.

CHAPTER 4

THE
Programmers

The Bubble-gum Bubble Complex

An oasis amid the dense student jungle of the University of California at Berkeley, the venerable Bancroft Hotel was designed by an associate of Julia Morgan in her Arts and Crafts style, with balconies or decks off all of the twenty-two airy rooms; its hallways are laid with Medi·terranean carpets, the broad-beamed ceilings hung with chandeliers. Off the front lobby a staircase descends to the bathrooms, and from there a fire exit ramp descends to a dark door. Push on the door, and you will find yourself in . . .

. . . cubicles.

The basement is packed with cubicles, and each cubicle is overflowing with computer equipment stacked on wood doors fashioned into desks, at each of which three to five young men are jammed elbow to elbow phoning, coding, assembling . . .

This is a business incubator, run by John Freeman, the

Helzel Professor of Entrepreneurship and Innovation at the Haas Graduate School of Business.

Freeman charges no rent and takes no equity. He requires only that the six start-ups pay their telephone bills. The start-ups are supposed to be for Haas students and very recent alumni, which is where the Big Network comes in. The Big Network's CEO, Steve Sellers, and its COO, John Hanke, graduated from Haas a couple years ago. Sellers is about five foot eight inches with brown hair; he wears pleated khakis and a faded blue cotton work shirt. John Hanke could step right into the pages of a J. Crew catalog and nobody would think he was out of place—six feet tall and slender, he has a swoosh of glossy brown hair that frequently needs brushing from his eyes. Both men are in their early thirties, and both are married with toddlers in the family. They've been working from the incubator for a year, and it's time to move along and find a proper office.

Freeman's annual class in entrepreneurship began five weeks ago, and all his MBA students have generated about fifteen business plans, several of which will actually get funded to the proof-of-concept stage by a donor fund Freeman has raised—and each of these start-ups will need a cubicle to work in. So every morning at around 9:15 A.M., Freeman walks down those stairs from the lobby and putters down the ramp to the back door. When he walks by Hanke's desk, Hanke eyeballs the black vinyl satchel Freeman is carrying. Every few days, that satchel grows thicker with student business plans, and Hanke knows he is about to get the boot.

Freeman is a solid man who looks to be in his fifties with a newly blooming gray beard. Hanke took his class two years ago.

"I swear, John," Hanke says, "we need just one more month. Then everything's going to be fine."

"I've got students who need to move in," Freeman says.

"I know, I know. We're working on a new Java version. We launch at the end of November. With that, we can grab our next venture round, and we'll be out of here."

The Big Network is a year-old game site in which Internet users can play simple board games such as chess and card games such as poker against other users. The games use a proprietary plug-in that has to be downloaded and stored on a computer's desktop—an obstacle to Internet-style growth. Sellers and Hanke had burned all but $20,000 of their first round of financing. Now they were taking a big gamble—holding off on raising a much-needed second round in the hope of reprogramming their system in Java, which would make the games thin enough and fast enough to be played from an Internet browser. With such technology, they could demand a much (much!) higher valuation and bring in "higher-profile" investors, that is, top-line VCs. If they didn't get the system working, it would take magic to get any kind of second round.

"A month?"

"Please, one more month."

"A month?" Freeman says again, not agreeing or disagreeing, just letting it hang there. He ruminates on it. His responsibility is to his new students. Then: "I'm going to get some coffee. You want something?"

It would be easy to glance at the surroundings and presume that John Hanke and his business partner, Steve Sellers, were neophytes to the Internet entrepreneurial world. In fact, they were both well seasoned. In the fall of 1995, when the Internet had very little of the functionality it has today, John and Steve's first company, Archetype Interactive, built the first 3-D multi-player fantasy world playable over the Internet, Meridian 59. It was way cool, and before they'd even advanced beyond beta they had sold the company, netting them each several million dollars (which at the time was considered a big score, particularly in the entertainment space).

Since then, the big money has gone away from cutting-edge fantasies, such as Meridian 59, and toward games that can draw bigger crowds—games that users can play on first glance, games everyone knows the rules of: chess, poker, backgammon. And the amount of money being thrown around now is at least ten times what it used to be.

So why, when they could raise a million dollars in a few weeks based on their track record alone, doesn't the Big Network just put out for a nice office in North Beach and hire a dozen full-time programmers? Why run a bone-dry operation out of a nonprofit incubator in which they have to beg for space every month?

The average gung ho, headstrong entrepreneur has convinced himself that his little start-up is always on the verge of being bought out for ten or twenty or thirty million. I call this mind-set the Bubble-gum Bubble Complex. You know how when you blow a bubble-gum bubble, it takes a heck of a lot of chewing and manipulating and tongue work to get the bubble started, but once it gets to be an inch in diameter it takes only the slightest effort, the merest discharge of air, for the bubble suddenly to be as big as your face? That's where the entrepreneur lives; he's always thinking his little bubble is on the verge of a sudden expansion. Having this belief is essential—it's the only way an entrepreneur would put up with the living hell of radical uncertainty that is start-up life. And it's not an unreasonable belief; some Internet companies do grow that fast.

Start-ups raise money by trading equity. Oh, that precious equity! To an investor, that little nibble of bubble gum is ten grand. But to the entrepreneur, that same nibble is on the verge of being the Arctic ice cap of his grand bubble! What's another three grand for a test server? Well, that's the Indian Ocean! What's five grand to employ professional testers? That's Africa! Every dollar of cash raised in the beginning will cost the entrepreneur ten times that when he succeeds. What's $75 an hour for a top-grade programmer? That's $750 an hour to the entrepreneur caught in the Bubble-gum Bubble Complex. (Think about it: by scrimping, the two founders of Yahoo! held on to 35 percent of their company. The four founders of Excite gave away all but 15 percent. As of this writing, the Yahoo! guys are worth more than a billion dollars *each*. The Excite guys are worth only $155 million *combined*.) It's simple: the greater the risk you take by being cheap, the greater the payoff.

Their first success gave Hanke and Sellers the confidence that in their next effort they could choose, at every junction, to take the path of greater risk. They had created a virtual company, with no actual cash-draining employees, giving away almost none of the bubble gum.

John and Steve had sought out extreme situations their whole lives. Before coming to Silicon Valley, John—who had been raised in a tiny town (population 1,063) in Texas—had been a press officer for the foreign service in Rangoon, Myanmar, during the period the military junta rode tanks through the streets, firing on student rioters. Steve, who had grown up in the Philippines, had been a foreign service officer in Lagos, Nigeria, and a peace observer of the Camp David Accords, flying over the Sinai in a helicopter, counting tanks. They bring that same spirit of adventure to Silicon Valley. "For our generation, this is really it," Hanke says. "It's the only place in the country where it's really happening."

With this transition to Java-class games, they had made what's called in this business a "bet-the-company decision." Everything would come down to the next six weeks.

The ABCDEFG Problem

Steve Sellers and John Hanke were pinching themselves as they drove from Berkeley to San Mateo that October evening. "It was like we turned the light switch on," Steve said.

No sooner had they started putting feelers out about their transition to Java than suddenly, *it* was happening. Suddenly, every big Web site decided it wanted to offer its users simple board games. Yahoo! bought one company, Classic Games, and Excite arranged a licensing deal with another game provider, TEN, the Total Entertainment Network. Infoseek and Netscape's Netcenter followed Excite's suit. Steve Sellers got hold of a producer at Snap, the fastest-growing search directory on the Web, who stepped up and offered the Big Network a contract.

There was only one problem . . .

Snap's representative, Dan Burkhart, had come to the Big Network's tiny underground virtual office in Berkeley, and Dan had to ask: *Where are the programmers?* Steve and John hemmed and hawed, not wanting to quite admit they were a virtual company, and then Dan Burkhart asked, "Well, are they employees, or are they just freelancers?" Snap wasn't going to do business with a ragtag company that couldn't handle its millions of users. Hanke had drawn up a schedule, and on his calendar he wrote the necessary milestones in a red pen. Then he had scrawled a big green "X" on November 16, launch day. Now that he had committed to this date, the Big Green X loomed heavily.

"Well, they're under contract," John Hanke said. Freelancers, but with some guarantees on availability.

So Dan asked the next logical question. "Do they have a stake in the outcome? Do they hold options?" Then he stated the point more directly: "How do we know they're still going to be here next month?"

"Oh, that's no problem," Hanke assured him.

"We've got a great relationship with these guys," added Sellers. "We've known them for a couple of years." This wasn't quite true.

John and Steve managed to get through the meeting without blinking, but as soon as it was over they got into the car and drove from Berkeley to Belmont, just south of San Mateo.

The Big Network did have five low-cost freelance programmers who had brought the company this far. In addition, Sellers's younger brother Mike, who was the company's creative director, could help out in a pinch. The company's chief technology officer, Arie Grossman, could handle site integration. The plan Hanke—ever intent on saving money—proposed was to fall back on that low-cost B team with the code that wasn't mission critical. For the code that was, they would go out and hire the best programmer they had ever known, Kevin Hester.

Sellers had known Kevin since they had worked together at 3DO. Steve would never have considered getting into the Snap deal if not for Kevin being between projects right now and available. A housemate of Kevin's, Mark "Max" Maxham, had just recently started doing some piecemeal work for the Big Network. He was proving to be just as studly as Kevin.

If by chance you've read *The Soul of a New Machine* by Tracy Kidder or any of its descendant reportings on deadline development, you know how the "signing up" session is supposed to go. A manager says to a programmer, "It will be hard work, thankless hours, for not a lot of pay. But it's the cutting edge—you'll have to figure out how to surpass the technology of our competitors. It's a job for only the best." And the programmer can't resist a duel, wants to prove he's one of the best, so he signs on. For pride. For the intellectual challenge.

That was the old way of working with programmers.

But, uh . . . the world's a little different now.

Top programmers are not nerds stuck in the back room anymore. They lead wildly imaginative lives. Kevin and Max are both pilots. One Saturday, they held a plane party on the tarmac at San Mateo Airport, everybody had just to bring $15 to cover the gas for an hour. Another thing they did was buy an old Wonder

Bread delivery truck and repaint it in pastel colors as the "Freezing Man" truck, which they equipped with massive freezer units and drove around the Burning Man festival in the Black Rock Desert, handing out ice cream sandwiches and Creamsicles to people in the hundred-degree heat.

Kevin and Max live in a place they call "Geekhaus," a five-bedroom, split-level ranch home overlooking the Sugarload Mountain preserve in Belmont. Every bedroom of the house looks to have been decorated by an earthquake: clothes, books, sporting goods strewn on the floor. The occupants seem not quite to have gotten the concept that certain things, such as artworks, may be hung from the walls rather than just leaned against them.

Max wears baggy blue jeans, a baggy, faded blue T-shirt, and sport sandals. His fingernails are cut excessively short, all in the pink; his fingertips swell up beyond the nail's end. Max is pale-skinned with faint freckles everywhere, and his hair, which used to drape onto his shoulders, has been buzzed off at a quarter inch. There are two thin hoop earrings in his left ear. He's the same age as Kevin, thirty; they've known each other since they were fourteen and growing up in Dallas, two young nerds who met on-line.

Kevin scuffles around the house in stonewashed loose-fitting shorts, Teva sport sandals, and a black Shiner Bock ("Go Texas!") T-shirt. He is six feet, one inch tall with precious little meat on his bones. He has pale almond skin with peach fuzz on his cheeks and dishwater blond hair that is accented, in back, with a stringy ponytail dyed purple and aqua. He has a face of beauty, kind, pale blue eyes, and a gemstone earring of the same color. Their laid-back appearance is mirrored in their dialect; their favorite adjectives are "foo," "large-N," and "blah." They can add a "y" to the end of just about any word that passes over their tongue, and for added emphasis throw in as a prefix "super-," "turbo-," or "giga-." So while Steve and John throw out market-savvy terms like "viral marketing," "CPMs," and "weighted-average ratchet clauses," Kevin and Max get a dismissive laugh out of that "turbobusinessy" talk. Kevin calls the whole Internet start-up thing "the lottery wheel."

Here is what you need to know about Kevin, which says a lot about the plight of programmers and what they struggle with today. Kevin is, by all accounts, a programmer's programmer, an *über*-geek. Studly engineers are always attracted to working with other studly engineers, and Kevin is a studly-engineer magnet. If you're lucky enough to know Kevin, you are tapped into a wide network of talented programmers who respect him.

In an economy like this, a guy like that should be fabulously rich, right?

Not necessarily. Two examples. Back when he was employed at 3DO, Kevin did some freelance work for a few friends at a start-up called Artemis Research. It was called Artemis Research only because the fitness studio that used to inhabit the building on Alma Street in Palo Alto had left a metal sculpture of an archer bolted to the brick exterior. They begged Kevin to join the company as employee number 7. He thought what they were doing was whizzy, but Trip Hawkins at 3DO convinced him that the future at 3DO was even brighter. Working at 3DO had always been "insanely fun," and Trip promised more. 3DO's stock was at $12 a share. In the following year, it dropped to $3. Meanwhile, Artemis Research changed its name to WebTV and sold itself to Microsoft for $350 million.

You come out of a situation like that not knowing who to trust, whose word to take, who to work for. So you rack your brain looking for a livable solution—freelance at a high hourly rate, fuck the options? Do you just focus on lifestyle and ignore the security a big payday would bring? Do you pore over *Red Herring* and *Upside,* hoping to kick-start your business savvy? Do you restrict yourself to working for managers whose companionship you enjoy?

This kind of thing, being so close to stardom without knowing it, has often happened to Kevin. The famous story about Kevin is a friendship he struck up with another pilot at Palo Alto Airport, back when he and Max owned a fabric-covered, 1960-model Piper Colt and Monday, Wednesday, and Friday mornings at 7:30 Kevin would go earn his instrument ratings. On cold mornings when Kevin had to wipe the frost off his wings, he would look with a little envy at another pilot who kept his fancy Malibu in a dry hangar. They struck up a friendship, talking strictly about planes, and all Kevin ever knew about this middle-aged guy was that he had retired from pro football. The guy had told him his name, but it meant nada to Kevin.

But one day, a cute girl at the office was talking about football, and Kevin offered up that he knew an ex-49er. Who? she asked. "Jeff somebody," Kevin responded. She was trying to think of a retired 49er named Jeff, but couldn't come up with names. "His last name is Montana," Kevin said. "That's it. Jeff Montana. Good buddy of mine."

Let's call this dilemma that good programmers face "The ABCDEFG Problem." I call it that because all good programmers have tons of choices to work on, A through G. Some choices seem cooler and some dumber, some possible and some improbable, but as to the payday lurking behind the door, they all look the same. They're just A through G, take your pick. Choice A may be 3DO, choice G may be $2 million of Microsoft stock, and choice C may be a quarterback with four Super Bowl rings, but *you just don't know.* It's sort of like choosing one million units of foreign currency according to which country's paper bills have the splashiest colors or making a million-dollar bet on the NCAA basketball tournament according to whichever team has the sexiest cheerleaders. The variables that programmers have to go on (A–G) are not the variables that determine the outcome (X, Y, and Z).

So when Sellers and Hanke sat down on the couch in the Geekhaus living room, Kevin and Max had the ABCDEFG Problem in the back of their minds.

Hanke tried to explain the situation: They had just signed a big deal on a project that would go live in a month. It would require a lot of programming to rebuild the system. A true challenge and all that. *Soul of a New Machine* stuff. The Big Network didn't have a lot of cash, and so it wanted to offer Kevin and Max options on a share of the company.

"Oh, no, thanks," Kevin said.

"Not for me," Max echoed.

John didn't want to tell these programmers too much for fear they might go right to Snap and charge more money for the work. But at the same time, he had to get across that *this is a real opportunity.* "It would be in your best interest," John tried. "It's with a very major player. If it flies, our company will become very valuable very quickly."

But Kevin and Max had their own secrets too; they really

didn't even want to tell Steve and John how they had been burned by options so many times before.

"We want you to be properly incentivized," Steve urged.

"We're happy to work at our hourly rates," they responded.

"Well, at least can we put you under a contract to guarantee us a certain number of hours?" John was aware that Kevin and Max were working for several other companies at the same time.

"I can help you for a little while," Kevin said. "I'll do the architecture. But from then on, it's more of a job for Max." Kevin is one of the rare engineers in the Valley who is really, really good at what is called "hardware bring-ups," the nether place where hardware and software meet. Most hardware guys have electrical engineering backgrounds and don't understand the importance of scalability. Kevin, who has a computer science background, can design a software system in sync with the hardware servers to be the Big Network's backbone. Being a freelancer was hard for Kevin—he was so much in demand that he constantly had to say no to people and projects he'd come to like. This angst tore him up. And whenever he wasn't working, he was thinking about how much money he *could* be making—how the opportunity cost of goofing off was $110 an hour. That was no way to live.

Kevin believed he had just solved the ABCDEFG Problem by taking a job at a reduced salary of $140,000 and working only four days a week. On Fridays, he rolls out of bed and scampers across the hallway to the Geekhaus garage, where Kevin is building his ultimate hack, an ultralight Dragonfly kit-assembly airplane. When he's done, he plans to sell Geekhaus and fly off to Geeksville, a friend's concept commune somewhere north, probably around Boonville, where they can live together and telecommute. When he needs to have meetings in the Valley, Kevin is just an hour away in the Dragonfly.

Max, though, was perfectly content being a freelancer. The longer he goes without a regular job, the less he wants one. He calls offices "cube farms." He has the opposite mind-set from Kevin's. He knows that if he worked full-time, he could rake in $150,000 a year. But he needs only a certain amount to live on every month, and at his hourly rate he knows how many hours he has to work each week: eighteen. With all the money he's hauling in as Contractor Boy, Max hired a "personal assistant," a friend named Chaya, at $15 an hour. She repainted the Geekhaus's kitchen an avocado color. She's sewing him a Willy Wonka costume for Halloween. He "commissioned" her to make two turbosized beanbag chairs for the downstairs rec room, each the size of a baby hippopotamus. His life now is "pretty zippy."

What thrilled Max was not the options but the surefire contract to go live on the Big Green X—the fact that his code would be out there for all to see, and soon. For a programmer, worse even than owning worthless options is the humiliation of having built great software that still sits in some dark closet, never having been implemented. By 1998, every programmer with a few years of experience knew the humiliation of "going dark," and it's become a bigger factor in how they decide the ABCDEFG Problem. Max says he has a "priority knob" that he can turn up at times. He was willing to turn it up for this opportunity, except . . .

"Don't forget, I'm going on vacation in ten days," he said. He'd been very up-front about his vacation all along. This was no surprise.

"Can you reschedule it?" John asked.

"We'll make it worth your while," Steve tried. There was so much Steve wanted to tell Max. He wanted to tell him how NBC had bought two huge chunks of Snap from C-NET, and how NBC had hired Saatchi & Saatchi to create a big advertising campaign for Snap that would appear during the American League championships, when 60 million Americans would be tuning in to watch the New York Yankees destroy the Cleveland Indians. He wanted to convey to Max that this was no ordinary opportunity; this was a chance to secure his future. Surely that was worth postponing a vacation for.

"My vacation is inviolable," Max insisted.

"Come on . . ."

"No. I won't reschedule."

"You must be going somewhere very important," John remarked.

Max wasn't even sure he wanted to tell them. Max was learning to draw boundaries in his life. He was not going to get overinvolved. He has never even been to the Big Network's offices.

Then he dropped the bomb on Steve and John. Max's cousin had a friend who had four hundred acres of land with nothing on it but the kind of vegetation that attracts deer, ducks, rabbits, and squirrels. "I'm going to Tennessee to go squirrel hunting with my cousin."

Squirrel hunting! Oh my! If ever there were a moment that signaled how the world had changed—a moment that signaled who was in power—this was it! This is not 1993 anymore, when game coders working on deadline were barked at, driven to exhaustion, and underpaid. This is 1998, and it's the era of the Internet, which has squared the complexity of programming, causing a paradigm shift in the market for talented coders. Never before have the few good ones had so much leverage. Talent! They *are* the talent, and it is *their* schedule we will adhere to.

My cousin and I are going squirrel hunting! A week in the mountains!

Hell, yes! The only time of the year to hunt squirrels is when the first chilly evenings of autumn scare those squirrels into panic mode, and those squirrels get so focused on their nut gathering that they don't notice humans with shotguns marching through the grove in camouflage suits. It's also mating time, and the male squirrels let out little mating barks for the females, giving away their position. So tell that to Snap!

Sellers and Hanke were at a loss. "You're leaving us hanging here," they said to Max. Even though Max would be around much of the time, his absence in the middle of the project meant he couldn't be the Go-To guy.

Max's friend Jason Tobias had been looking for a freelance project on which to work. Max said they could look Jason up and talk to him.

"Is he good?" Steve asked Kevin, trusting his old friend's judgment.

"He's studly," Kevin said.

"I'll look him up," John said. "I'd like to get him involved right away."

Code Re-use

Jason Tobias is a twenty-six-year-old programmer who lives a couple miles south of Geekhaus. He is five feet, seven inches tall, wears hard jeans and fashionable heavy-soled black leather shoes and a burgundy short-sleeved cotton buttondown. His downy hair is buzzed down to five-millimeter length, and just under his lower lip is a wispy tuft of peach fuzz. Jason spent most of his life in Texas and says "folks" and drives a gray four-speed Ford pickup. He looks even younger than he is, and his demeanor is as soft as his peach fuzz. He rents a room at the back of a house on top of a hill in San Carlos, which is where he spends this day trying to resolve his employment situation. Jason calls this part of his work "out-of-band noise" ("band" as in "bandwidth"; anything that is not programming is "out of band noise").

Jason is willing to promise the Big Network that he will give it ten hours a day for the next month, for which it's willing to pay him $75 an hour. In order to make the Big Green X, Jason has to finish the game system's "core class library" and post them to the server by . . . tomorrow. Jason doesn't want to think too much about the World Series/NBC/Snap/Big Network cascade because, as he says, "I've had fancy names whispered in my ear a few too many times."

The only problem with this arrangement is that Jason . . . has a job. Jason hasn't even quit his job yet! Last Thursday he went to the VP of engineering at his employer, Optical Networks, and tried to resign, but it was worse than breaking up with a girlfriend; the company kept begging and making counteroffers, and the more he said "no" the more it ratcheted up its offer, making it harder for him to leave.

"Jason, what is it that you want?" his boss begged. "What bugs you?"

Jason had already told him that he simply just wanted to leave. So this time he added, "I hate the drive, it's a full hour."

"We'll get you a corporate apartment," his boss said and an hour later called back with the specifics: five minutes from work, free maid service, fireplace, et cetera.

"No."

"We'll think about it and get back to you," his boss said again.

A little while later, his boss called, this time offering a $15,000 bonus and ten thousand stock options, on top of his regular pay, if he would stay for just forty-five more days.

Jason was turning down a wad, but he knew that in the long term fifteen grand wouldn't matter. He told me, "That's the luxury of being a good software programmer in this market—

the ultimate luxury—the luxury to not compromise my integrity." He knows he's lucky.

So once again he said, "No."

It finally started to dawn on the guy: "You're not just playing us for a better offer, are you? You actually want to leave."

Finally, Jason could say, "Yes."

"All right, then."

Jason was gambling. He'd only met the Big Network folks four days earlier—they'd shared a pepperoni pizza at Kevin's house.

Jason took the contract with the Big Network because he trusted Kevin's judgment.

"Kevin can give a two-sentence synopsis of anybody, and usually he's very accurate," Jason said. The summary of that two-sentence synopsis comes down to one word: "Clueful."

Jason was working on his own solution to the ABCDEFG Problem. On the side, he had been developing Internet tools that help telecommuters and virtual companies work remotely. He now wanted to work from home in order to exercise that muscle. Fairly soon, he was going to buy a house in Austin and work from there—something the Big Network had no trouble with. When he had refined his virtual office tools, he would found his own start-up to sell them.

It took Jason several hours to decompress from all the stress. Tomorrow was now only two hours away. His home office is the western hemisphere of his bedroom, where he has a desk that looks out over the back fence into the wealthy hillsides of San Carlos. He slipped his headphones over his ears, put on the Beastie Boys' new album, *Hello Nasty,* and hit the "Repeat All" button. The lyrics became a wall of sound keeping out the industry noise that for several days had been shattering his mind. He concentrated.

If there were a rap about programmers, it would go something like this:

> *Living in this valley of gum bubble*
> *Who's gonna keep you outta trouble*
> *G F E D C B A*
> *Make your move or you'll get jumped,*
> *The kinged go that way,*

The queen is trumped.
Who writes the rules?
Who gets to play?

IT TAKES A bit of explaining to communicate how a mere card game can be such a programming challenge. It's always been easy to program something to work in an individual case, the instance. It's always been tremendously harder to program it to work in the general case, universally. To program a card game to run on a *particular* computer is really easy. To get it to work on *any kind of* computer is exponentially harder. To have thousands of users playing the game at the same time, each of them on any kind of computer, is exponentially harder still.

When programming was confined to the computer desktop (before the Internet), it was always pretty easy to hide the fact that its guts/architecture might be mangled. We, the modern masses, have always judged software by its features, or the way it looks on the surface, ignoring its guts. The era of the desktop didn't expose the gap between programmers who are sucky and programmers who are truly studly.

But in the transition to networks, guts are everything. You can no longer hide ugly guts. On the Internet, ugly guts will crash the system under the stress of multiple users. When a Web site crashes, the whole world knows about it. In the era of the Internet, the gap between the studly and the sucky is suddenly very conspicuous.

Of all the projects going on in the Valley in the fall of 1998, I chose this particular project to follow because it's a pure programming play. By this I mean that it's a test of guts, not of features. The games are set in stone. Yahoo! can't one-up Excite by inventing a new chess piece, for instance, or by changing the rules of checkers. Seven-card stud is seven-card stud and always will be. On all the sites it will look pretty much the same. But the guts are different.

That's the test of programming today: build a system that will scale from hundreds of users to millions.

Build a bubble-gum bubble that won't burst.

The core class library is the building blocks of code from which games are assembled. When you're linked over the Internet, the less that has to come across the phone line, the faster the game will play. The key concept is called code re-use. If a game is assembled from core blocks the shared blocks can be reused when an Internet user switches between games. It's sort of like being Spiderman for Halloween one year and Superman the next: you can reuse the blue tights and red boots and have to pop out to Wal-Mart only for a cape.

What blocks could Jason make? Some were obvious, such as the fact all the board games have some sort of move of the game pieces. There are only three subclasses of moves, which Jason called "Slide," "Jump," and "Plop." For instance, checkers uses a combination of Slide and Jump moves, and the board can be set with a number of Plops.

What is less obvious are the ways in which board games and card games are similar. Sellers and Hanke were hoping that finding generalizations here would give them an advantage over their competitors. Steve knew that his biggest competitor, TEN, had started with card games and only later added board games—so it was likely that its hierarchy of code logic was not optimized, that very little code was reused when switching between backgammon and spades.

Jason realized that a card table can be represented by a blank game board and cards are no different from game pieces—the cards ace through king are just like the chess pieces pawn through queen. Playing a card is the same as jumping from your hand to the center of the board. In addition, both card games and board games pass the turn around the table, both keep score, both use black-and-red color schemes. Jason wrote the code to define all these general maneuvers, which he called a "turn array." Both card and board games would be descendants of the turn array.

One of the customs of programming is that unless the time is specifically stated, a deadline for delivering on a certain date is 23:59 on that day—*anytime* before midnight. The Big Network has a development server in its cage at Exodus Communications, the Internet hub in Santa Clara. Sometime between two and three in the morning, Jason Tobias posted his core class library to the development server.

Not Caring

*Modelviewcontroller*modelviewcontroller . . . it was all bunched together inside Mike Sellers's brain, slurred, his mind foggy, unable to sleep. He couldn't quite grasp this programming concept. Java code can't slop from one category to another, it needs to be modular, and Mike's code was full of slop. His code was still interdependent. *Modelviewcontroller*. Model view controller. MODEL. That's the hunk of data. VIEW. That's code to look at the data. CONTROLLER. That's code to control the data. Gibberish.

Nightmares.

Mike is the Big Network's visionary. He's writing a book about the rules for on-line communities, and he's written articles on topological reasoning, whatever that is. His older brother Steve describes Mike as "unrestrained creativity, a guy who has no downtime—he's just lying fallow." Mike spends a lot of time driving around Pleasanton, waiting for his muse. But Steve wishes Mike had just 1 percent of his own type A personality.

Mike hadn't done any serious roll-up-the-shirtsleeves coding in four years, but as soon as the Big Green X was etched into the calendar, he was enlisted in the effort. He wouldn't touch the guts, he would just extend the functionality of some features.

Mike had spent five years coding in C++, but he'd never written Java code before. Never.

So Mike went out to his local chain bookstore and bought a copy of *Teach Yourself Java in 21 Days*. Twenty-one days? No problem. Except . . .

John Hanke's schedule gave Mike six days.

Mike sat down at the big oak rolltop desk in his bedroom and started to log the hours. He tried one little test applet to give him faith the code worked. He picked up the Java syntax in a couple of hours. He picked up the class structure before the sun went down. But his coding was still like this:

10: read Java book for half hour.
20: write one line of code.
30: repeat.

Mike worked twenty hours a day for the next week. "I've had five hundred-hour weeks in my lifetime," he says. "Two of those five are this last week and this coming week." He was besieged by nightmares about Java principles. He's a Mormon by marriage who lives at the end of a cul-de-sac in a planned development in Pleasanton, which is exactly what the town name implies. Mike's five feet ten, a little taller and a little stockier than his brother Steve, and at this time of year his house is heavily decorated for Halloween by his six kids. His own personal ghost is the model view controller method.

Kevin had taught me about the second key overview concept of Java programming, "Not Caring." The less a building block of code has to care about what other blocks of code are up to, the less likely the bubble-gum bubble will burst. Code that "slopped" was code that was too interdependent, code that made the mistake of caring.

One of the particular agonies about programming for a network is that the programmer can't compile and debug his code in private, on his own, "locally"—before anyone else sees it. Mike had to upload it to the team's server, where it would plug into everyone else's code immediately. This can be quite an embarrassment, sort of like getting dressed in public. On Saturday night, four days into it, Mike made his first try at posting to the server.

In no time he got a telephone call from Max (who hadn't yet left for Tennessee), followed by a flurry of flaming e-mails (which came to be known as "Maxgrams"): "You're going to make me rip my hair out! You're killing me! I'm going crazy—what the hell? I'm going to pop an aneurysm!" Mike's code was causing havoc.

"I never pretended I was an ace coder," Mike said.

"I thought you were smarter than this!"

Only then did Mike explain that he had tried his first line of Java only four days ago. Suddenly, Max understood. He taught Mike some Java philosophy. It helped.

Max was not as calm. Max was a strong proponent of "egoless programming," which means that coders have to swallow their pride and defer to the most senior geek. That Mike would have changed the code on him—without even telling him first—

suggested an ignorance of the proper process, which was worse than an ignorance of Java.

With Kevin mostly on the sidelines after writing the initial server architecture, Max was the most senior Java geek. The team would have to take its lead from him. This habit of just posting to the server, what was with these guys?

Arie Grossman, the Big Network's chief technology officer, had already given Max some unwelcome feedback on Max's recommendation of a system called Perforce for source code control. This management software allows a team to track all of its generations of code and "roll back" to previous versions if they evolve in a direction that proves troublesome (like being able to backtrack in a maze when a route hits a dead end). According to Arie, Perforce cost $600 a user, and he had urged as an alternative a shareware product called CVS, which was nearly free. Without even telling Max, Arie had installed CVS on the server. Max had been furious—Arie was wrong! The first two users of Perforce were free, and only additional users cost $600 each. Max and Jason could use Perforce for free. Max had to burn a day installing what he wanted, not trusting Arie anymore.

At Max's hourly rate, it was costing the Big Network almost as much to fix the problem as it would have to pay for the license. Max believed Hanke was taking a strategy that would cost more in the end. "Cheap programmers cost more than expensive ones," Max told me. "They work slower, produce more bugs. It adds up."

One of the advantages of being "Contractor Boy," as Max calls himself, is "I can shout my mouth off about things that would get me fired at any company." Most of his shouting off is directed at the B team. He hasn't looked at Mike Sellers's code in the last few days, "I'm afraid of what I might find." Of Arie's work, he says, "Being able to administer a Unix box doesn't make you an engineer." Of David Dies's code, he says, "It made me want to vomit when I saw it." But Hanke didn't have much of an alternative to using the B team—Max was heading off to Tennessee.

The Piece of Cheese

"These are the gates to the kingdom," Arie Grossman says as we walk into the Internet hub Exodus, where many Valley companies host their Web sites. Arie is here today to install two new servers into their cage. It's 10 A.M. Sunday. The equipment is locked in cages with sliding doors. The room is lit by fluorescent overheads, and air feeds in briskly through grates in the floors. Everyone's equipment is bolted into seismically braced racks. Some are protected by fingerprint-reading security locks.

The driving principle behind this place is the speed of light. Theoretically, on a fiber-optic line a signal can cross the United States in virtually no time at all, and so where you host your servers shouldn't matter. But even at the speed of light, it takes far less time to send a signal across the room than across the country. In order to make sure their Web sites are responsive, companies pay top dollar to store their equipment here.

"We skimp on a lot of things, but not on Exodus. We get what we pay for here."

As we stroll through the cages, Arie oohs and aahs over other Web sites' hardware.

"We're over here, in the low-rent district," he says. Cage 62, over by the east wall. Arie calls this his server farm. We slip two Intel Pentium II tower cases into the racks. Each cost only a thousand bucks. "We're on the budget design," Arie says. "What we give up in quality, we make up for in quantity. If one of these goes down, hey—we just buy another."

Arie is five feet nine and about 145 pounds. He wears blue jeans with a beaded belt that matches his watchband, Stan Smith sneakers, and polo shirt. He is thirty-six years old and, like all of his partners at the Big Network, has a couple of young kids. When he is otherwise still, his eyelids twitch and so does his hand, almost vibrating. Arie is a very aggressive listener, always asking questions in a way that can feel like an interrogation. Fundamentally, he has a huge brain, and a lot of the time it doesn't have much to do but worry about other people's responsibilities.

For all but Arie, Kevin Hester's principle of not caring is the dominant attitude for all parties involved. Snap doesn't know the Big Network's programmers don't have skin in the game. Jason has no idea that the Big Network's supposed "big venture financing" has been held off until after the Snap launch. Max doesn't even know that the Big Network's "offices" are really just two doors laid flat over sawhorses. Everyone's just doing his part. But not Arie. He's intrusive with his caring. He's loud with his caring. Very loud. He butts in. At times he seems unable to move forward on his own work for fear other people haven't got their details worked out.

Today, he has two concerns on his mind. He's just learned that the contract with Snap is still not quite signed.

Did I hear that right? I thought the whole point of this crunch was to meet Snap's deadline. Max and Jason might never have accepted this job without the assurance that the fruits of their labor would go live. What will happen when they find out?

"I trust Steve," Arie says carefully. "I do, I trust him."

But?

"Well, the damn thing is *not signed.* I know all the terms have been negotiated. Snap said they would sign it. I'm sure Steve's got it covered, but from the looks of things, it appears that Snap is leading us on."

Does he really have doubts?

"We know they're still talking to other developers. We know they were talking to TEN, which delivers games for Excite and Infoseek. Snap assured us they were no longer talking to TEN. Ours is better, a lot better, no doubt. But I won't stop worrying until it's actually signed."

His hand is doing the high-vibration tremor.

Just a few years ago, Arie was an astroplanetary scientist with a Ph.D. from Cal Tech. He worked at the world's largest radio telescope facility, the Very Large Array in the middle of nowhere, three hours southwest of Albuquerque, New Mexico. "Basically, my job was to stay up all night and baby-sit the telescopes," he says. Nothing ever went wrong with the telescopes, so Arie had a ton of free time and some of the most sophisticated computer equipment at his fingertips. The Internet was just becoming a new thing outside academia.

What Arie would do was to visit the Internet game sites, solve the brain-stumping puzzles, and win all the free prizes. Between his big brain and the Very Large Array's computer, "it was like taking candy from a baby." Arie Grossman won everything. He won a Toyota Rav 4. He won the hovercraft from the movie *The Fifth Element* from Sony Pictures. He won lots of cash—over a hundred thousand dollars! If anyone tried to renege on the prize offer—anticipating, for instance, that they had come up with a puzzler that nobody could solve (the fools!)—it helped that Arie's wife was a Harvard-educated attorney. When Procter & Gamble decided to get its feet wet on the Internet, it created a contest to promote its new orange drink, Sunny-Delight. It was a treasure hunt—every day for ten weeks, contestants had to find the little Sunny-D bottle hidden on a Web page somewhere on the Internet. After ten weeks, the top ten finishers were to have a one-day finale and race to be the first to find the Sunny D. Arie had written little bots to search out the orange bottles, which miraculously wasn't against the rules. Arie had read the rules very carefully—"It was just stupid; if they'd known anything about the Internet, they would have anticipated this"—and also found no rule prohibiting him from being multiple people or using his brother's name and friends' names. So on the day before the grand finale, Arie telephoned Procter & Gamble and said, "Look, there's no need to have the race tomorrow. I'm all top ten finishers." He took home ten grand and ten video arcade systems.

Finally, it occurred to Arie that he could do a lot better at creating on-line puzzlers than these jokers, so he created his own Internet site, Play-4-Prizes, and gave up his job baby-sitting telescopes. He funded his start-up by winning more prizes from his competitors' sites. Need a server?—go out and win an SGI workstation. Rather than paying for advertising, Arie "convinced" Procter & Gamble to hide one of its Sunny-D bottles on his site (it had gone on to more rounds of the game), and all of the treasure hunt game players instantly found his site. He quickly established a registered user base of 85,000, and last year he merged his company into the Big Network's—strength in numbers.

Arie now goes by the nickname Arie-Claus. When U.S. Robotics introduced the 56K modem, it gave away fifty-six modems a day for fifty-six days. He won hundreds of modems, which he would resell for a $150 a pop on the on-line auction sites.

Just recently, he won a slew of videoconferencing camera

balls. About that contest he says, "Something went wrong. I'd worked out the math, and I anticipated winning 31.4 percent of the modems. But I only won 30.6 percent of them. And I've never been able to figure it out." He's given one to every Big Network programmer so they can have some visual contact.

Arie's story sounds sort of happenstance, as if he ended up here on a Sunday morning beefing up the hardware only by a few haphazard turns, and with all that brainpower he's got I wonder if there are big dreams behind those twitches he's not talking about. My questions to this point sort of freeze him midworry.

"No, I . . . I don't dream much. These days there's just too much reality to deal with."

He looks at the two servers he just added, now making it six in the cage. He will install three more next week. Currently, the Big Network's peak load is three hundred simultaneous players, which usually occurs during the lunch hour and just after work. John Hanke has made estimates that in the first week of the Snap launch, the load will instantly triple . . . and steadily climb.

Arie says, "We have no way to know how it will hold up. We've made estimates that these servers can handle two hundred to four hundred simultaneous users each. But what if we're wrong? What if they can handle only a hundred each? We have no plan."

The only way they can even try to anticipate the load is for Max to write a program that simulates hundreds of users hitting the system at once. Last week, Max said that writing such a program was "a piece of cheese." When Arie heard that, he didn't know what Max meant. Did "a piece of cheese" mean it was easy, like the phrase "a piece of cake," or did it mean something stinky, meaning the simulation would be a rotten program?

"He said a piece of cheese, and we had no idea. Was it Brie or was it Limburger?"

Keiretsu

Steve Sellers called up Dan Burkhart and asked what the hell was going on. Were they, or were they not, going to sign this contract? Burkhart jumped on his motorcycle and buzzed across the Bay Bridge to explain the situation in person. He was new at Snap as the director of business development, and the deal with the Big Network was his first.

Steve wanted to know if Snap was still negotiating with competitors. He extracted a strong promise that Dan was not negotiating with any other game provider. Snap was having a party the next night to celebrate the opening of its new headquarters building. Dan asked Sellers and Hanke to attend.

I entered the Snap launch party with Steve Sellers, but no sooner did I attach my name badge to my shirt than I was sucked into a maw of loud gossiping chatter, a kiss-kiss hive of cross-pollenating portal players. The party was so crowded that in seconds I lost sight of Sellers. I gave it a few minutes, but it only got worse. I pulled my mobile phone off my hip and dialed Sellers's phone number.

"This is Steve." I heard the crackling maw in the background. It was almost, but not quite, the same maw as around me.

"Where the hell are you?"

"I'm over by the soundstage."

"Don't move, you're not twenty feet away. I'll be there in under five minutes."

On the way, I bumped into John Hanke. He yelled into my ear that Steve was looking for me. I followed him. We passed a wall of television monitors endlessly replaying the new series of Saatchi & Saatchi–created advertisements for Snap to run on NBC. We caught up to Steve and shuffled off to a corner to observe the party from a distance. Steve introduced me to Sean Timberlake, Snap's artistic producer, who is working closely with Dan Burkhart. Sean is about five feet six and ultrahip—brassy yellow dyed hair, plush purple velvet sport coat, round glasses with thick frames. It's too loud to hear each other.

Mike Sellers showed up too. Nobody said anything for a while. We just watched the whirlpool of lithe bodies, of grown-up frat men in Sisley shirts and long-haired women in Bebe minisuits— and the same thought occurred to all of the Big Network guys at just about the same time:

"Man, when did all these gorgeous women start working in this business?"

These guys have been so busy working for the last two years, and on top of that they all have young children, so they haven't been on the hopping high-tech party scene since 1996. And it suddenly dawned on them how radically the business has changed in that time. The people are different. There's not a programmer in the room except them. They're all business development VPs for one Web site or another or marketing directors or PR flakes or CEOs—and they all have graduate degrees and come from good schools and used to work in management consulting. They're not all blond and blue-eyed, but that's the dominant strain. They all have firm handshakes and can look you in the eye and have big plans to go away on the weekend and aren't absent-minded and know to come out with a laugh when the conversational gambit is meant to provoke one. It's like the Valley crowd was given an en masse *Cosmo* makeover, given "that MBA look," gentrified just in time for the big Silicon Valley dramatizations and book deals. I looked at the scene, and I thought about how NBC bought into the company, and then it hit me: the party looked like a scene from *Friends*. As if every actor who hadn't made the cut had been given a job in the Internet division.

This is the cultural scene of late 1998. Programming used to be the bread and butter of high tech, but the in crowd now prefers chapati to bread and crème fraîche to butter. It's all about synergy deals and branding and national advertising.

I got talking with Robert Silverman, the loquacious silver-tongued PR flack for NBC, and he explained strategy from the 30,000-foot view. Silverman tossed around newly minted buzzwords like "convergenced" and "advantaged." In the dialect spoken by portal players, there are "parities" and there are "differentiators." Parity is now a given—it's called keeping up with the Yahoo!s. They've got free e-mail, we've got free e-mail. They've got travel reservations, we've got travel reservations. "Parity is so assumed that it's not even part of the story anymore," said Silverman. Parity is not sexy. The story is exclusively about differentiators: special tidbits that guys like Silverman can repeat endlessly.

That's about as close as any conversation dipped toward programming all evening.

Standing on the far fringe of the party, Steve Sellers noticed that there were several people at the party from TEN, Total Entertainment Network, which delivers games to Excite, Infoseek, and Netscape.

What are they doing here?

Dan Burkhart came over to talk to Steve to tell him the news before he hears it from anyone else: "C-NET just inked a deal with TEN."

This frightened Steve. C-NET owns a majority of Snap, and the two companies are tightly linked. TEN is backed by the venture capital heavyweight Kleiner Perkins, and Kleiner Perkins is notorious for using its behind-the-scenes leverage to break the will of independent-minded deal makers. KP had created a family of firms called the *keiretsu*, after the Japanese model of doing business. These closely knit firms give first preference to each other on contracts. They call this "co-development," which is too nice a way to put it. Start-ups are forced into working with each other, adopting each other's standards. Suppliers and vendors (such as landlords, office furniture outlets, and computer stores) will give reduced rates to start-ups who drop their VC's name in hopes of being the main supplier for all of that VC's affiliated start-ups. (That this economic model helped to bring down the Japanese economy by sheltering unprofitable firms from reality hasn't seemed to discourage KP.) The *keiretsu* has tremendous strong-arm muscle. The most dramatic story that I have heard occurred in late February 1996, when the McKinley search directory was one day away from filing its S1 prospectus; it would have been the first search engine to go public. KP called McKinley's bankers, Robertson Stephens, and "convinced" them to drop McKinley in favor of KP-backed Excite.

If KP now had an in with C-NET, it would not hesitate to leverage it on Snap.

"So Dan, what's the deal? Are you or are you not negotiating with TEN?"

Dan insisted that he had not been talking with TEN. But his boss, Sam Parker, might have been. It was Sam Parker who was refusing to sign the Big Network contract. Dan was not happy about the situation either, because he had taken the job at Snap on the promise of being vested with autonomy to make deals. "Sam's a big TEN fan."

Dan urged Steve to get the project done.

"We've shown you a demo."

"We've got to see a card game."

They agree to a demo of Spades the next Friday. Max would be back from squirrel hunting tomorrow.

With so much on the line, John Hanke gave the responsibility for Spades to Jason.

Java Pollution

Friday morning: John Hanke has to decide whether to go ahead with the afternoon demo for Snap.

John said, "I don't know what Jason did since last night, but it seems to have made things worse." Jason was frustrated with having to rush Spades—it didn't give him time to think through the card games' core class library. The proper procedure was to program the generalities, then work down into the instances—to create an infrastructure that could be refined into any game, from Spades to Uno. Now he was programming just the instance, and he kept making mental notes: "Fix this later." "You can't develop quality software inverting your schedule to make all these demos," he'd complained.

It will be what Hanke calls a "pulling-my-hair-out demo." At 11 A.M., John Hanke, Mike Sellers, Jason Tobias, and Max Maxham gave the system a mini–stress test, hoping they can find out under what circumstances the system breaks down—and then, maybe, they can tiptoe through a Snap demo by avoiding those circumstances.

John and Mike were in the basement incubator in Berkeley, where they have three computers between them, while Max and Jason log in from their homes.

Blitzing the system from multiple browsers, typing nonsense at full speed into chat, and resetting games, they found a pattern. The chat features work fine until the game begins, then they freeze. Spades worked fine with Microsoft Internet Explorer but crashed with some versions of Netscape Navigator. Only the first game of Spades can be played to completion; when a user hits the "Restart Game" button, everything freezes. It's noon. Jason and Max have maybe two hours to try to debug these problems. Except . . .

. . . they've got to go. Got another freelance job they need to be at. Sorry.

That's how things get done in the Internet era. The Talent has its own plan. The A team comes prepackaged with liabilities.

Got to go! Didn't you see my schedule?

Who knows if Max and Jason would have been able to debug the problems in two hours? Probably not. But it begged the question once again: When the day came that the Big Network would *really, truly, inviolably* need the A team to come through, would they be there? Would their hourly rate be enough incentive?

In the chat window beside the Spades game, John begged Max to turn his cell phone on in case of an emergency. Max typed back in rap:

I know ya planned it,
gonna set it straight,
this Watergate.

This problem of the system not quite working with either Microsoft's or Netscape's browser is one of the pervasive frustrations of coding in Java. It's a problem that should not exist. Microsoft was being sued by Sun Microsystems for violating its Java licensing contract by adding to Java and, in effect, polluting it. (Less than a month later, the judge presiding over this suit stipulated a summary judgment in Sun's favor.) Two strains of Java have evolved, one developed by Microsoft and one by Sun, making it harder for browsers to be compatible with both. As a result, Web sites have to be fine-tuned for each brand of browser.

The team hadn't had time to do this fine tuning.

After signing off to Max, John Hanke conferred with Steve Sellers over whether it would be worse to proceed with the Snap demo or cancel it. Since it was Friday afternoon, they wondered if they could just flake out and not even call.

John said, "I just have a fear that they'll lose confidence in us if we don't call."

"Is it a *we call them* situation or a *they call us*?"

"Fairly, it's a *we call them.*"

Steve suggested, "Well, it's lunchtime now. You could probably call and get their answering machine. Then it would be a *they call us—*"

John finished the thought: "And we just not answer the phones the rest of the day?"

"We have to think of a way to artfully put this off until Monday."

John said, "I could beg off for personal reasons." He is moving house this weekend and hasn't even packed yet.

There was no way they could go through with the demo. John suggested that he make the call and leave a message. He would hedge—not quite beg out but say he had certain other appointments and there was only a small window of time available, one that he secretly hoped Snap couldn't make.

"I'm going to go outside to do this," John said, taking his cell phone with him.

Steve explained, "He hates to lie in front of other people."

An hour later, John was still playing the Spades game, trying to discern its failure patterns. Suddenly there were two other players in the parlor lobby. Who could they be? John knew that Max and Jason were off on another job. Arie, maybe? John tabbed over to the directory of on-line players.

It was Sean and Dan from Snap. They had logged on for a spot inspection. John never bothered to turn on the security features that would have prevented them from accessing the system.

This was particularly troublesome. It was one thing to give a demo presentation in person, to an audience, in which the demonstrator can click in all the right places and be careful to avoid crash-inducing circumstances. Letting Snap have the run of the house was something else altogether. What if they were using Netscape Navigator? What if they tried to reset a game? What if they tried to chat while playing Spades?

I expected John to start pulling his hair out, but he was cool. He pulled Mike Sellers over. They began to chat on-line with Sean and Dan. Mike demonstrated many of the chat features while John tried to start a Spades game. The first three attempts, it would not load. Finally, it came up. John picked up the telephone and called Sean. The other three players joined John's Spades game. Sure enough, the chat feature stopped working. But luckily, the telephone line had taken its place as the means of communication. Sean and Dan didn't seem to notice. John began playing his cards. Sean was actually having a very hard time remembering how to play Spades, and this was taking all his concentration, distracting him from the kind of nitpicky comments he had made before. Amazingly, the game proceeded smoothly. Sean and Dan must have been using a Microsoft Web browser.

Just don't hit that Restart button.

To slow the game down, John Hanke began asking about Sean's and Dan's Halloween plans. Then Sean said the system wasn't letting him play the card he wanted to play.

"I keep clicking, it's not going," Sean said over the speaker-phone.

"What card is it?" John asked.

"I'm not going to show you my hand!" Sean joked.

"Are you trying to play a spade? You can only play a spade if you've used up the other suits first."

"Oh, right."

John looked at his watch. Now he really did have an appointment. The four players end the game without quite finishing up the cards or having to restart another game.

"Well, that's a pretty good start," Dan said.

"It's a huge improvement," Sean added. "You've come a long way." They sounded excited and began to one-up each other with compliments.

"We love the look with that new art—"

"The difference you've made is extremely visible—"

"We'd love to show this to some other people here—"

"I'd like to show it to them next week, if we could."

They're going to get their day with Sam Parker.

Everyone said good-bye.

John Hanke sighed with relief. "We dodged a bullet there."

Single-Applet Architecture

John Hanke is drawing heavily on his experience of being a diplomat in managing some very hotheaded coders.

It's Tuesday and the Snap demo is Friday and Jason is in Austin making an offer on a house. The code is broken again. Everything is broken. It's a big problem.

Kevin had built a dual-applet architecture. One applet brought up the gaming room and the seating arrangement around the gaming tables. When the user chose from the menu of games, that started a second applet; the latter *didn't* have to care about the former. This made an easy server-farm arrangement—one server per game, and the gaming room applet on yet another server. Unfortunately, some users were getting disconnected when they clicked on a game to play, disconnecting from one server and attempting to reconnect to the appropriate game server.

Anytime you jump servers, you're taking a chance. That's the unpredictable nature of the Internet. Overnight, Max e-mailed a possible solution in which each server would have both a lobby and the games on them, so the user would never have to disconnect. A single applet would run both the lobby and the game. This would be a fundamental shift in the architecture, and the Snap demo is only three days away.

Meeting with John Hanke the next morning, Arie is hopping mad. His fingers are twitching, and his effort to control his emotions is actually making the twitching worse, because he's bottling up everything—not just his anger but his ability to communicate. "It's a *bad* idea," he says curtly.

"Why, Arie?" John begs.

"It's just a bad idea, John!"

John tries to get Arie to elaborate. But Arie is so upset, he can't explain what he predicts will happen. ("He was having kittens" is the way Max and Jason describe Arie's fits.) Instead, he barks commands at John, hoping John can think it through and figure out the problem himself. His barks are, in effect, clues to steer John's thinking.

"What happens if the user reloads the page?" Arie barks, and John thinks about that but can't see what Arie is getting at.

"What if there's only one applet per page?" Arie barks again, but John still doesn't get it.

Then Arie says, "From the beginning I never understood why we went with that architecture! I tried to argue that they were going to have this problem, but Max's response was 'I've got four more years of experience than you, go fuck yourself!' "

"I don't think he used those exact words," John said.

"Yes, he did! Kevin told me I needed to learn to 'suck eggs.' "

"I doubt he said 'suck eggs.' "

The team held a meeting at Geekhaus at the start of the project, and Arie managed to "suck eggs" for an evening and listen with his mouth shut as Kevin and Max explained the architecture. Recalling this, John says, "I thought you left that meeting with your questions answered."

"Kevin had assured me that this networking protocol would

work, but of course it hasn't!" Arie doesn't like Max's new solution either. Mainly, he just doesn't trust it—if Max was wrong once, isn't there too great a possibility that he'll be wrong again? Every solution brings with it new problems.

John was in a very difficult spot now. He had two programmers, Max and Arie, arguing over a deep-seated technical issue. (Imagine a judge who speaks only English presiding over a trial deliberated in Spanish.) If they could explain it clearly, Hanke has enough technical expertise to make a decision as to who is right, Max or Arie. But neither programmer has the interpersonal skills to walk him through an explanation. Max once told me that when he was eight years old, his mother had taken him to a psychologist, who had determined that he was sixteen years old intellectually but emotionally only four. Max makes no secret of the difficulty he has picking up on the subtle signs that are clues to people's thoughts.

John feels that the code architecture is Max's turf. But there's always the possibility that Arie, with his huge brain—that brain that can solve every game puzzle on the Web as easily as stealing candy from a baby—it's possible that Arie might be right.

John Hanke realizes he has no choice. "We may fail by going with Max's solution," he says, "but Max is our guy. We will win or lose with our guys. We have to respect everyone's area. Your area is maintaining the hardware system and the HTML frames, Arie. The Java architecture is Max's area"—then he throws in some diplomatic phrases—"though it's very healthy to have this kind of debate. A dialectic about these issues is good. I'm glad you raised your concerns."

The tremor in Arie's hands is an 8.0 on the Richter scale. It's impossible not to sense his unease.

John says, "Arie, I really believe that Max knows what he is doing."

"I have my doubts, John!"

Arie doesn't feel that this deep-architecture issue is strictly Max's turf. It would involve putting all the code on each of the Big Network's server computers at Exodus, rather than dividing the code among servers. The calculations that each server should be able to handle two hundred users at a time may now be worthless. Maybe they need eight servers, or ten. What's making Arie's hands shake like a chandelier in an earthquake is the possibility that his server farm won't be able to handle the load—and that he will get blamed for it.

"It's going to be okay, Arie."

"I have my doubts, John."

"Do you think we're hanging ourselves?"

Arie takes a fifteen-second pause. He's thinking, and the question rings in the ear.

Do you think we're hanging ourselves?

Changing the architecture three days before the demo!

Do you think we're hanging ourselves?

Three days!

"It's hard to say without testing it," Arie responds.

This seems to be the least contentious statement Arie has made yet, and John wants to get out on this note. With tremendously diplomatic kindness he begs Arie to calm down: "As a practical matter, we have to go with what Max has got. That will be version 1.0. Why don't you send me an e-mail explaining what you propose, and maybe that will be the direction we take for version 2.0."

The only good news, in a perverted sort of way, is that Max's cat got poison oak on his fur and then slept on Max's face, and now Max has open welts on his lips and a bubbly rash on his forehead and doesn't want to be seen in public. His skin is "hyper-supersensitive," but he also has a reaction to cortisone shots—they keep him up for three days without sleep—so if it weren't for Kevin's "gigasteroid" ointment, he'd be in the hospital. Kevin has the gigasteroid ointment only because his skin has developed a burning allergic reaction to the epoxy used in lacquering his Dragonfly.

"Max's not running off to play ultimate Frisbee every afternoon," John says. "So I feel confident he'll devote himself full-time to working through the problems."

Code Freeze

The demo for Sam Parker was a disaster.

At eleven last night, the system was working perfectly. Max's new single-applet architecture significantly speeded up the games. It gave them false confidence. The night before a demo, there is supposed to be a "code freeze," allowing time only for testing and debugging.

But the system was working so well . . . it was hard to resist further tinkering.

And in one of those tinkerings, at eleven that very morning, Arie Grossman inserted a cool little feature allowing the user to change his name and select a cartoon head to represent himself on-screen.

When it came time for the demo, several Snap people played with this feature, and then, when they joined the games . . .

. . . the system crashed.

Disaster.

John Hanke roused Arie Grossman on his cell phone and instructed him to disable the feature. When he did that, the system worked perfectly. John called Dan Burkhart on the phone and showed him, "See? See? It works perfectly!" But the damage had already been done. Dan had been badly embarrassed in front of his bosses, who had seen all they needed to see.

John remarked, "Even a week ago, I kept wondering, 'Can we do this?' I wasn't sure if we could build this system. But now I know that we can. So the question I'm wondering now is, 'Can we convince anyone else that we can do it?' We really put Dan Burkhart in a bad position there. We made him look bad in front of his boss."

Steve Sellers asked, "So Arie never should have added that feature so late?"

John wasn't so sure. From 11 A.M., when Arie added the feature, to 1 P.M., the time of the demo, there should have been plenty of time to test and fix. But Jason's Internet connection had been nearly dead that morning, painfully slow, and he had been unable to post the rebuilt code to the server until exactly one o'clock. There had been no time to test. John Hanke said that there were always mistakes in code. Insufficient testing time was at fault, not Arie. Nobody was to blame, really, except for the untimeliness of Jason's Internet service provider going on the fritz.

But Max was livid. Max believed that Arie had nearly sunk the company by making a critical change to the system a mere two hours before the most important demo. But was it any wonder that if the two didn't get along in person, their code wasn't going to get along?

Max sent e-mail: "I can't believe I work so hard on something that can be totally ruined by the CS equivalent of a three-year-old with matches."

It was beyond the point where Max was just blowing off steam. Not so jokingly, Max and Jason began to talk between themselves about what would happen if they said to John Hanke, "It's us or Arie, you can't have both. We won't work with him any longer." Max began to talk about Arie's background—Max had just learned that Arie had a Ph.D. from Cal Tech. "How did a guy who should stream intelligence get to be such a fucking moron?" Max objected to Arie's $150,000 in prize winnings, believing that hackers like Arie gave programmers a bad image.

To Max, the root cause was clear: B-team thinking, the constant effort to save money. Max brought up any number of corner cuttings that bothered him. They were using a statistics gathering tool for which they hadn't even bothered to pay the minimal $30 license fee. They had never hired professional testers to find bugs. The B-team game programmers, Greg Shaw and David Dies, hadn't been able to complete their respective games, Chess and Backgammon, by the scheduled time.

At one point the team had decided to set up two test servers—one from which to run demos with only stable code installed, a second to be the developer playground. If that had been done, this blown demo would never have occurred. In fact, at one point Arie said that he had set up a second server when he had in fact only partitioned the single test server into two—a solution that *just wouldn't work* (because every computer can have only one of what is called a "well-known port").

"It made me insane," Max said. "You can't build something great without the right tools." He had warned that the effort to save money would cost them in the end, and it appeared that it had.

John Hanke realized he could not afford the risks associated with using the B team again until the contract was signed—even though this meant being that much more vulnerable to the A team's schedules. John called Jason to ask about Max, "Is he on our side? Is he on the plan?" Jason was the only A-teamer actually under contract. John told Jason to finish up Chess and Max to start over with Backgammon. John was giving more responsibility to the Talent, even though they had no skin in the game, and Max was probably going to be very pissed off when John told him the Snap contract had never been signed.

The Halting Problem

John and Steve got one last chance with Snap. This time they would demo in person, at the Snap offices. They would be meeting Sam Parker for the first time. Sam had been described as "very intense," "very inquisitive," with no qualms about putting people on the spot: "He can 'go rottweiler' in a second."

John asked Kevin and Max to attend the demo to field technical questions. John told him it was "a demo for all the marbles." Nobody put it to him straight, but Max understood that this meant the contract wasn't signed.

How did he handle it? Did Max "go rottweiler"?

He said somberly, "That's what happens in this business. The big guys like Snap string along the little guys. Why? Because they can. It's always been that way."

In the beginning the Big Green X had meant everything to Max. But by now he was too heavily invested in his code. In the end, pride in his work resurfaced as the X factor, the thing that kept him up at night giving it all he had.

The vulnerability of this project to freelance programmers who might bail in the clutch—who might run off to hunt squirrels or buy a house in Texas or work for someone else—never became a factor. Though there was smoke, there was no fire.

After one all-nighter working on the stress-tester simulation program—the infamous "piece of cheese"—Max invited me to Geekhaus for lunch. We drove to the San Mateo airport and rented a "superwhizzy" Katana training plane, reminiscent of a gnat. Weather check, breeze out of the north 15 knots. Carb heat off. Choke on. Flaps good. Fuel pump on. Trim neutral.

"Good to go," Max calls. We accelerate up the runway. At 65 miles per hour, Max pulls back on the joystick and we pop into our climb, buzzing over Oracle and heading north with the 101 Freeway below us.

"Kick ass!" Max bellows.

We quickly get up to three thousand feet. Only then does Max bother to tell me what happened on the way to Burning Man over Labor Day weekend.

Max borrowed his friend Matt's classic, fully restored 1949 Cessna 120 "tail dragger" to go to Burning Man. He expected to be a big hit, landing that two-seater on the Black Rock Desert floor. But somewhere over Sacramento, the engine started vibrating, he heard a crunch, and the plane started leaking metal chunks. It had blown a rod, the crank had failed, and the propellor had disengaged. At nine thousand feet it would lose five hundred feet a minute. Max radioed an airstrip in Auburn. Max overshot the airstrip slightly, but he got the plane down without body damage, rolled it out of the way, and immediately called Enterprise rent-a-car to get to the desert.

As a way of talking about the load simulation on the Big Network's system, we discuss the Halting Problem. The Halting Problem is a logical conundrum that every programmer who has studied theory has learned. Basically, you can prove that a certain program will halt, that is, crash, but the inverse is not true: you can never prove that any certain program won't halt.

In other words, you can prove that a plane's engine *will* blow a rod under certain conditions, but you can never prove that it won't. You're just lucky until it does. Or in other words again, the Big Network can run its system, and it may not crash during any simulation, but that is *no proof at all* that it won't crash when it goes live.

And a thousand feet above the bright vermillion suspension towers of the Golden Gate Bridge, Max dips his right wing and spins the Katana like a top. My stomach is down somewhere near my knees.

"Kick ass!" Max whoops.

Fifteen minutes later, we land in Half Moon Bay to grab some lunch at Maverick's Café.

Max confided how he had been confronting his issues about commitment. He had thought that his freelance status was a way of keeping his priorities straight and protecting himself. He had outrageous fun and brain-candy work, what more could a young guy want? But now he was reseeing it as a lack of attachment in every direction: no job, no kids, no marriage, no love. Did owning a portion of a house and volunteering for a San Mateo Big

Brother program count as commitment? His freelance contracts explicitly stated, "Either party may terminate this relationship at any time." "I consider these things and wonder, have I found new and valid lifestyle alternatives, or am I simply a coward?"

Odd how these feelings surface. The five-year saga of the TV show *Babylon 5* came to an end with the most recent episode. It was time for all the characters to say good-bye to one another. Max spent more than a third of the episode in tears. "It really dragged out some feelings of loss and left a sadness hangover that lingers eight hours later. But it made me think: if your experiences tell you that nothing lasts, it's safer to avoid attachment. Few people go to church; nobody—in my business anyway—stays with a job; you move, neighbors move; nothing lasts. Nothing lasts. It seems only natural, in that light, that no matter what, people keep one eye on the door."

Without knowing that this is what is running through Max's mind, it's easy to underrate his involvement. In fact, he wasn't thinking of leaving, and it didn't bother him that he might not profit grandly from the outcome. "I'm not taking a risk. John and Steve are getting paid to take the superrisk." He seemed to be understanding that the "value added" was Steve and John's willingness to tolerate the living hell of uncertainty. "Anyway, if they land this big, juicy deal, I can raise my rates."

He still says, "It'll be a while before anyone can get me back on the start-up bus—I have a visceral fear of doing stuff for no money." About equity/options, he says he is "superbitter." He's been burned, but he knows part of the blame is his.

"I just have no intuition for what will sell," he explains, listing one product after another that he presumed was roadkill yet got bought for millions. He doesn't understand the role non-programmers play. As he calls it, the "canonical" example is the Big Network—"Where is the value add?" he asks aloud. "I don't get it. I like John and Steve a lot," Max says, "but I'm not sure what they really bring. We're the ones doing the programming. If anyone asked me, I'd say they're roadkill."

Then, in an ironical twist, Max's logic goes like this. "But since I am always wrong, it follows that if *I* think they're roadkill, Big Network probably will be big money."

When he got home to Geekhaus less than an hour later, Max began the stress test. When his simulation got up to 250 users, he reached a comfort level, and a mere twenty-two hours before the showdown with Sam Parker, John Hanke opened up the games to a beta test, with all regular users of the Big Network being invited to jump over to the new Java-class games. That night, after simulating 100 users chatting as fast as possible, Max rewrote a code function to make chat scrolling much more efficient.

The next morning John Hanke began to get error messages that he hadn't seen in weeks. At 11 A.M., with the demo three hours away, he called me to say that the demo was "TBD," to be determined. He put the chances of it working properly at fifty-fifty. Max and Jason began to search desperately for the cause of the errors, and just before he got into the car to drive up to the city, Max decided to "roll back" the code to the version that had been working before he rewrote that one chat function. It was a complicated rollback, because Jason had since fixed a few things that Max wanted to keep. He hoped it would work. There was no time for testing. He jumped into the car and sped north.

Scalability

The team had been told to rendezvous at 1:30 across the street from the new Snap building on Pier 39, at the Burger Café, a chrome-and-neon diner with red vinyl chairs, sparkly Formica tabletops, and checkerboard black-and-white floors. The television above their table is playing the movie *Apollo 13*.

Before they arrive, I confront Steve Sellers: "You've got a buggy product, no contract, thirty days of cash in the bank, programmers with no stake in the outcome, and you're getting kicked out of your office in two weeks—how do you possibly sleep at night? How do you possibly stare that situation down? How do you keep going into the *living Hell of radical uncertainty?*"

Steve has a smile on his face, and it's not a nervous smile—he looks as if he's enjoying himself. He laughs at my summary of his plight and says, "Actually, I kind of think we're in a very good position."

But he admits the risk level would probably seem absurd to most people. "Eventually, it becomes a lifestyle. There is a saying which I think is true: 'What doesn't kill me makes me stronger.' "

Steve got his undergraduate degree in anthropology, and he is an astute observer of the world. He sees his life in a panoramic perspective, always able to step back into theory, philosophy, or literature. He says he is indeed enjoying himself. He tells me how Nietzsche advocated being warriors, but *happy* warriors, cheerful—comfortable in our skin. Get him talking about Nietzsche, and he can go all day. The spirit of the entrepreneur is exactly the sort of thing Nietzsche celebrated.

"In the end it comes down to will. That is my value added to this equation: I can't code a lick and I've never contributed a creative idea, and though I've arranged funding, what I really add is the force of my will. My will to never give up and to make this happen no matter what."

As his Big Network team huddles over a table in the Burger Café, the one person who is conspicuously absent is Arie. They couldn't risk Arie taking offense and pissing off Snap. Max looks as if he's about to crack. Kevin is smooth and highly verbal. John Hanke, as usual, is calm enough to provoke wisecracks from his teammates about Prozac consumption.

This meeting is billed as one on scalability. They've been told that Sam Parker is very concerned about signing a contract with a garage outfit that is completely unproven. So what if the games are stable with four players in a demo—can they handle the load of several thousand users at once? Deal makers at his level think in terms of "building the brand" and "spending the brand," and a system crash would most definitely spend Snap's brand. In Dan Burkhart's words, "Sam puts a very high value on the risk premium."

So they've got to convince him that Snap's traffic is safe with them, which is very much like a bank convincing you that your money is safe. This is why banks have grand granite arched fronts and marble floors and hardwood teller windows and security guards. The money isn't even there, the money is no more than an electronic signal in the Federal Reserve computer system, but the formidable front-end presentation helps convince Joe Q. Depositor that his money is safe. Sam Parker is a VP, not a technical guy. No matter what Max or Kevin says in the meeting about diagnostic tools and beta tests and Jitterbug reports, Sam Parker is still going to be thinking in the back of his mind, "These are a few cowboys who don't even have an office—can I risk it?" He's going to be thinking, "If I sign a deal with TEN, at least I will be able to sleep at night."

Steve Sellers uses this chance to tell everyone on his team that TEN, their dreaded powerhouse rival now backed by Kleiner Perkins, moved into on-line card games by buying a small company called Webdeck, which was just one ex–Oracle programmer working out of his garage. Just one guy! Not so long ago this all-important revenue producer for TEN was a lot smaller than the Big Network. So no thinking, *We can't do this.* No thinking, *What are we doing playing with the big boys?*

Then Steve points everyone's attention to the movie playing overhead. It's the scene where the *Apollo 13*'s capsule's heat shields are damaged. If the capsule doesn't slice down into the earth's atmosphere at exactly the right angle, it will bounce off the atmosphere and veer forever into oblivion. Down in Mission Control, Ed Harris turns to the news media and boldly says, "Ladies and gentlemen, this will be our finest hour."

What perfect timing. Before they depart for their appointment, Steve says to anyone within hearing distance, "This is what life is all about. This is really living. There's just not many times in life where it all comes down to one moment."

Epilogue

Programmers have a favorite saying, a sort of Murphy's law as interpreted by M. C. Escher, called Hofstadter's law: "It always takes longer than you think—even when you account for Hofstadter's law." Both the Snap deal and the launch continued to progress without ever actually being completed. Snap had seen the sausage being made, and it had scared them from having the confidence to be the first implementation of the Big Network's Java games. They wanted someone else to be the guinea pig. That guinea pig turned out to be TheGlobe.com, which during this same period had both canceled its planned initial public stock offering due to the weak market and then reattemped the IPO with fabulous success, posting the greatest first-day gains in stock market history. Not having witnessed blown demos or programmer tantrums, TheGlobe had nothing to fear.

CHAPTER 5

THE Salespeople

IN THE OFFICIAL history of this industry, there is no chapter on selling. The idealized entrepreneurial life-cycle begins with an idea; ideas become products, products become start-ups, and if a start-up can grab a few early adopter beta users, it gets bought out for millions. End of story, back to hunting for the next idea. Let whoever acquired the company ramp up the customers.

Bill Kellinger is a career salesman. He was at Oracle in the late '80s, he was at Netscape back when it was Mosaic. Now he's landed here, on just another arterial street in Santa Clara inside just another ordinary office park at just another very ordinary high-tech start-up on the verge of facing the Reaper.

Most entrepreneurs scurry around this industry totally in denial of the fact that one day, the Grim Reaper will be at their company's door. They can be the buzz of *Internet World* and send everybody home with a pocket full of decoder rings, but still the Reaper knocks. They can float a public offering and create a balance sheet so top-heavy with cash it wants to stand straight up in the air, but still the Reaper knocks. They can pay Yahoo! millions to get their share of eyeballs, but still the Reaper knocks. The time has come.

Someone has got to move units.

At Manage.com, Bill Kellinger has been brought in as employee number thirty to ramp up his firm's sales organization. According to the business plan that is about to get its second round of VC financing, he is supposed to bring in $1.5 million in sales this year, which with a $3,000 price point breaks down into five hundred closes. The average sales cycle will be thirty to forty-five days. He gets to hire one telesales rep and one field rep, both of whom will be coming over from Netscape when Bill gets the okay.

Kellinger offers me a media-savvy menu of product explanations—the *Wired* level of detail, the *Information Age* level of detail, the *MIS Journal* level of detail.

"I'll take the *Wired* level of detail."

In the *Wired* level of detail, the new firm he's just joined, Kellinger says, "is a plane up in the air." And this plane has been flying around for nine months—basically, completely removed from society. The programmers had to build the plane, and the system engineers are the air traffic controllers, and it's his job just to land the plane.

You can read that explanation again in case it was too technical for you.

The only problem with this is that Bill Kellinger's firm doesn't officially exist yet. It won't announce its existence for three more weeks. There's not even a Web site to produce leads for him. Founded by engineers, the company has been paranoid that if it announces its existence and idea, its product will get copied by someone else. They've been up in that plane refusing to identify themselves on the radar screens. Employees one through twenty-nine are actually quite nervous just having Bill Kellinger around; they eye him suspiciously over the rim of their cubicles. They've asked him to come in only half-days. "They're terrified of me," he says. He's too high-energy, talks too fast, and they're afraid he will sell their wine before its time. Their product is basically 98 percent done. To a salesperson accustomed to selling vapor, 98 percent done is 100 percent salable. But engineers are perfectionists, and to them salable is a far cry from shippable.

This is the X axis of the psychic space that divides engineers from salespeople: technical elegance versus pragmatic compromise.

So Kellinger has to get started on his $1.5 million without any product to sell, without even a company to announce. This doesn't seem to bother anyone but him, and to tell you the truth, it doesn't seem to bother him that much either. The reason is, his product has a clear niche for an established need. Basically, over the last few years, all these Fortune 1,000 companies bought way too much intranet software, primarily from Netscape, and now can't manage it all. Kellinger's new company (which doesn't yet exist) is selling software (which doesn't yet exist) that manages the logistics for department-level network administrators. It's sort of a real-time CAT scan for the bloated body of network systems.

Maybe this is just the *Wired*-level-of-detail explanation, but it sounds to me as if Bill Kellinger oversold a bunch of customers some intranet software when he was at Netscape, and now he's come to another firm to sell them a solution to the problem he helped create.

Kellinger insists, though, that it would be unethical to raid his old client list from the Netscape days. No argument from me there.

Just in case any of this seems out of the ordinary, I should explain how this company that doesn't exist got its quota for the year of $1.5 million—progressing to $8 million next year and $20 million in year three. Bill says, "The marketing director looked at the business plans of ten other start-ups. And the common denominator for all ten was that their first-year expected sales were one and a half million, then eight million, then twenty." Then Bill takes another peek at the cover of my novel, which I set down before him at the beginning of the interview. Its title is *The First $20 Million Is Always the Hardest*. It's just a novel, but Bill looks at it and says, "Yeah, twenty million. That takes about three years, doesn't it?"

It is the coldhearted imposition of top-down/product-indifferent quotas like this that makes engineers so distrustful of sales. So deep is this collective distrust that the sale of the new machine is routinely kept hidden from the general public. We never hear about the salespeople. The bias is so entrenched that a recalcitrant coder with purple hair, nose ring, and hands heavily callused from his punk guitar is considered a more acceptable public figure—he better represents this industry—than an overfriendly family man in a Nordstrom's suit who carries the company bag. What's going on here?

The guardians of the official history suggest that the real brilliance in the software business is in strategic decision-making. It's all about cutting the right deal—reserving a crucial right in the contract or partnering with the company that's on the cusp of becoming the protocol standard. Product. Marketing. Deals. These are all cunning solutions that demonstrate virtuoso brainpower—and there is nothing more esteemed in this industry than virtuoso brainpower.

But sales is not about brainpower. Sales is about manpower. While chip speed has been doubling every eighteen months, an average face-to-face sales call still costs $400 and takes half a day. It's labor intensive. The methodology of sales is still fairly much trial and error—you knock on fifty doors, you find five good leads, you close one sale. Don't like it? Go hide in your cubicle.

Dare you do more than peek over the cubicle rim? Dare you risk learning what really saves the software industry's ass, quarter after quarter? Can you stomach confirming your worst suspicions, all of which have to do with sales being sleazy, in order to go where you're only unofficially allowed: into the soul of the sales machine?

Field Call

The most notable characteristic of Mars Garro is his voice: it's the resonant pitch of a television sports announcer, quick to lend exuberance to ordinary dramas. Sometimes he does his own play-by-play commentary, offering observations to the other half of his broadcast team, an imaginary presence whom Mars addresses as "Jim." If you are one of the worker bees deep in the honeycomb hive of a downtown city, a visit from this human bumblebee will take the lull out of your day. His love for life is infectious.

Mars, a pseudonym I'm using to preserve his anonymity, is a field rep for Oracle. In the last week before he was to leave town for another region, we called upon a division of Wells Fargo. Rep territories are always being divided and repartitioned, and reps are frequently moved around so that they don't have to live with the consequences of overselling an account. There is an opportunity for Mars to do that today—to load up Wells with software it could go without. He blew out his annual number three months ago, so he'll earn a triple commission on any orders taken today. When I ask him what his income is, he replies, "Tasty." I do know that he's been looking at open houses on Sundays, and a mortgage is an option, not a necessity. Last week, he went house shopping one night, found something he liked, and put an offer in at 10 P.M. The next day, he drove by to take another look, and with the benefit of daylight discovered that the trim and siding he thought was slatted wood was really faux plastic. He had the realtor on the phone right away.

This division of Wells Fargo is the Ad Hoc Reporting Group. They are green berets who wear green eyeshades. They report directly to the CEO. What they do is independently verify all of the department reporting that gets sent to the CEO to make sure some department isn't covering up red ink with cooked books. They need a safecracking tool that can penetrate the internal network and raid all of these wildly divergent types of databases scattered around the firm.

Mars is going to demo just such a tool that Oracle has ready. Well, kind of. It's almost ready to ship. Really, quite close. Give or take a little time. Close enough to suggest to the Ad Hoc team that it is safe to put an order in now, before the end of the quarter. Well, at the very least we can say that it's ready to demo, which is more than we could say three weeks ago, when Mars failed to get it working in front of this same audience. The point here is, Ad Hoc has been begging for this tool for years, and if Mars can make it look like it works smoothly and handle the supervisor coolly, the rest of the sale should be easy. Ad Hoc so wants this tool to exist that at 7:30 A.M. on a Friday morning the conference room is full. There are no stragglers.

There seems to be a slight problem, though. Mars is trying to dial into the Wells network through a phone jack, but his laptop can't establish a connection. He tries another jack, and then another.

"Murphy's law seems to be prevailing, Jim." Mars laughs anxiously.

Mars is pretty sure that it's a problem on Wells's end, but it still looks bad for him. People head out to refresh their coffee and check e-mail. One of the Ad Hoc supervisors scratches his head. He tries to call the sysadmins, but can't reach them, so he puts out a page. In the meantime, Mars trolls cubicles, fielding technical questions from the Ad Hoc team about other software he's already sold them.

One of the things that makes Mars such a great rep is that he came out of tech support at Oracle. This taught him all sorts of practical, hands-on solutions to the everyday problems users have with software. Since buyers can never understand all the technical issues that distinguish one software package from its "me too" competitor, at some point the deciding factor shifts to some entirely different proxy variable. That proxy is the rep. Which rep would you rather do business with? Which rep would you rather have chatting you up every month, taking you to lunch, trouble shooting your system, and bothering your staff? The Ad Hoc team has been happy to have Mars, and he'd like this to be their lasting impression—that he was helpful.

At 8 A.M., one of the sysadmins finally calls back. "Oh, yeah," he says, "it looks like some bozo turned that network machine off last night." He powers it up, and in no time Mars is able to dial in without problems. He fires up the screen projector, which blasts a picture of his desktop onto a dry-erase whiteboard that covers the wall. The Ad Hoc supervisor calls his entire team back into the room, someone dims the lights, and we're ready to go.

Except . . . another tiny little problem. Mars goes to the dry-erase board to wipe away all the formulas that have been written on it, so he has a clear surface to project on. The red ink won't seem to come off. Some bonehead has accidentally written all over the board with indelible red ink. Suddenly this roomful of semiprogrammers attack the problem. The only thing that seems to work is a ton of elbow grease. One of the Ad Hoc guys uses a blue dry-erase pen to draw a matrix over the board, and he orders everyone to take their square and start rubbing. Fifteen guys, burnishing a wall.

"Talk about drama!" mocks Mars.

It takes about five minutes, and most of the ink comes off, except where the blue dry-erase pen crisscrosses the red—that chemical combination seems truly indelible, leaving the whiteboard pocked with these purple hatch marks. Everyone's palms and thumbs are bright pink.

Except for those forty minutes of minor inconveniences, the demo goes smoothly. The software works beautifully. Unfortunately, the Ad Hoc team has to meet with the CIO at 8:30, so Mars is cut short before he has a chance to really let the program show off. The programming team at Oracle that wrote this software would abhor the oafishness of this scene—the lack of precision, the shortage of time, all the cool features that go unshown. But the Ad Hoc team is nevertheless impressed. The Ad Hoc supe says what he always says: "Why don't you send me a free copy to evaluate?"

Mars gets maybe twelve minutes in, and could squeeze in another three but he wants time to find a proper good-bye. The Ad Hoc supervisor breaks the ice for him: "Well, guys, some of you may know this, but Mars is moving to a new region and this is his last visit to us."

One of the guys brings in a cinnamon roll festooned with a lit birthday candle. Nobody knows what to sing, so they just applaud a little. Mars, who is a natural showman, croons in a Frank Sinatra voice a few lines of Cole Porter's "I Get a Kick Out of You," then breaks down in embarrassment. He tries to cover up his unwanted exhibitionism with forced chuckles, saying, "Aw, shucks, hold your applause, please." Then watches are glanced at—okay, token moment over—and the room clears. It's just the Ad Hoc supervisor and Mars (and me). What about the sale?

We make our way to the elevators.

Normally, the time span from demo to close takes a month, during which the product is evaluated and contracts are negotiated. Going for the close so soon after the demo is a procedural faux pas, an awkward unseemliness in a timeworn, step-by-step exchange designed to make buying and selling pleasantly unsleazy. Also, Mars doesn't want his very last impression to be forced. But hey—Mars is a salesperson. I'm not sure he can help the words from coming out of his mouth.

Mars tries what is known as the reverse close. I'd heard that the reverse close is a very dangerous pitch line, not many can pull it off, but it works fast if it's the last day of the quarter.

He says, "Look, this is my last week, I don't have time to close you. And if I did, you've seen all my techniques. So let's not jockey each other that way. I know you need this new software as soon as you can get it, and you know I need the letter of intent this week. So the question is, How much room do you have in your budget? You tell me. I'm going to give you the CD. How many seats can we write now, and how many will we just wait until next quarter for?"

The Ad Hoc supe pushes the elevator button. "Well, I'd like to take a look at it."

Mars throws the next line out jokingly, but it rings with wishfulness. "Not feeling like giving me a little going away present, huh?"

And the elevator arrives. Time's up. They return to the comfortable ritual of highly starched male barbing.

"Go get 'em out there," the Ad Hoc supe jousts, plugging Mars's shoulder with a softly thrown fist.

"Work on that golf swing," Mars parries. "Next time we play I don't want to take all your money."

The doors come together.

I look at Mars and he's a little sweaty. He shakes his arms out and rolls his shoulders. "Oh boy," he says. He's giddy. He's helium. "Last time in this building, Jim."

"Too bad about the sale," I say, steering him back to the topic.

His mind is elsewhere, but he still responds. "No worries. He's a good guy. He'll buy as soon as the software's ready. I'll call him."

He hits the front doors at a clip. "Oh boy," he says again. The bumblebee is free.

Some Translations

Hockey stick disease: Picture a hockey stick: _/ This is the line graph tracking sales volume chronologically over the quarter—none for two months, then a steep incline at the end. It's not uncommon for 45 percent of the deals to close in the last two days of the quarter.

"Me too" product: Software that is pretty much the same as another company's software.

Dropping your pants: Lowering your price to close a sale.

Overhanging the market: Promising that desired features will be designed into future upgrades.

Seats: Seat licenses in volume selling, that is, number of paid users.

Mindshare: As opposed to market share. When a salesman says, "I'm building mindshare," what he means is he hasn't sold a thing.

The Cycle: The average length of time it takes to make a sale. This can be as long as nine months, which makes it hard when there's a new upgrade and new pricing every six months.

"The Queen Mary *has turned around":* Said when a reluctant client finally is ready to buy.

Spiffs: The bonus incentives that software firms offer top resellers—mountain bikes, a BMW leased for a year, et cetera.

Motivation

Salespeople are motivated by money. They'll admit this right up front, which is quite refreshing—it's not taboo to them. They don't fabricate some cockamamie motivational flowchart to imply that, after all, money is just status, or how it's in the best interests of the firm for them to pursue their own personal self-interest. They want money so they can buy cars and houses and private school education for their children, and maybe a sailboat or a trip to Tahiti. It's not an equity game—they want "W-2 money." Cash. They don't want promises. Income this year, right now. They don't have the net worth of company founders, but their take-home pay makes up for it.

Money is also what pulls them through the bad days, the days when customers are reneging and the sales manager is carping about why more deals that were rated last month as "85 percent likely to close" haven't closed by now. To drown out this chatter, they singlemindedly focus on hitting their number, and once they hit it the lure of two-times or three-times kickers spurs them to blow it out.

Their number is their quota. Most software salespeople have quarterly numbers, but some are monthly, and in the real chop-house atmosphere of a regional reseller it's "put out or get out" on a weekly basis. The quotas come directly from the business plan, which is to say they may have no discernible relationship with reality. When a salesperson meets quota, every additional sale above that quota pays double, then triple the commission. Quotas are skewed down intentionally, so salespeople feel good about themselves averaging 120 percent of their number.

The dollars earned determines your career. Walk into a pre-interview and hand over your résumé and the first thing the headhunter will do—the first thing—is get out the HP35 calculator and add up the running totals of two figures: how many years you've sold, and how much money you've earned selling. It's that simple. As soon as you've made $50,000 in qualifying leads, you'll have job offers in telesales for $90,000, and a year on the horn will land you in the field, working face-to-face for $140,000, minimum. If you prove you're any good, expect double that.

So if it's all about numbers, do salespeople really believe in what they sell? "Do they," to restate the question in their own terminology, "drink the Kool-Aid?"

If it were a multiple-choice question, the answer most frequently checked would be: n/a, Not Applicable. I encountered the complete bell curve of optimism, from bitter cynics to earnest evangelists, but nobody pretended that this was essential. What salespeople need to believe—and all they need to believe—is that they can sell the product. Not necessarily that it works, just that they can sell it. Before you roll your eyes at that, consider that selling unworkable software is far less common than the inverse—being given a quota on software that works fine but that nobody needs. That's the salesman's migraine. Just give 'em something they can sell.

Listening

Jim Yares is a rover, a specialist who targets crucial strategic clients for the Vantive Corporation, which sells high-end customer databases. His average purchase order, combining the basic software and the seat licenses, runs in the mid-$300,000s.

By now, you are probably expecting Hades himself. The guy who sells Fuller brushes to the wife of the guy who sells Florida swamp real estate to the bedridden. But Silicon Valley is in Northern California, after all, and the *Glengarry Glen Ross* sell just doesn't go over well here. We need our touchy-feely. So a majority of the most successful salespeople are ones who create a touchy-feely buying process, who can make you feel comfortable and reassured with your purchase decision.

Yares used to be a goal-oriented Machiavellian, but he burned out on that and has learned to turn sales into a process. He's thirty-five—for men, an age of introspection. Before he came to Vantive, he took seven months off with his wife to sail off the coast of Mexico. Now he's got a baby who's walking but not yet talking, and his daydreams as he drives up and down 101 are mostly about being on that sailboat again. He recently reread *Zen and the Art of Motorcycle Maintenance,* and considers its author, Robert Pirsig, one of his heroes. What makes Jim Yares so Northern Californiaesque is that he grew up in the South, where congeniality is so nurtured it seems natured. Jim Yares is touchy-feely, but he's not sticky. He doesn't ooze any vibe. He is a porch, a wicker chair, and a summer breeze.

Executive summary of what I found when accompanying Jim: Selling is all about listening. Listening is a euphemism for keeping your trap shut. When you walk into an account, what you're asking for, at the very least, is a meeting—which better go well. Customers' satisfaction with a meeting will be directly correlated to how much they get to speak. (It is the tendency to interrupt that hinders engineers who try to sell. Even when they try to listen, engineers-turned-salesmen give in to the irresistible desire to impress the client with their brainiac ability to anticipate needs through logical deduction rather than allow clients to spell out their needs themselves.)

Yares uses a highly empathic conversational method that is much like echoing or mirroring. He merely repeats the essence of what he hears, resisting all temptation to ask leading questions. The dialogue that ensues sounds more like marital conflict counseling than a sales call. Yares often ends up moderating the bureaucratic grudges between technical engineers and their department managers.

Technical Engineer/Husband: She thinks I'm lazy.

Department Manager/Wife: He ignores what I ask him to do.

Jim Yares: It sounds like what I hear you saying is that you agree you need a better customer database, but you have some differences about how difficult it is to implement such a database.

Yares can see where they're headed, but it's important he let them voice it. It's sort of like a twelve-step program; they can't solve their problem until they publicly admit they have a problem. That's why it's very important that Yares meet with more than one person. In private, people will always confess their problems to salespeople. At that point, it's still a personal issue. But to get them to confess in front of a coworker is to make the problem an organizational issue. Unfortunately, some people— once they feel they're being listened to—can't shut up.

Jim Yares (facing the woman): It sounds like you have some staff who might be resistant to change.

Department Manager/Wife: Well, yes—

Technical Engineer/Husband (interrupting): Can your system work on Palm Pilots?

In the afternoon, Yares finds himself in a tough jam with a tiny department of a very large engineering conglomerate. I promised to disguise its name, so I will call it Colonel Electric. The Boss Hog of this Colonel Electric divisional subdepartment has just purchased from Yares a very limited module of Vantive's software with a very limited number of seat licenses, a baby system. Now he hopes to get the system customized by Vantive "consultants," that is, programmers. Software consulting normally runs about $1,500 a day. Yares would love to sell Colonel Electric a month's worth of consulting, but he can see that's not going to happen—this Boss Hog doesn't have that kind of money in his budget to spend.

Boss Hog tries his own kind of sell. He explains that if the system is adapted to run well in his department, it will probably be adopted by some of the other dozen relevant departments. The subtext of what he's saying is, "Why don't you give me the consulting for supercheap, that is, free, invest in my system, and it'll pay off with more seats in due time."

But is this just a bluff? What if he actually has very little influence in all those other departments?

How to refuse the Boss's request for free consulting without just saying "no"—that's the question for Yares. If this were a one-on-one exchange, it might be easier for Yares to bury the request in the bureaucracy: "Why don't you put that down on paper and my managers will consider it." But, unfortunately, Boss Hog has brought his entire engineering staff with him—there are seven men in the room, all now serving as witnesses. Yares can't expect him to back down in front of his boys.

This is a situation that an engineer-turned-salesman probably would blow. Engineers are notoriously too fast with the solution to the customer's problem. They don't show empathy. Making the problem seem too easy to fix is to make the customer feel stupid for not having fixed it earlier.

What Yares does is very delicate. If he can't draw the huge consulting fees out of the boss, he'd like to encourage all the Colonel Electric staff to enroll in the cheaper Vantive training classes where they can learn to customize the system themselves. But if he offers the training classes outright it will sound like a blunt "No. You're not getting any free consulting." Also, Yares senses not to address each of them directly, since their boss is running the show.

So Yares starts mirroring Boss Hog, counselorlike, with the deep focus of a hypnotist: "It sounds like you personally have some system needs you'd like to be met." In no time this gets him to cough up a complaint: When the system prints out a certain report, the layout doesn't include fax numbers.

"I got nuthin' without those fax numbers," Boss Hog admits.

Yares gets out his laptop. He intends to train the Boss, right then and there, how to customize the layout to include fax numbers. If the Boss can do it, then the staff will follow. This is a very high-risk maneuver, because if the Boss embarrasses himself in front of his staff Yares will never be forgiven. As Yares had said to me in the car (as sweetly as if he were quoting Robert Frost), "to sell software is to ask people to willfully become temporarily incompetent"—and men hate to look incompetent.

Yares demonstrates, but Boss Hog is reluctant to risk making a fool of himself. It's dawning on him, though, that he's not going to get that free consulting.

Now, this is what is known in closing as the Wait. The Wait often transpires with a letter of intent in one hand and a fountain pen in the other, poised to secure a signature on the dotted line. But the Wait can take any form, over any issue. The salesperson has to simply sit there and outlast his client. The skill of waiting is in being stubborn without betraying any of the confrontational chin-thrusting of stubbornness. The salesperson can't provoke his customer to defiance.

Yares, the expert listener, is also a terrific lingerer. Minutes pass. The conversation in the room veers toward other issues, but Boss Hog and Yares are hanging in there, mute. Yares is still that wicker chair, he's not leaving that porch. Yares could spend days watching grass grow.

Eventually, Boss Hog just can't stand not doing anything, and his idle hands turtle-creep toward the keyboard.

Leads

It is raining bad leads in the software business. The hurricane of shitty leads is ten miles off the coast and bearing down. Every software firm's 800 number rings off the hook, but it's always another grandma in Arizona with the wacky idea of selling hand-knit baby socks over the Web, and she figures she can spend $49 before her second husband steals the checkbook again. Every firm's Web site is being dented with a barrage of e-mail from rogue developers angling for a free trial copy of the software. Every convention yields a fishbowl crammed with business cards, mostly from people who want to sell to you, not buy from you. Every direct-mail house has a catalog of brokered lists, compiled by housewives in Omaha who poll 10 million businesses with such micromarket-defining queries as "Is your company A) 1 to 50 employees, B) 50 to 1,000, C) 1,000 to 10,000 . . . ?"

Salespeople have an inextricably snarled love-hate relationship with leads. On one hand, the number one complaint of salespeople is that they don't spend enough time actually selling, and spend too much time doing the bullshit—writing contracts, begging engineering for fixes, and chasing bad leads. I found this complaint to be true across all price categories. Too much downtime.

On the other hand, most salespeople insist on seeing all the leads, on the off-chance one of those droplets falling from the sky might be a diamond, a lead that's worth working.

The dilemma in the software business is lead qualification. A good system screens all those rinky-dink leads then traffics the good ones right away to the salesforce. The problem is, nobody wants to get on the phone and do the dirty work. With all the jobs open in Silicon Valley today, anyone who can speak in full sentences has got better offers. Calling people—it's just so damned low-tech, it's antithetical to why people join this industry in the first place. Telemarketing services can do the job, but small firms don't have the volume to meet the contract minimums.

So El Niño of crappy leads continues.

Quarter End

I hate the silence. There is something wrong. There is something evilly wrong. I am on the road again this morning with a salesman from a major software firm. I hooked up with him in the parking lot of the McDonald's on Bowers Avenue in Santa Clara, got out of my Jetta and got into his Porsche, and now we are on the way to a major bank to close a sale. He is silent. He has never been silent before. There have always been words coming out of his mouth. His silence is a wall I am afraid to climb.

Caffeine dizzies. The subtle noxiousness of rush-hour traffic exhaust. A whisper of carsickness from my stomach. His cellular jars us with its ringing. He doesn't look at it. It rings six times then cuts off. A moment later, he reaches to his belt, removes his pager, and sets it on the dashboard.

We have found a mutual respect, he and I. In my mind, I have nicknamed him the Burn Artist. From our first meeting I had always enjoyed him for his excessive character, in the way one has a sick fondness for John Malkovichian villains. After that first meeting, I wrote this description of him in my notes: *The Burn Artist drapes over his seat like a casually tossed leather jacket, other places to be. His face is stubbled weekend ruffian, and his wrist flashes a $7,000 Rolex. He is of medium build, but his Ego, which rises up behind him, wears a 46.* What that description doesn't convey is how much I have come to respect his cunning.

I'm beginning to see what he has done. I told him I wanted to learn about sales, and he told me some sensational stories about deals he had closed. Example: he sold seat licenses to regional divisions, when he knew that the customer's headquarters had already bought enterprise-wide licenses for that region—idiotic bureaucracies make such double-sales possible. (He also some-times manipulated his commissions: he sold software but turned the purchase order in for consulting services, which pays triple the commission of software.)

Let me tell you how a salesman gets into this position. If you're a public company, you can be a growth company or a ma-ture company. A growth company trades at a very high multiple of earnings, and the Street will ho-hum losses as the natural con-sequence of heavy investment in growth. A mature company trades at a very ordinary multiple and if there's a loss the Street executes the CEO. All the tech companies that want to be growth companies have a powwow with their stock analysts every quar-ter, and the analysts look at last quarter's revenues and say, "Well, if you still want to be a growth company, this quarter you've got to get your sales up to here." And the analysts give them an exact figure. Meet it or watch your stock drop by half.

It's a treadmill that a firm can't get off. Grow, grow, grow, every single quarter, every salesperson's got their share. A firm is under intense pressure to make sales.

"Sometimes a product that we know doesn't work very well should be dropped," I had got him to say at our second meeting. "It will burn the customer, and it will create support nightmares for us for years." Might this be the situation today? The Burn Artist is expecting to close a sale of an E-Shop Merchant System. It will be an enterprise-wide sale, thousands of seats. He is going to drop his pants from $15 million to $10 million to make the close. He's already over his quota for the quarter, so the commis-sion he's expecting would be two points, $200,000.

We arrive at the parking lot of our destination. His cellular rings again, in vain.

He seems uncomfortable. He tells me to wait in the car. He says, "All year I've been telling them we should drop this product. Now that I can close the deal they don't want me to sell it. But when the money's on the table, they won't be able to say no."

When he went in, I sat alone in the car for a while. The phone rang twice more, then I got out of the car and went for a stroll. I thought about my friend in marketing who had put me in touch with the Burn Artist, and about the baby boy she'd had five days earlier, who was still under the sunlamps at Mount Zion Medical. I walked into a Denny's and sat at the counter and drank decaf. In the booth behind me, there were two young guys in suits, one of whom was playing with a laptop and saying, "You remember last quarter, at Orange County? God, that was something."

Sales stories are always funnier afterward. On the way to a sale, salesmen tell little Aesopian parables, reminding themselves what to do and not to do. They're like little red pills, these stories—pick-me-uppers. The time I almost didn't chase that lead, the time I almost asked for too low a price, et cetera. On the way home from a sale, the stories take on satirical dimensions. There is no lesson. The client was always as ugly as Godzilla or as dumb as a stick. Moments of agony become moments of high humor. "Boy, what was with her? The look on her face was like, 'How much more of my time are you going to waste, because I don't want to be late for my doctor's appointment at four o'clock to get this broomstick pulled out of my ass.'"

I walked back to the Porsche. In some time, the Burn Artist returned. His first six words all started with F. He stashed his laptop and we were on the road again.

"All I had to do was drop my pants," he said. "They were expecting it, I was expecting it. But I didn't do it. My boss would have kicked my ass. But he can kiss that ten million good-bye." (A few days later, the Burn Artist told me that his firm had officially stopped selling the product.)

"I gotta get out of this business," he says, aggressively downshifting as the Porsche hits standstill traffic.

Schmoozing

It doesn't happen very often. This industry is a sorry sad-sack bunch of no-funners. Oh, sure, field reps do some dinner and drinking, and if Macworld's in town you can stand outside the Mitchell Brothers All-Nude Theater and watch conventiongoers unpin their hologram badges and slip their wedding rings off their fingers, but the stories I've heard and scenes I've seen are mere cardboard cutouts of the real thing that goes on in more established industries. Where are the reps who racked up three Gs on the Amex in one night, renting a limo by the mile to go night skiing in Reno, where at the Canasta table around 2:00 A.M. they met the princess of Albania, who took them to her chalet to pet the polar bear chained up in her backyard?

People are working too hard on such short sales cycles, grinding away in their cubicles, trying to save their firms—they don't even know how to boondoggle a golf game now and then. The mock-casual eloquence of sales is largely missing. Everything these days is Solution Sell, meaning every bit of sales karma is invested in getting customers to like the product. And that's a smart strategy, because in the Valley of Revolving Doors, both the seller and the buyer are likely to be employed elsewhere soon. Big schmooze budgets, the crowbar of the Relationship Sell (always cracks clients open), aren't very common here.

Firms do have entertainment budgets, but that's allocated for marketing, not sales. Marketing usually blows 90 percent of it on a big party at a trade show, the success of which is carefully measured against the industry-standard Tylenol Index—that is, the severity of one's hangover. The money is spent on the party because there the CEO can see where it goes ("Gosh, look at the size of those defrosted prawns!"), as opposed to when it's spent by reps in the field.

And one of the main reasons money isn't thrown at clients is that it doesn't have to be. Geeks are patsies for a baseball cap. Even if you're selling software to, say, the Plumbers Union, you're still selling to a geek who works in a closet in the back of the Union Hall, and he'll drool over a T-shirt. What pushovers! I have seen so many coffee mugs passed out I can't help but roll my eyes—this is the best you could come up with? I'm astonished to watch how greedily these cheapo mugs are taken in, and by the long faces that appear when there haven't been enough mousepads for everyone in the room. Like they don't already have a mousepad, or a drawer full of mousepads, or enough mousepads to wallpaper the hallways with tiled cushions.

The Drift-off Moment

It's time to answer the really big question on everybody's mind, in regards to the technology industry.

Can it keep growing so fast?

Because it seems, sometimes, that these high-tech firms are just selling their stuff to one another.

And they are. When I was with Jim Yares at Vantive, he'd been having trouble breaking into 3Com, which his firm had determined would be a key account. Yares couldn't get anybody at 3Com to return his calls. So how did he finally get a meeting? He did some hunting around his own company, and found that Vantive regularly buys a lot of 3Com network equipment. So he called that salesman at 3Com and in the nicest, sweetest, most low-pressure way possible implied, "HEY—BUDDY! SCRATCH MY BACK AND WE'LL KEEP SCRATCHING YOURS!"

Four different sales reps all told me a version of the embarrassment of walking into Dell Computer carrying a Compaq laptop, or vice versa. They never got away with it. There's a loyalty test: We'll only buy from those already buying from us.

So it is very important that when Paul Mans walks into Oracle to sell the software giant a service called Surveybuilder.com, Mans is running Surveybuilder on an Oracle 8 database back in his Sausalito office. It is the first question out of the Oracle team's mouth, and it is also questions two through four. "Are you running Oracle 8? Good. Are you a partner? Oh, you're not. Why aren't you? You'll want to correct that before you make a pitch to Corporate."

Meanwhile, Paul Mans gives a truly fascinating demo to Oracle. Surveybuilder.com is a tool for Webmasters to get feedback on their Web pages: a little pop-up balloon asks every tenth browser of a Web page to take a survey. The answers help improve design, but more important, this gives a clearer profile of the average user, which Web advertisers are insisting upon. In order to get users to take a minute to fill out the survey, what Mans has found works best is to offer to make a donation to one of twenty-two charities, such as the World Wildlife Fund or the American Cancer Society. Fill out the survey, and a donation will be made.

How big a donation does it take? For an average visitor, it takes a donation of $2 to arouse good compliance. But if they are trying to poll executive types, it usually takes a donation of $50 to make it worth their while. I don't know if that makes the executives more stingy or more generous.

So selling Surveybuilder.com is a real joy for Mans. Mans

made a huge bundle in the headhunting business when he sold his partnership in a firm that had grown in three years from eight people to forty offices. He's deeply at peace now, and he's found a niche where he thinks he can really help people, since so many Webmasters are being hammered on by their bosses to justify why so much money is being sunk into e-commerce. His product is cool enough and engineered so well that he could easily be sprinting for the quick acquisition/embrace, but he's not giving in at all to that hundred-yard-dash mentality. He's got a staff of only nine, has turned away venture funding so far, and doesn't want to push Surveybuilder on clients who aren't ready for it— even if that means he'll get copycatted by other entrepreneurs willing to play the game at burnout speed. He motors down from Sausalito in his old Porsche Targa, wearing film producer clothes, and the mood is more Sunday Drive than Sales Call.

When Mans gives a demo, what he's waiting for is what salespeople call "the drift-off moment." The client's eyes get gooey, and they're staring into space. They're not bored—they're imagining what they could do with Surveybuilder. All tech salespeople mention this—they've succeeded not when they rivet the client's attention, but when they lose it.

The beauty of Mans's sales call is that he saves the donation part until about twenty minutes in. He makes no mention of it. And then, right about when the client is expecting to be told what Surveybuilder costs, he pops the donation thing on them. I watch this happen with the Oracle team. In an instant, their internal monologue shifts from "I bet this is pretty expensive" to "Wow, think how much money we can give away." And this juicy, soulful idea is incredibly appealing to the average philanthropist stuck in a misanthropic cubicle ecosystem. That the $2 donation makes the cost to them $2 more expensive per survey result doesn't faze them. What Mans is really selling here is the opportunity to be altruistic while still doing one's job.

This is exactly why Mans's own soul is so contented—he's breeding altruism while simultaneously selling.

For the four Oracle staffers listening to his pitch, the gooey-eyed drift-off into daydreams of generosity and munificence was as instant as clicking on a TV.

Price

In today's environment, selling vapor is less common than the opposite problem: customers who want to pay vapor. So many software firms have given away so many valuable programs in an attempt to gain market share that it's really hard out there for the salesman who's still charging money. I'm not just talking free browsers and plug-ins; some big-ticket firms are giving away what they used to charge five figures for, trying to book revenue on installation fees and consulting hours attached to the fire sale.

One Netscape field rep was asked by Lockheed for those terms—free server software attached to a generous purchase order for consulting. His response: "Sure, you can have the software for free. Hey, by the way, can I have a free jet?"

Again and again, software firms have to convince customers that the work they do is "Not Trivial," that their product wasn't just whipped together yesterday with a few Javascripts and can't be customized to their liking by tomorrow with a few more. Salesmen defend the efforts of programmers. It does not help that the salesperson's efforts to substantiate the price are regularly undermined by his own firm radically discounting the software every six months, trying to clear inventory to make room for upgraded versions.

That said, there are a few standard price points in the industry that seem to hold firm, the "Magic $99" being the lowest. Below that figure, there's not enough margin to pay for direct mail, advertising, or telemarketing. Put it on a shelf or give it a half-page in a catalog and pray. There are hidden costs there, though. CompUSA will charge you a $5,000 "product testing" fee; the catalogs want advertising surcharges. Make no mistake: retail selling is an expensive investment. A minimum three-across shelf-space for ninety days, supported by an end-cap display and a window poster, will cost $35,000 to $50,000, with no guarantees that most of your product won't get returned.

The next category up is "Fits on a Credit Card," meaning somewhere in the upper hundreds of dollars. There's enough room in that to cut resellers in on the action, creating a whole network of dealers who host open houses and give demos. This multitiered distribution infrastructure is called "The Channel."

Above that, it's "Department-level Discretionary," about three grand. At most Fortune 1,000 firms, all purchases above three grand have to go through a purchase requisition manager, who is someone who has taken classes and been trained to sit on a department's purchase order until the very last day of the quarter, when he knows the salesperson will call back and offer an additional 20 percent discount just to make his quota. Just as salespeople are paid commissions, these purchase requisition managers get quarterly bonuses based on how much they save their firms. Keep the price under three grand and handle the transaction over the phone, a series of calls spread out over thirty to forty-five days.

Then you get to the direct sale. Face to face. Category name: "Whatever the market will bear." Or how long the salesman can bear: In the early days of Netscape, when the company had far more leads than sales reps to close the leads, they didn't bother negotiating. Salespeople were free to drop their pants as far as they had to drop them to make a sale, and in a slash-and-burn method that got their sales cycle down to three days, they would customarily quote a price one day and cut it in half the next. (Now they're on a shorter leash.)

All of this is to say that the price of software, according to those who sell it, has everything to do with what buyers are willing to pay, and nothing to do with what the software costs to develop.

The Sale

Jonathan Harris had such fond memories of the extended-family feeling at Macromedia during its pre-IPO years that he recently jumped to become the sales manager at another start-up, Cosmo Software, hoping to find that magic again. Cosmo makes very cool VRML software tools for building 3-D Web spaces.

VRML's been the next big thing since 1995, which is a kind way of saying it's never become the big thing. Cosmo's sole investor, Silicon Graphics, has hung in until now, but the rumor I heard is that SGI, which has its own losses to bear, needs to find a new investor for Cosmo by the end of the quarter or it will pull the plug. A new investor will come in only if it sees actual hard sales—if there's proof the Web is finally ready for VRML. To make matters even harder for Jonathan Harris, Cosmo's flagship product, Worlds 2.0, shipped only two weeks ago. So he and the seven other sales staff who work for him now have a ten-week window to save the company.

Let me restate that more succinctly: the bosses have reluctantly let the programmers take three years to turn an idea into a shrink-wrapped product, but to turn that product into a market they're allowing the salesforce ten weeks. Not exactly that extended-family magic Harris was after. A seemingly soul-robbing situation, until we hit the road.

To check the pulse of VRML, Harris and I fly to Bellevue, Washington, to check in on NW Tech, a hard-core dealer that sells workstations and software to the real bleeding-edge user. When we arrive, we're sniffed out first by Mathilda, the office dog, and then by a Billy Bob Thornton look-alike named Big Dan, dressed head to toe in black canvas. NW Tech is a family-run outfit, so also on staff are Mom, Big Brother, and Uncle Rog. This is strip-mall turf, the office equivalent of trailer park livin'. Harris knows the family from his days selling at Macromedia, and when he and Big Dan greet, I half expect Mom to holler at Big Brother, "Go skin one of the rabbits and drop it in a pot, our boy Jonathan's back." We plunk down right inside the front door with Big Dan, and rather than Harris hard-selling the virtues of Worlds 2.0, Big Dan is the one with his mouth flapping.

"Oh yeah, we get calls about VRML every day. I'm going to kick it. No problem. Worlds fits on a credit card—we love it. You're way ahead of your competitors. Win-win-win. Attach Worlds on to all my 3-D Max sales, make another seventeen points? I want some of that. Hey—it's a chance to take someone's money. Yup. We'll make some bucks together."

NW Tech is legendary for its ability to move new technology. The office walls are smothered with plaques from various software companies honoring them as Number One Dealer, Million Dollar Club, Platinum Reseller, et cetera. If you live in the Northwest and you design Web pages or draw 3-D graphics for a living, at some point you have probably talked to Mom, and she hasn't forgotten a thing about you. She is around sixty years old, her name is Oma Kemmis, and because of a lifetime smoking Parliament 100s she's got one lung left, fights emphysema, and a tube runs from her nostrils down to a portable respirator at her side. She's got the hand-knit button-down sweater draped over the back of her chair.

Now here's something you are probably not expecting: Mom is known as the number one closer in the software business. Software firms track this data—they pass on leads to dealers and track the percentage that end up in sales. Mom has a close rate of 80 percent, and what's particularly amazing about that rate is that NW Tech doesn't drop its pants to make sales. In fact, customers often pay a slight premium to do business with her.

Why is she so damn good? Because she's a mom. People trust her when she rasps, "Nope, nope, that's a hobbyist tool, if you're working for clients on deadline you need to spend some bucks." If Jonathan Harris kicks it, and Big Dan pounds it, then Oma Kemmis kills it. Oma says, "Young salespeople today . . . [*inhale*] if the customer's shopping them for price . . . [*inhale*] too many young guys give up . . . get beaten up . . . [*inhale*] I think the problem is . . . they enjoy the game . . . [*inhale*] I only enjoy the kill."

Big Dan says he lives for the occasional pat on the back from Mom. He gets misty-eyed talking about her. It used to be that he couldn't close. Big Dan was just a demo jock, and for the twelve years they'd been in business he'd left all the closing for Mom. He had the classic techie's disability: He couldn't ask for the sale. He could line up all the dominoes but couldn't tip that first domino over. He could talk about a product 'til the cows came home, but he just couldn't ask for their money.

Then a year and a half ago, Mom went into the intensive care unit with pneumonia. NW Tech got in debt and their investors were begging out. Big Dan had to make sales. He was nervous as all get-out, but his first sale was for $400,000 at a 25 percent margin, and suddenly it was "Hey, I can do this."

"I'm not in Mom's league, but my close rate is up there," he says with tremendous pride. He talks with his hands, which are as big as hams. Last week he closed nine sales on the trade show floor, standing right in the aisle—"They handed me their business card, but I took their credit card." He's gotten the hang of keeping his margin at a healthy 25 percent: "When I write up that invoice, one line's got the retail price, the next line's got a cool discount that makes 'em happy, but a third line for an install fee puts the net right back up there."

No matter how much sales lingo pours from his mouth, I can see that Big Dan's not doing it for the money, or for a promotion, or to take a vacation in Tahiti with the commissions—he's doing it for Mom's love.

Now he sells all the time. He loves it. He loves to help people. At lunch, standing in line at Boston Market, he'll just turn to the next person in line and say, "Hey, you having any troubles with your computer?" The answer is always yes. Last week, he did a career-day demonstration at Kenmore Junior High, and before it was over he was selling animation software to eighth graders.

Our conversation is cut off when the phone rings. Mom wants Big Dan to take the call. "Gotta go," Big Dan says. "Can't turn down a chance to take someone's money."

I listen in for a couple minutes as Mom and Big Dan work the phones.

Mom rasps into her receiver, "Sounds like you needed this yesterday and want it installed no later than tomorrow." Without giving the customer a chance to think twice, she follows this closely with, "So, does your firm use purchase orders? No? Good, then why don't I take down the delivery address."

On the other line, Big Dan is defending his price. "Yes, this sale is lucrative for me, but it'll be lucrative for you, too. Think of how much more work you'll be getting done." He meets a little more resistance, but nothing he can't handle. He works an angle on the reverse close—I know what it's like to be a buyer. "Listen, when I'm buying a product, I appreciate clarity and full explanation. I like to know what I'm buying. We'll see that you have the same." He reaches for the order slip.

As we depart, Jonathan Harris's mood is buoyant. An hour with the family has completely restored his faith in Worlds 2.0. "It feels real good," he says, unlocking the car. "Sometimes being on the road is so much more affirming than hanging around the office. . . ." His voice drifts off, then comes back. "Sometimes selling doesn't make you question what you're doing, in fact it's the very opposite: nothing makes you truly believe more in what you're doing than watching a customer like Big Dan's eyes light up."

Postscript: the VRML market did not emerge in time to save Cosmo. In the second week of July, Cosmo was closed down.

Closing

You might think the hardest part of selling is asking for the sale. The unpleasant transition from talking about the product to talking about the price. Coughing up the line, "Do you have enough money to get yourself out of this problem you're in?"

But that's not so hard. The lines are scripted, the staging carefully orchestrated. Selling can have its phony niceties and feigned kindnesses, but hey—I'd rather be nice than rude.

What's hard—what's really hard, the hardest thing—is after you've closed a sale, to say good-bye quickly. That's when you have to be rude, you have to cut conversations short at the very time when the natural human reaction is to linger, to further make nice as a sort of flash penance for having just closed the sale. The longer you linger the more time you give the client to rehash the decision to buy, and the more chance your sale is going to kick out. Linger and they will change their mind. Leave.

Oh, but it's so tempting to stay. So tempting to try to end on a good note. Good-byes are never scripted, always improvised—trolling for an authentic moment so that your customer's last impression is not a disingenuous one. "The Long Good-bye," this weakness is called: the unbearable temptation to seem, in the end, not like a salesman at all.

And I feel that urge, after spending six weeks with salespeople. I want to search for one last anecdote to share, one more moral quandary or one more standout character who demonstrates the nuance of selling.

Instead, I'll make my good-byes short: Give salesmen their due respect. They're keeping a lot of companies afloat and dreams alive. Sometimes we get frustrated that the version of the future we'd like to buy is never quite the version of the future they are selling. But at least they have it in stock. Or will soon.

CHAPTER 6

THE Futurist

GEORGE GILDER'S WIFE prohibits anything stronger than Lipton tea at home, so when his connecting flight from Chicago O'Hare to Vancouver, British Columbia, is delayed, he takes advantage of her absence to hit the Starbucks for a bolt of caffeine or two. Or four. Four cappuccinos! Gilder is on turbodrive all the way west. But when he tries to sleep that night in his Vancouver hotel room, all he can think about is the speech he's supposed to give the next morning to an association of Canadian phone companies. Figuring exercise might burn the caffeine out of his system, he goes down to the health club and jumps on the treadmill, selecting the Pikes Peak option, which means the front of the treadmill rises a foot off the ground and he runs straight uphill for twenty minutes. Sweaty and tired but not sleepy, he goes back to bed and waits out the night. In the morning, he's groggy and figures the only thing that will resuscitate him is a brisk run in beautiful Stanley Park. He starts out from the hotel at a fast pace, but something's wrong with his left knee—a dull, bloated stiffness caused by the treadmill. Frustrated and saddened, he turns around and limps back to his hotel.

His speech goes badly. Uninspired. Scattered.

The next morning he's in San Francisco, and he's worried that today's speech to the Millennium Conference will be another clunker. He's being paid almost $20,000 to speak, so he has to be on. These people are expecting a glimpse of the near future from him, but right now he has a hard time thinking past breakfast. He looks sadly into his cereal and can't find verbs to go with his nouns.

"I gotta . . ." he starts out. Then he pauses, searches for his next word, gives up on that sentence, and starts another. "Sometimes if you do badly . . ." This one, too, stalls. Finally, he raises his finger at the waiter, signaling for more tea.

The Millennium Conference is a block away in Yerba Buena Gardens' Center for the Arts Theater. The men in the crowd are wearing gray suits and polished shoes, which suggests that they're not Valley techies—they're just ordinary businesspeople who walked here from Montgomery Street. They've all forked over $375 to get in; they've paid that much to hear Andy Grove and Peter Drucker speak. Gilder is just the warm-up act. The crowd becomes restless when the moderator tells them that Drucker—the godfather of all management theory—has been scratched from the card and replaced by Lester Thurow, a mere economist.

The audience probably doesn't realize it, but the event organizers have picked speakers from the full political spectrum. Thurow is the most liberal, if you can ever call an economist liberal. A liberal economist is one who thinks the government had better do something about American illiteracy. Andy Grove, as a businessperson, is the "practical" speaker—he gets the middle ground and is therefore guaranteed to come across as reasonable. He gets to make irrefutable remarks such as "Government should do more good than harm." Gilder, by contrast, is way off to the right of the other speakers. If you were to plot them all on a chart, when you came to plotting Gilder's coordinates you'd have to get another piece of paper. He believes that government-run education is to blame for declining American literacy. Compared with the other speakers, Gilder will probably come across as shrill, as an extremist. In a way, he's been set up to fail.

The lights dim. Gilder is to speak first. A blue spotlight focuses on center stage. The podium is a big brushed-steel cone, narrow at the base and flaring out as it goes up. When Gilder strides in from the right and stands behind the cone in the blue light, he looks like a scoop of blueberry ice cream, and the ball microphone dangles in the air like a maraschino cherry on top of his head.

Gilder starts to speak about the coming revolution in sand (silicon), glass (fiber), and air (wireless). The millennium promises a billion transistors on a single sliver of silicon, seven hundred bitstreams in a single thread of fiber, and a cellular infrastructure a thousand times cheaper than today's. Taken together, these phenomenal advances will topple all centralized institutions. His sentences flow easily, his voice starts to boom, and his body language becomes animated: his arms thrust forward and back, pumping *chugga-chugga* as if he's doing the Locomotion dance on *Soul Train*. People in the audience sit up in their seats. Some reach for their pocket pens, trying to scribble down the telling statistics Gilder is delivering. Others glance at their programs, checking Gilder's profile and wondering to themselves why they haven't heard of this guy before. The bio of Gilder is a full page long, but it lacks telling detail; it's all mumbo jumbo about places he's taught and titles of books he's written.

Gilder doesn't pause—he's electrified, practically speaking in tongues, testifying to the coming doomsday for cable television programming, which is being made obsolete by DirecTV satellite. Forty minutes later, when the monitors in front of Gilder flash, "Your time is up," he's still going strong, and the audience is in a state of frightened shock. He's convinced them that the future will be a very different place, but they can't think what to do about it other than to call their travel agents and cancel their vacation plans.

One of the few technology writers to really do his homework, George Gilder is a real thinking man's thinking man. Wait, that's not quite right. He's a real man's kind of thinker. Or a thinker's kind of man. Well, let's just say he's a man, and he thinks a lot.

Alvin Toffler—another guy who thinks a lot—takes the stage a few speakers after Gilder. Onstage Toffler looks like a scarecrow: he's about seven feet tall and no thicker than a broomstick; his white shirt cuffs hang far down out of his coat sleeves, and his bony hands hang far down from his shirt cuffs. Toffler is perhaps the most famous futurist of them all; Gilder is often categorized with Toffler (they both get described in the press as advisers to Newt Gingrich, though Gilder was actually a supporter of presidential candidate Steve Forbes). But when Toffler starts to talk, the difference between him and Gilder becomes clear: Gilder is, well, more specific. Toffler seems to lump all technology together as a "force" altering politics and business. His sentences are strung together with words such as nation-state, NGO, and subnation, which is to say that his remarks are sufficiently term-laden to sound important but sufficiently vague as to be untestable, meaning no one can accuse him of getting things wrong. That's the fine art of futurism: sounding predictive without actually making the mistake of making hard predictions. The audience gets off on the brainteasing tickle, the sense of wonder and imagination. For years, that's what futurists have done: tickle our brains. We pay to be tickled.

But that's not what Gilder does. He's a new generation of rogue futurist, contentious and dangerous: he's the Tupac Shakur rap master of futurism. Sure, he's old enough to be my father, but he's still got the rebel soul of youth. Gilder bothers to delineate which technologies will disappear and which will prevail; his sentences are peppered with such snappy statements as "Working at four percent efficiency, these thin-film solar collectors would generate ten megawatts of power." He makes *hard* predictions, predictions that we will be able to look at a few years down the road and ask, Was he right? He starts out tickling your brain, and then, just when your brain starts giggling, he delivers it a stiff spanking: *Pay attention!* In so doing, Gilder is appealing to a whole new generation in the Valley that has had it up to here with futurists and their vague, blowhard conference-speak, workers who dismiss management theory as just so much psychobabble. Gilder is their man, and he does it not by being ironic or postmodern in his style but by being daring.

Unfortunately, not many of them seem to be here today. This is the San Francisco suit-wearing crowd.

Late in the day at the Millennium Conference, all the speakers gather on the stage to be cross-examined by Andy Grove, who in Drucker's absence has adopted the role of godfather. It can't be by accident that the stagehands point Thurow to the chair farthest on the left and Gilder to the chair farthest on the right. To get the conversation off to a fast start, the huge screen behind them flashes a recent *Wall Street Journal* article titled "Futurist Schlock," which shows futurists making the same rosy predictions about the Internet today that were made about the telephone a hundred years ago. Starting with Lester Thurow and going around the circle, all of the speakers chip in to confess that, yes, the Internet is overhyped and has its share of problems—all of the speakers, that is, except Gilder.

He says sharply, "Unknown entrepreneurs will invent new technologies to solve the current problems that hex Internet commerce, including encryptions, viruses, and nanobuck transactions. The Internet will multiply by a factor of millions the power of one person at a computer."

A factor of millions? The crowd gets a little uncomfortable. It seems as if Gilder is not playing by the rules here. I mean, he had his forty minutes alone to make wild predictions; now's his chance to cool down a little bit, to pull back on the reins. And then we can all go home. Doesn't he get it?

Sensing the tension, Andy Grove makes a move to rope Gilder in. Knowing that Gilder hates government tampering with high tech, Grove asks Gilder to concede that the military was the primary market for early transistors and that the Internet was also subsidized by the government.

Well, that seems reasonable, doesn't it?

But Gilder holds firm. "The Internet and the microchip only took off after the government withdrew from those markets and let private companies in."

This makes the crowd laugh nervously: Gilder is taking on the godfather! He's challenging Andy Grove, of all people, the very guy to whom just about everybody in computers owes his job! Suddenly they all hate Gilder with a fervor. Somewhere, the airconditioning system clicks on.

Lester Thurow sees his opportunity to defend Grove: "It may surprise you, George, but America doesn't lead in everything." It's not much of a zinger, but the crowd claps and laughs. It's the spirit of the comment that counts: be reasonable, be worldly, above all be tolerant of others' ways. Thurow adds that it would be smart for all of us to learn some Spanish and maybe some Japanese and even—God forbid—learn to play soccer.

Well, that seems reasonable, doesn't it?

Gilder, though, scoffs, "My kids aren't learning Spanish. They're learning C++."

That does it. This is a liberal town, a multicultural mecca—even the name of the city is Spanish! The crowd snickers; there are even some hisses. Forty-year-old men and women in suits, hissing! Gilder doesn't mind. Hell, they're on the edge of their seats. They've been sitting for about five hours straight, but not one of them wants to go home. They haven't had this much fun at a conference in years. Most important, they've gotten their $375 worth. Like all writers, Gilder has a little bit of the performer in him (he got his start in speechwriting, so he knows the value of a good line), and if it takes hyperbole to stir up some excitement—well, so be it.

Afterward, the crowd retires to a banquet of extravagant hors d'oeuvres and microbrews. Most of the people still have their name tags on. I remove mine and go incognito, sliding up alongside a small circle of people from Pacific Bell who are, pitifully, talking about their work. They glom onto my foreign presence and pretty quickly ask me what I do for a living, hoping for an answer that might provide some conversational stimulation. But I don't want to talk about myself, so I tell them I'm an accountant. That usually does the trick. I ask them what they thought of Gilder.

"Smart," one says.

"Really smart," says a woman.

A third adds, "But I'd never trust my business to him." This comment provokes a flurry of nods.

"I tell you what I really want to know," says the woman who seems to like the word "really." "I want to know, does he *really* believe all that stuff he says? I mean, does he *really* believe the CMOS chip will not survive the century? Does he really believe that five years from now the poorest schoolchildren will be getting a better education via computer than today's richest schoolchildren?"

Heads start nodding again.

"Right. We're *geeks*," the woman adds. "So when he says 'a factor of millions' or 'five years,' well . . . you just don't use numbers that way. Well, we don't, anyway. I mean, does he *really* think he knows better than Andy Grove?"

That does seem to be the question with George Gilder and the new rap masters of futurism: Do they *really* believe their wild assertions? Or is it just showmanship—is it just daring to grab attention, the equivalent of rock-'n'-roll stars trashing hotel rooms and ordering bodyguards to whup journalists? Is it image, or is it real?

What the audience didn't know, and what this small circle of people didn't know, is that George Gilder is actually a huge fan of Andy Grove—so much so that Gilder devoted a huge chunk of his book *Microcosm: The Quantum Revolution in Economics and Technology* to the story of Grove's early days at Intel. Gilder is also, ironically, an old friend of Lester Thurow; in fact, the two planned to take a limousine to the airport together after the conference. So the day's all been a bit of an act, it seems: George's hyperbole, the speakers' mock squabbling, et cetera. Ha ha. No harm done, old boy. *Good show for the customers!* All in a day's work.

There's only one problem with that explanation. When George gets back to his hotel, he goes looking for his black limo, but it turns out that Thurow has left for the airport without him. Ditched! With old friends like Lester, George has no need for old enemies. But alas, have them he certainly does. Oh, yes. And there are quite a few things that his enemies would like his audience to know about him.

Deliverance

Meanwhile, the day after his speech, Gilder is back in San Francisco, and from the airport we drive into the East Bay netherworld. Gilder is under pressure to come up with his next grand theme. His last nine-thousand-word article for *Forbes ASAP* (in which George is the headliner) was all about emerging Internet software. Now he's promised his editor another nine thousand words on Internet hardware—who's inventing it, who's hot, and who's barking up the wrong tree. The article is due in just ten days; he has done a lot of the technical research, but he's held off writing anything until he gets hit with a way to tell the story—either a big theme or a personality to hang it all on.

Gilder's articles will make up a book called *Telecosm,* which will be put out sometime in the future by Simon & Schuster. *Tele-cosm* is the ultimate vapor book; every year since 1993, the byline on Gilder's *Forbes* articles has promised the book "later this year," but now it's looking like a fall *1999* publication. It's just very hard to write a book about emerging technologies, since by the time the book gets copyedited, typeset, printed, and shipped, the subject matter isn't so emerging anymore. Gilder swears this piece on Internet hardware will be his last to include in the book. Except maybe just one more on the physics of the electro-magnetic spectrum. Nevertheless, it will be worth the wait; there are dozens of books on the potential consequences of all the new technologies, but Gilder's is the best-grounded in the specifics of the technology. Like other firebrands such as Camille Paglia and Lewis Lapham, Gilder has a knack for supporting his fore-casts in such a way that even if you disagree with him, merely by reading his work you come to know your own opinion better. For instance, his Internet software piece landed on subscribers' desks the same week as the launch of Windows 95—*launch,* as if it were an Apollo mission. While pundits around the country were weighing in with their opinions about whether Win 95 was a worthwhile operating system, Gilder's piece raised the question whether operating systems en masse might be made obsolete by "dynamically portable" software—programs that compile line by line in real time.

Gilder drives into Contra Costa County, a maze of look-alike office parks and anonymous brown foothills. He gets lost for a while and has to call ahead to get directions. Eventually he pulls into the parking lot of Livingston Enterprises, a little ninety-person company that has gained a huge share of the market for Internet servers and routers. Importantly to George, these guys have grabbed that market merely by having the best products—they have no well-known figurehead, they haven't accepted any outside investment, and they don't even have a public relations department. Gilder doesn't normally care to hobnob with CEOs, since they're usually too high up in a company to really know what's going on, but Livingston's CEO, Steve Willens, still has a hand in product development.

Steve greets George in the lobby and takes him into a confer-ence room.

Every time Gilder meets an engineer, they go through a sort

of cascade of language syntax, negotiating like two modems, trying to find the most efficient level of conversation they can hold. It ends up sounding like the dueling banjo scene from *Deliverance:*

> GEORGE: Hi, nice to meet you. Hey, that's a sweet access router over there. Wow, both Ethernet and asynchronous ports?
>
> STEVE: Yeah, check this baby out—the Ethernet port has AUI, BNC, and RJ-45 connectors.
>
> GEORGE: So for packet filtering you went with TCP, UDP, and ICMP.
>
> STEVE: Of course. To support dial-up SLIP and PPP.
>
> GEORGE: Set user User_Name ifilter Filter_Name.
>
> STEVE: Set filter s1.out 8 permit 192.9.200.2/32 0.0.0.0/0 tcp src eq 20.
>
> GEORGE: 00101101100010111001001 1101100001010-10100011111001.
>
> STEVE: … … … .. … … … … .. .. … … .. … … .. … … … … .. ..
>
> GEORGE: Really? Wait, you lost me there.

Willens has never had a writer ask about his machines in this much detail before. Pretty soon he's spilling his guts about the history of the company, and several times he has to stop himself before he reveals confidential information. The two men talk for about three hours, until just about every Livingston employee has gone home for the night and Willens begins to yawn. George is still pumped up. He loves to learn. Reluctantly, he gets steered toward the door.

When he reaches the car, Gilder looks worried. He has only nine days left, and he realizes he still has a ton to learn. At one point in the interview, Willens told him that he believes there are technological problems with piping the Internet into the home via coaxial cable. Until that time, George had been of the opin-ion that cable is the natural and obvious hookup, and he had been going to predict that cable modem manufacturers will be hot. But George respects Steve; Steve clearly has the right stuff, and if Steve says there are problems, well . . .

"I'm really going to have to bear down on the science," George says while looking at his electronic day calendar, hoping to find some free time in the days ahead. Unfortunately, he has to give a speech in Hollywood the next day and from there fly on to Aspen for yet another conference. He looks exasperated. "I can't . . ." He tries again. "It's hard for me to write, even to think, on days I'm giving speeches." I get the feeling he wishes his public life would disappear for nine days, but he has no one to blame but himself: he makes his own schedule. Unlike other prominent consultants, George has no publicist and no assistants—nobody speaks for George Gilder but George Gilder. This is an admirable attempt to keep his life his, and it suggests that Gilder is not just an act— which goes back to the real question: Does he really believe the Internet will increase the power of a person at a computer by "a factor of millions"?

Daunted by the coming weekend in Aspen, George focuses on a few bright spots. "There's a digital satellite company near Aspen . . . maybe I'll stop in for a visit. And there's Ajax . . ." Ajax is the ski mountain looming above Aspen Village, which at this time of year makes a great hike. "I wonder if my knee will be better by Friday."

The Jetsons

Back in the early summer of 1981, George Gilder's supply-side treatise *Wealth and Poverty* made it to number four on *The New York Times*'s best-sellers list and was being called "the bible of the Reagan revolution." Reagan kept telling the public that government could raise revenues by cutting taxes, and as this seemed an inherent contradiction, everybody bought George's book to have the riddle explained: cutting taxes, he said, would stimulate entrepreneurship, thereby increasing the taxable base of the economy. (As a reference point, Reagan also insisted that federal mental hospitals were merely group homes for idle bums, predicting that if we closed the hospitals it would stimulate the lazies to get jobs.) The sudden attention was more than a bit of a surprise for George, since the book's first printing had been a mere five thousand copies. He was trotted out on all the talk shows and asked to express his views in crisp sound bites, which he did somewhat reluctantly. What nobody knew was that George was already hot on a new topic and had a secret ambition.

He'd read Tracy Kidder's *The Soul of a New Machine,* and boy, that was really "it," that was the stuff. What a book! Then George found himself talking with a friend, Peter Sprague, who back then was chairman of National Semiconductor. Peter told him that not only could scores of transistors be put on the head of a pin, but scores of transistors could be put on the *tip* of a pin. The tip of a pin! That did it.

George looked up *The Rosen Electronics Letter,* found a list of semiconductor manufacturers, and picked the one at the bottom of the list, Micron Technology. George wrote an article on Micron for *Forbes,* and he was hooked. Then he called Ben Rosen to ask for a free subscription to Ben's newsletter.

By chance Ben had read George's piece in *Forbes,* and Ben had gotten the mistaken impression that George knew a heck of a lot about semiconductors. So Ben said, "No, you can't have a free subscription, but how about you report on semiconductors for the newsletter?" George jumped at the chance. He wrote nine pages every three weeks for about a year and a half. He attended classes at Cal Tech with Carver Mead, who became his sage. He got neck deep in the science.

What emerged from those years was *Microcosm,* a detailed history of the semiconductor industry. The book stands up as well today as it did when it was published in 1989, partly because Gilder devoted a major portion to Andy Grove and Intel, who have since emerged as real giants. Ironically, George had been intending to write the book about Robert Noyce and Intel, but George got scooped by Tom Wolfe, who wrote a sensational profile of Noyce for *Esquire.* Gilder wasn't going to compete with one of his favorite writers. Grove was his second choice.

Even his profile of Micron—a company he picked nearly randomly—looks prescient today. Stock analysts have written off Micron many times in the last decade, but the firm keeps fighting back. George has repeatedly stood by its side.

After *Microcosm,* George got a gig as a featured writer for *Forbes.* His cover stories garnered a lot of attention and a wide readership, but he wasn't proud of his work. His pieces were being rewritten by his editors behind his back. Frustrated, he went to Steve Forbes and asked for a new outlet, something more like his old arrangement with Ben Rosen. Steve Forbes tried to purchase the business and technology magazine *Upside* for him;

when the deal failed, he started *Forbes ASAP* from scratch. A sympathetic editor, Rich Karlgaard, was hired away from *Upside,* and Gilder was given the room to write.

When bandwidth became a front-page topic, Gilder was already an expert. He's never really managed a business, and he's never really coded a program, but—as they say at Microsoft about Lotus 1-2-3—"he got there first." Because there are so many journalists covering high technology these days, many are new to their beats and haven't developed their own sources. They read Gilder's pieces for guidance, and they even call Gilder for quotes. (A Nexis search on Gilder turned up more than four hundred quotes in just the last two years. One thing George certainly learned from the Reagan era was how to give a good sound bite.) This way, Gilder drives the debate. In the PR business, it's called "leverage." The danger is that many people hear George's hyperbolic sound bites without ever reading his books or *Forbes* articles, so he sounds to them like the boy who cries wolf, willing to say anything to get some attention. Among more cynical high-tech insiders, the word "Gilder" verges on being used as an adjective, as in "How Gilder of you to believe the quality of life is improving." There is even some debate as to which form of the adjective will prevail. If Orwellian is everybody working for the government, then Gilderian would be nobody working for the government. If Kafkaesque is waking up as a cockroach, then Gilderesque would be waking up as George Jetson's boy, Elroy.

Let's Make a Deal

Building the hardware revolution with sand, glass, and air often seems to require tremendous faith. If we put a hundred satellites in the sky over Asia, will Asians buy phones to use them? Should we adopt this protocol standard, or will a better one emerge tomorrow? If we extend fiber-optic pipe into the home, will interactive entertainment emerge to take advantage of it? George Gilder has that kind of faith in the unknown. If he ever got onto the television show *Let's Make a Deal,* no matter how many times Monty Hall offered him the Cadillac Seville or whatever's behind the curtain, Gilder would always choose the curtain.

HALL: I'll give you the Seville and ten thousand dollars cash . . .

GILDER: I'll take the curtain.

HALL: I'll give you a Senate seat and three million dollars cash . . .

GILDER: I'll take the curtain.

What's behind the curtain, Gilder knows, is nothing more than a rather ordinary geek—an unfashionably dressed electrical engineer, preferably an immigrant with a Ph.D. who's hungry for success. All the better if he's God-fearing and has a family to provide for. Give enough engineers a problem, even a really big problem such as "Find a way around operating systems," and one of them will have the right stuff to figure it out eventually. That's what Gilder loves to write about, engineers like Steve Willens who have the focus and drive to be making front-page news a few years from now.

A few years out is where supply-siders like Gilder are most at home. The classical definition of economics is the study of choice under scarcity, such as "I have to choose which animations to drop from this CD-ROM since disk space is scarce." But in Gilder's world, scarcity is only a temporary problem; things we normally consider to be scarce, such as bandwidth, will soon be plentiful. RAM will not be scarce, the electromagnetic spectrum will not be scarce, solutions to our problems will not be scarce. All those things will be "supplied." In the long term, Gilder is always eventually right—engineering ingenuity unfailingly comes to the rescue. Gilder's advice can be invaluable to a strategic planning committee that has to formulate a five-year plan, but it's usually no help to a product team that has to ship in time for peak Christmas sales.

As a writer, Gilder likes to boil down technological advances to loose-fitting "laws" for his readers to keep in mind. Inspired by Moore's Law—that the density of transistors on a computer chip doubles every eighteen months—Gilder came up with his own Law of the Microcosm: Every n increase in the number of transistors on a chip results in an n^2 increase in the chip's performance-to-price ratio. Recently he added to this a corollary for the wired Web (based on Bob Metcalfe's similar hypothesis), the Law of the Telecosm: Every n increase in the number and power of computers on a network results in an n^2 increase in the network's performance value. He doesn't intend for these principles to be mathematically strict; they just help make the point that the rate of social change is occurring exponentially, not algebraically. So if you want to be as successful tomorrow as you are today, you'd better get back to work.

If any of this has lost you, I've made up a simple mantra that combines Gilder's affinity for exponential theorems with his conviction that the future will provide answers to today's problems. Let's call it Gilder's Axiom: Assume Utopia is some time away. In one year, if we get n closer to Utopia, in the next year we will get n^2 closer to Utopia. This way, we keep getting closer and closer without ever having to actually get there. Which is probably for the best. I mean, Utopia would be great, but only if we could turn it off now and then.

Seinfeld

Another day, another speech. This time Gilder's addressing a breakfast club of entertainment heavyweights at the Radisson Hotel in Beverly Hills. The event has been organized by David Horowitz, a onetime leftist organizer turned conservative critic who, along with his Second Thoughts Books, brings attention to the destruction caused by 1960s radicalism. The ostensible theme of this morning's breakfast is to celebrate the reissue of Gilder's book *Visible Man: A True Story of Post-Racist America;* copies are being sold on the way in, and the book stands upright in the center of each breakfast table. *Visible Man* is a biography of one young black man living in Albany, New York, who, despite his charm and intelligence, continually gets in trouble with the law. His story conveys a political message: that the cause of his criminal behavior is the pandering welfare system that creates and corrupts the underclass. Gilder blames the very people who try to help. The book was first published in 1978, and if there's one book Gilder's old enemies would have the world read, this is it. Unfortunately for them, not many people have: it sold only eight hundred copies in the first year.

A revealing moment occurs shortly after Gilder takes the podium and begins his speech. "Among people of influence in

America, racism is dead. Racism has virtually nothing to do with the plight of black America," he says. "If you adjust for age and credentials, black women earn 106 percent of the wages of white women. If you adjust for age, IQ, and gender, black full-time workers earn 101 percent the wages of white workers." The audience is politically conservative, so George could go on like this for an hour without raising any eyebrows. But George's tone is flat and unenthused; compared to the Millennium Conference, he looks bored. So he starts to wrap it up after just five minutes! He suggests that people buy the book and consider its ideas carefully. He pauses. The silence is uncomfortable. George starts talking about the coming death of television. He then segues into the "Sand, Glass, and Air" speech he gave at Millennium.

He switched subjects!

Even though he's supposed to talk about *Visible Man,* George would much rather talk about how new technology is going to change the power structure of Hollywood. These are pretty heady days in Tinseltown—Disney and Seagram just bought half the town on a shopping spree, and the locals are being reminded that "content is king" every time they open their morning paper. But George has a contrary opinion, and he'd like to voice it.

Slowly and painstakingly, he makes the case that the expensive economics of television and movies is primarily a function of the technology used to produce and distribute them; as the technology changes, the costs will come down dramatically, shattering the business's biggest and oldest barrier to entry—the fact that it takes money to make money. The market will be flooded with the high-quality work of low-budget auteurs. And someday, sooner than you think, consumers who want to watch something other than PG-13 flesh and blood will be able to. We will move from a society of lowest common denominators to a first-choice society, and Gilder has faith that everybody's first choice won't be Heather Locklear's short hemlines.

It's this last part where Gilder loses his audience. These men have built empires by manufacturing name-brand stars. The conventional wisdom in Hollywood is that when the market fractures into a gazillion digital channels, consumers will be so disoriented by the huge selection that they will cling desperately to familiar faces. Several audience members raise their hands and express this opinion. But Gilder scolds them: "Don't underestimate the intelligence of the public. Those who do will go broke."

One minute George is defending the intelligence of the American public, and I want to cheer him. But then I recall that he just denied the existence of racism. Remember that *Seinfeld* episode where Elaine falls in love with the guy who moves her couch but then, as a test of their compatibility, asks him what he thinks about a woman's right to choose, and he turns out to be a prolife fanatic? Despite her love, she had to break up with him.

George Gilder's past presents just this sort of problem to the many fans of his technological prophecies. Because amid all the people who hold libertarian views on technology, there are still deep chasms under the surface that yawn open the minute the topic of conversation switches away from technology.

"I'm not trying to avoid my sociological work of the seventies," George says to me later. "I stand by those views. It's just not . . . Well, I'm focused on something else these days." Still, it's hard not to connect the dots:

- George is so media-savvy that it would be fair to say he's an expert on being an expert.
- Some portion of his current fan base would take exception to his sociological views, were they better known.
- George switched subjects.

It would seem that Gilder has a plan for who gets to know what. There's only one problem with jumping to that conclusion. A few days after this speech, in response to the Million Man March on Washington, George writes a long op-ed piece for *The Wall Street Journal* that repeats the conclusions of *Visible Man:* the welfare state renders husbands superfluous, and young black men—their role as providers undermined—become predators on the streets. If George Gilder were trying to divert attention from his controversial opinions, he certainly wouldn't have revealed them to several million readers.

Starstruck

After the breakfast in Beverly Hills, when the room clears out, George goes from table to table, downing all the untouched glasses of orange juice. On the way to the airport, he eats a package of dried fruit and contemplates his article. During the week, he's seen the Canadian phone companies, the boys at Livingston, and now some honchos from Hollywood. And there was such a difference. At Livingston people were actually doing something, while at the other two, well—they were still just talking about it.

"I've got an idea for the article," George tells me. It goes something like this: If the phone companies were smart, they'd be offering flat-rate Internet service to every one of their customers. But the phone companies are distracted by the rush to own a piece of Hollywood. They're starstruck. Meanwhile, hundreds of Internet service providers are busy capturing this lucrative, booming market. In addition, if Internet telephony (long-distance calls for the cost of local) becomes popular, the Internet service providers will "hollow out" the regional phone companies. This is vintage Gilder—little guys against the big ones. It's the kind of grand theme that will separate his Internet-hardware article from just another buyer's guide to servers and firewalls. But he knows that the merest intimation that the phone companies are vulnerable is sure to be dismissed as just more hyperbole unless he can argue his case persuasively.

When Gilder tells me this—we're on Highway 405 headed south, the two of us in the backseat—it's a defining moment. I've caught George Gilder on the cusp of formulating his next prediction, the kind of prediction that will make people wonder if he really believes it, and even he doesn't know whether he believes it or not.

Gilder carries this idea with him for a few more days as he travels around. Five days before his deadline, he shows up at the offices of *Forbes ASAP* in Redwood City. He's cleared a hole in his manic schedule and booked a room at the chichi Hotel Sofitel down the street. He intends to work around the clock until he gets the article done. Forbes lends him an office and a computer. By chance another columnist, Andy Kessler, happens to be around. He is a partner at the investment banking firm Unterberg Harris and, in George's estimation, a supersmart guy. So George runs his grand theme by Andy, about how the Internet service providers may hollow out the phone companies.

To George's dismay, Andy thinks that just isn't going to happen. No way. The phone companies are too big to roll over and die. If anybody ever starts making big money in connecting users to the Internet, the phone companies will just jump into the market and squash them. Andy points out that the phone companies already have all the technological and billing systems to offer Internet dial-up networking. And if for any reason they can't squash the Internet providers, then by God they'll buy them.

The conversation puts George into a funk. It's partly because he now needs a new theme to write about Internet hardware, and partly because it's agonizing that the Internet revolution is still dependent on the bureaucratic phone companies. It just doesn't seem like much of a revolution if the Baby Bells profit from it.

While we're there, the October issue of *Forbes ASAP* arrives from the printer. I flip through the glossy pages. Ten of them are devoted to letters from industry notables, all responding to Gilder's previous Internet-software article. Scott McNealy, Andy Grove, Scott Cook, Larry Ellison, they all wrote a response. Most of them agree with the gist of his piece—that the network is becoming more and more important—but most also take exception to the language Gilder uses. In particular, they take offense at his prediction that the network will "hollow out" the personal computer. Andy Grove starts his letter, "George, George, George—you haven't met a new technology you didn't like." Letter after letter, they keep coming. On the ninth page, George finally gets to respond: "I will concede . . . that the use of the term 'hollowing out of the computer' . . . is hyperbolic, even misleading in an absolute sense. But they should acknowledge that in relative terms, the balance between desktop and network is shifting sharply."

As I read this, I'm thinking: If they didn't like "hollowing out the computer," they sure won't like "hollowing out the phone company."

George closes the door to his office. When everybody else at *ASAP* is gone for the day, George is still in there, reading and thinking. To get inspired to write, he rereads passages of Tom

Wolfe's *The Electric Kool-Aid Acid Test,* which to him is "all about religion, all about transcendence." George says his best writing comes to him only after he's been sitting at the computer terminal for four or five hours straight—only then do all life's distractions fade away. But tonight he can't seem to actually write any of his article; he just can't get it going. The dream fails to take him. Instead, he doodles notes to himself and random thoughts and arguments countering his critics. He doesn't walk back to the hotel until 3 A.M.

Religion and transcendence infuse both George's style and his substance. He has a missionary's drive to teach others what he knows, and he speaks with a preacher's fervor. He believes that moral values translate into entrepreneurship and technological development.

When George and I talk about religion, he says that someday he would like to write a book about how technology has its roots in the mystical and the spiritual, but that (1) he hasn't figured out how to write it, and (2) if he attempted it and it was anything less than "just right, or right on target," it would be discounted or brushed aside, and maybe people would even laugh at him.

George Gilder has a valid reason for being careful about writing a book connecting religion and science. *Wealth and Poverty* described the way business is compatible with religion. George pointed out that businesses succeed by serving their customers' needs, and he noted how similar that is to the Christian ethic of living your life in service to others. Give, and you shall receive. Invest, and you shall prosper. Reagan loved it, but Ayn Rand— whose work Gilder had read and admired—was enraged. Here was this Gilder wonk being touted as a libertarian, and he was telling people to serve others! It was an outrage! Life should be spent serving your own vision, not the needs of others. She devoted the last public speech of her life, at the Ford Hall Forum, to denouncing Gilder, and among Ayn Rand libertarians he became an outcast.

So for every Reagan trumpeting Gilder, there is an equal and opposite Ayn Rand condemning him. For every book of his that's made the best-seller lists, there's another one that has sold only eight hundred copies. In 1974, the National Organization for Women named Gilder its "Male Chauvinist Pig of the Year" for his book *Men and Marriage.* In 1981, he was giving a commencement address at American University when fifty students wearing white armbands turned their backs to protest his writings on race. In 1991, Susan Faludi allocated a section of her book *Backlash* to portraying Gilder as a guy who despises feminists because he can't get a date, and then, perhaps even more bitingly, she accused Gilder of spouting antifeminist polemic just to get on TV.

I don't know how he does it. He's so thick-skinned, he should have a cattle brand on his shoulder.

The next morning, George looks out the window of the Sofitel at San Carlos Ridge, which divides Highway 101 from Interstate 280. He puts on his running gear and we drive about a mile west, to the base of the ridge. He doesn't need to stretch. He was a runner in college, so he has perfect elbow-pumping form. Gilder is one of those rare guys who can still wear the khakis he wore in college, and maybe he does. He explains that he can't run very fast on flat land anymore because his knees are too arthritic, but he loves to run up hills—there's no pounding running uphill. Then the street we're climbing gets very steep, so he stops talking to focus on his breathing. I start to fear I'm going to be left behind. After about ten minutes, I'm relieved to see that the road ahead levels off. I give it one last burst to catch up with him before the intersection, but when we get there I see that we're not at the top after all—if we take a left turn, there's another half mile to go. Gilder, of course, takes a left.

He has a favorite running route in every major city but rarely a running partner. Most of the time, he runs alone.

Dallas

After the run, George Gilder takes a two-minute shower and heads down the valley to Netcom On-Line Communication Services, an Internet service provider that is outgrowing its office space exponentially. George has set up several appointments with key people from throughout the company. He arrives a few minutes early, so he ducks into the cafeteria to get a Snapple tea.

"I want to be pumped up for this," he says, downing the tea. When he puts the empty bottle down on a copy of that morning's *San Jose Mercury News,* a news item catches his eye—apparently,

AT&T has just announced that it will offer Internet service within six months and it intends to own half the market within two years. George can't believe it—Andy Kessler's prediction is coming true! The phone companies are jumping in with every intention of squashing the little guys!

George meets first with Netcom's marketing gun, John Zeisler. With some resignation, George asks him about AT&T's entry into the market—what does he think this means? Zeisler only laughs. He laughs! Zeisler explains the difference between Internet years and human years: a human year is about five Internet years. So if AT&T expects to offer service in six human months, that's two and a half Internet years! A lot will happen in two and a half Internet years. AT&T will never catch up.

In his next meeting, this one with Netcom CEO Dave Garrison, Gilder gets more good news. Of the approximately $20 users pay as a flat fee for their Internet account, only $1 goes to cover the phone connection. It's too small a slice for the phone companies to be able to get a price advantage. Then Garrison details where the rest of the $20 goes, and it turns out that one of the biggest chunks is for twenty-four-hour person-to-person customer service—not just some infinitely branching voice mail system but a live techie on the line. Garrison points out that it's just too much of a stretch to imagine a Pacific Bell operator editing your config.sys file. When he says this he grins wickedly, knowing he's proved his point, and suddenly he looks exactly like Larry Hagman playing J. R. Ewing on *Dallas*.

Gilder is getting jazzed. Andy Kessler's got it wrong after all! These guys at Netcom have hunger, they have focus, they have drive. They're not afraid of AT&T! They give their customers exactly what they want, nothing more and nothing less. If that's not a formula for success, then what is? George begins to size up all the people at Netcom he meets. I can sense what he's doing: he's looking for one person to hang the story on. He's looking for one guy who can demonstrate the difference in culture between AT&T and Netcom. He's looking for his protagonist.

The obvious possibility is Netcom's founder, Bob Rieger, except that Rieger recently retired from involvement in day-to-day operations. It's hard to say a guy has focus and drive when he's retired. Then George hears about one of the chief engineers, Bob Tomasi. Tomasi used to work for Timenet, then for MCI, and now for Netcom. He has lived Gilder's grand theme: he's moved from the bureaucracy to the rocket ship.

"I gotta meet this guy," Gilder says.

Hell, yes, George Gilder believes. *Really.* When he looks hard enough and long enough, he finds a place where his affinity for hyperbole and his passion for the nuts and bolts of engineering are not a contradiction—they are in line. The dream and the reality are one. And when he gets there, when he finds that unique place, he is finally ready to write.

Before he leaves, George wants to spend some time in the control room, the physical place that all the Netcom customers connect to. It's on the second floor, in an air-conditioned room stuffed with rack after rack of U.S. Robotics modems, Cisco servers, Sun SPARC stations, and Livingston routers. George dives in amid some wires where he sees an engineer tinkering away.

"Livingston routers, huh?" George says, beginning his cascade of syntax. "Hey, an RJ-45 connector!"

CHAPTER 7

THE
Dropout

00:00:00 The Curious Thing Danny Hillis Has Been Up To

The legendary designer of computer architecture Danny Hillis has given up computers for a while. A Disney Fellow and vice president at Walt Disney Imagineering in Glendale, California, he has devoted himself to a mission that at first glance seems beyond wacky: he is building a monument-sized mechanical clock that, if it is erected and started according to schedule on January 1, 2001, will continue ticking and counting time through the year 12000.

Considering that the pyramids of Egypt and Stonehenge are only about five thousand years old, Hillis's objective is so off the charts that it annoys the mind even to attempt to think about how long that is. As if this were not challenge enough, Hillis has set himself to what seems an even more formidable aim:

He wants us to take him seriously.

Danny hopes that these two ingredients—the clock and taking it seriously—will combine to lengthen the technology industry's short-term time framework. In essence, he wants us to stop thinking about what's for lunch and start thinking about how to feed the world. An admirable objective that no one will contest, but it's not apparent what a mere clock can accomplish.

00:01:00 What He'd Like Our Sense of Time to Be

Danny Hillis would have us execute a sort of back flip with twist on the way we have learned to think about the environment, which is to recognize that our negligible year-to-year impact on nature has added up to devastating consequences over generations. The back flip is to stop carping about the negative and to imagine what we might accomplish over generations with minor year-on-year positive efforts. The twist is to apply this type of thinking beyond nature to the rest of our lives.

It turns out that the sense of time has indeed been altered in this way for the fifteen or so people whom Danny has inspired to join his effort,* smart people who have dedicated the better part of three years to pondering such design questions as:

- In what language do we create a manual to explain to people, several thousand years into the future, how to repair the clock?
- What counting mechanism will survive erosion for ten thousand years?
- If we put the clock in a city to get visitors, will the city even exist in thousands of years?

Reflecting upon these almost unanswerable problems carries over to the rest of their lives. At work, these fifteen or so people find themselves less interested in coming up with the next cool Web site and more interested in advancing artificial intelligence. "Deep time" is how they describe their state of mind.

---

*00:00:20 Hillis is to techies what Robert Altman is to actors. Cool, famous people who could make a lot more money doing something else get drawn in to his projects: his Tinkertoy computer, his Connection Machines, and now his Millennium Clock have all read like a Who's Who of the day.

00:02:07 How Seriously the Rest of Us Are Supposed to Take It

However, most of us won't get to work on the clock. What we will get is an opportunity to visit the clock monument, the way we visit a museum. That's why the taking-it-seriously part is so important. Inevitably, the visiting hours of the clock will end at around 5 P.M. on any given day, and at 4:15 some tourists will show up at the gates and decide to get it in quickly and then go have a beer. They will rush through the monument, never take it seriously, and leave by five, their time frame defined more by their forty-five-minute viewing allowance than by the clock's ten-thousand-year ambition. Only by taking the clock seriously— in the way the fifteen people currently working on it do—will the experience of visiting the clock cross over to have a beneficial impact on visitors' time frames.

Danny intends to accomplish this by making the monument a grand puzzle to be solved, perhaps treating each visitor as an anthropologist who must figure out the clock's very purpose. The analogy that Danny likes is the Vietnam Veterans Memorial. The almost sixty thousand names of soldiers etched into the black slab of rock are listed chronologically, not alphabetically, so the effort of finding a friend's name requires scanning hundreds of names, in which time the gravity and enormity of the loss sinks in.

Danny has his own criterion of success, a $.10^3$ test: "It'll be worth building the clock if I can inspire 10 percent of the engineers in Silicon Valley to spend 10 percent of their time thinking about problems whose solution is more than 10 years out into the future."

00:03:31 What Danny Hillis Achieved, During the Early 1980s, That Provoked Full-Page Articles About Him in <u>Time</u>, <u>Esquire</u>, and <u>The New York Times Magazine</u>; That Is, Some Evidence of Genius[*]

Using a radical architecture he called "massively parallel processing," Hillis built supercomputers that were in some applications

---

[*]00:00:09 If I'm going to call someone a genius, I don't want the reader to have to take my word for it; I want to be able to show the reader a moment of genius.

up to one thousand times faster than anything else the world had seen.* This was shortly after the Japanese government boldly announced the 5th Generation Computer Project, a national effort to dominate computer technology the way the country had taken over cars, steel, and memory chips. In an information economy, the argument went, those who can manipulate information fastest will run the world. In the same way as the race to the moon had become the symbol of U.S.-Soviet Cold War military competition, the race to create the world's fastest computer became the symbol of East-West economic dominance.

Massively parallel processing was so radical because everyone had assumed it was impossible, as scoffed at as cold fusion. The conventional wisdom was the acceptance of a mathematical proof called Amdahl's Law, set forth by the senior IBM system designer Gene Amdahl. Amdahl's Law is awfully technical, so perhaps it can be best understood through this metaphor: Imagine a family trying to eat as much food as possible. The mom is running back and forth between the refrigerator and the dining table, dumping food onto all her kids' plates. Seymour Cray built his supercomputers by making each component bigger and faster: bigger refrigerators, faster moms. Danny's proposed innovation was putting thousands of kids around the table. The naysayers pointed out that at some point, the mom will be at her limit, exhausted and screaming and ready for a Xanax. Just adding kids wouldn't make a difference; she wouldn't be able to get any more food to their plates.

But Danny understood better than anyone else the consequences of memory and processors being made of the same material, etched silicon; there doesn't have to be an artificial distinction between storing and computing. In my kitchen example, the refrigerator is the memory, the kids are the processors, and the mom is the chipset shuttling between the two. But Danny understood that kids aren't just mouths. Kids can go to the refrigerator and get the food themselves; they don't need mom!

---

*00:00:23 Just to underscore how much a thousandfold leap is, around the same time as Danny's first supercomputers were sold, the personal computer world was being radically altered by the introduction of the IBM-PC AT with the Intel 286 chip, which was only three times faster than the IBM-PC.

Danny Hillis was heralded as a hero of the Information Age, a Neil Armstrong for the business class. He was only twenty-eight. In the photos that accompanied the stories about him, Danny inevitably posed with toys.

00:05:52 What Danny Hillis Is Really Like, in Person

He speaks the way our eyes read poetry: a few words to a line, then a pause, then a few more words, then another pause. He always gets the beginning of the next thought out before pausing, so there's sort of a tease that more is to come.

There's something about Hillis that's different from every other high-tech bigwig I've interviewed; he didn't try to convince me or win me over or spin me. I have found that Silicon Valley executives thrill on debates of the hairsplitting variety; they love Socratic dialectic. To the CEO brain, arguing is what the whetstone is to the edge of the knife—it keeps it sharp, ready for action. They don't answer my questions so much as debug them, correcting the mistaken presumptions inherent in the questions.

Compare them with Danny Hillis. When the thread of our conversation had enough momentum that it could continue without eye contact or head-nodding affirmations, he would often physically disengage. We would keep talking, but he would go lie down on the floor and stare at the ceiling, maybe stretch his back.

He articulates wonderful metaphors and purposeful anecdotes, each one offered as sort of a gift to the air, floating in space like a cartoon thought bubble. He likes to talk about solving world hunger or how to achieve interactive storytelling or "Which will last longer, Mickey Mouse or Walt Disney Incorporated?" These are not solvable queries so much as they are koans to contemplate. Koans free the mind of the rule that everything has to make sense, allowing us to accept the world more for what it is in all its contradictions. A typical quote from Hillis:

> In some sense, we've
> run out of our story, which
> we were operating on, which
> was the story of power taking over nature—it's not

that we've finished that, but
we've gotten ahead of ourselves, and
we don't know what
the next story is after that.

00:07:49 The First Thing Danny Hillis Did When We Met

The first thing Hillis did when I arrived at his Spanish villa–style home in Hollywood was slide a microchip under a microscope and have me look at it. Really look at it. He had designed the chip using new MEMs technology and had just gotten the chip back from the foundry in a UPS shipment that he was signing for as I walked up. To the naked eye, this pinky-nail-sized chip was the color of any other, a muddy copper. But at 400 power the strata of polysilicon and silicon dioxide and aluminum were a well-organized translucent kaleidoscope of tints, a stained-glass window in gold and blue and amber and pink.

"Isn't it nice?" he observed.

I said it was. He wanted me to see it as a very, very small work of art, a thing to be appreciated for its physical beauty. This is very important to him, that technology be appreciated on a physical level, and he was expressing something there that would repeat itself numerous times as I heard the story of his life. Moreover, he wanted me to see that even though the chip was electronic and its logic gates were infinitesimally small, there was nevertheless a mechanical, leveresque cause and effect at work.

Danny's mind has the ability to scale to an extent I have never seen in another person. By "scale" I mean the conventional industry usage, that something works just as well in small quantities or huge ones as it does in the test-sample quantity. Danny can scale down or scale up, and his brain never goes fuzzy with vertigo; he never loses track of the levering mechanisms. In the version of Disneyland's Tomorrowland I visited when I was eight years old, one ride traveled slowly into the microscopic dimensions of a snowflake, until I was as small as an atom. That's what Danny's brain does.

If chip design can transport him into the miniature, on the other end of the spectrum there's the clock monument, which will have one of the world's longest pendulums, sixty feet, and three-ton sandstone dials that you can sit on and carve your initials into. Furthermore—and this is where Danny's brain is really exceptional—Danny can scale not only in spatial dimensions but in temporal dimensions.

When he was designing the massively parallel Connection Machine supercomputers in the 1980s, his brain had to be able to think in subnanoseconds. Like traveling back out of the snowflake at Tomorrowland, he was able to amplify a nanosecond until it seemed human-sized. A nanosecond is a billionth of a second, and in that period light and electricity travels one foot. The Connection Machine was five feet wide, tall, and deep, so an electrical impulse traveling one foot away had to be phase-locked with a simultaneously sent impulse that might have to zigzag as far as thirty feet. And since the Connection Machine had 64,000 processors, each of which could send and receive impulses, synchronizing all these impulses took an extraordinarily imaginative design.

How can I better explain this challenge? Imagine 64,000 people in a stadium, all trying to clap their hands at once. It's hard, particularly because the speed of sound is slow enough that one person clapping on one side of the stadium hears the opposite person's clap some time after the opposite person has actually clapped. Now spread those 64,000 people all over the city and try to get them to clap in rhythm just by shouting instructions at them. That's about what Danny was able to manage. He was able to scale his mind down to billionths of a second, get creatively comfy with subnanoseconds, and engineer a solution to synchronize the electronic impulses.

I looked at the microchip a little longer to assure Danny that I had truly admired it, which seemed the only way not to offend him by asking the most obvious question:

"Great, so, uh, what is it?"

"Oh, I was just trying out the MEMs design system, so for lack of anything better I made an antenna. I also calculated how long a string I could compact onto a single chip. Fifteen feet."

In other words, the chip wasn't going to be used at all. It was going to remain in his study, just another exhibit in his small chip collection, which he keeps in a drawer. This, too, was a very

Hillisesque trait: that a thing's usefulness—or lack of it—not be a reason not to give it a try.*

This trait is both frustrating and admirable: admirable because he is motivated by curiosity, which seems far purer than what's motivating Silicon Valley these days; frustrating because one can't help but wonder how much he might accomplish if he would devote himself to practical challenges.

00:12:18 Quiz

Following is a list of some friends of Danny, and a separate list of things they said about the clock. I offer these quotes as evidence that even some people who are close to Danny, think he's brilliant, and are even willing to work on the clock will let slip now and then that they can't quite take it seriously.

Match the person to the quotes:†

1. Paul Saffo, member of the clock's board of directors
2. Doug Carlston, member of the clock's board of directors
3. Marvin Minsky, mentor of Hillis at MIT and current Disney Fellow
4. Anonymous, off-the-record old friend

—"It's a nice hack, but it would be a shame if it were all he were known for."
—"I don't know if I get it. I'm not great on symbols. They strike me as tourist sites."

---

*00:00:32 This reminded me of an anecdote about a meeting Danny had with the U.S. military. (Since the military purchased so many of Hillis's supercomputers, he has a very-high-level security clearance.) At the end of the meeting, all those in attendance passed out their business cards, while Danny offered to give out a little vial. In the vial were chains of DNA encoded with his contact information. For most people, it's interesting enough to merely know that one can encode DNA with information. Danny actually does it.

†Quiz answers: 3, 2, 1, 4.

—"The way to make something last ten thousand years is to create an oral tradition. We don't need the clock so much as we need to start the myth of the clock."

—"I'm very annoyed that somebody with the genius of Danny is wasting his time on something as silly as this clock."

00:13:05 Other Than Our Opening Moment with the MEMs Chip, Why the Remainder of My First Attempt to Interview Hillis Was Almost a Complete Failure

At the time, Hillis had just accepted the position at Disney, and Disney's public relations department had just approved the text of the press release announcing the establishment of the Fellow program. As the first Fellow, Danny had little idea what he would really be doing. In the meantime, he was being used around the corporation as a consultant, dispensing advice in brainstorming sessions called charrettes. Though Danny had been thinking about the clock design for several years, the project was not yet on Disney's radar.

Danny was also wary of disclosing anything that wasn't officially authorized by public relations. I wasn't allowed into the Imagineering model shop, Danny couldn't share any of the ideas he had for theme park rides, and he certainly couldn't tip me off on what Disney had planned for the divisions Disney Online and New Technology.

In order to accommodate me despite these strict limitations, Danny and I arranged to have lunch at Disney headquarters and then spend the rest of the afternoon going on rides. The idea was that Danny was such a unique individual that his "Dannyness" would be as vibrant when he was discussing the design of Frontierland as it would be when he was discussing the design of supercomputers. Just having lunch with him, I imagined, would reveal an original character. This was the fallacy of the objective correlative: the presumption that the moment (of Danny) could speak for the whole (of Danny).

Danny tried his best. He was the only man in the Disney executive dining room in a short-sleeved shirt, but there was just no way to infer geniusness from the way he dipped French fries into ketchup.* At Disneyland, we met up with his twin four-year-old sons, Noah and Asa. "Cute" doesn't begin to describe them—they're a Johnson's baby shampoo commercial waiting to happen. We took everyone's favorite rides. In conversation after conversation Danny tried to express an exuberance about Disney intellectualism, lecturing on transcultural notions of beauty and the master-apprentice labor model behind early animation. None of it had anything to do with him, and none of it demonstrated any particular "Dannyness." In truth, we both seemed a little burdened by the expectation. The "Fear and Loathing in Disneyland" angle wasn't producing a ripping experience. Several times Danny apologetically commented that he didn't feel as if he'd given me anything to write about. The fact that he'd become a walking encyclopedia of Disney banter didn't demonstrate any genius, only homework.

Months later, when I understood him better, I saw that to subject him to the moment-speaks-for-the-whole literary device was contradictory to the gist of his work, which is all about emphasizing the whole and deemphasizing the moment. In this sense, any article about him should show the clock in the context of his whole life, not just the moment.

00:15:52 What Is So Upsetting About the Clock to Fellow Futurists

Perhaps the most defining and controversial design principle of the clock is that the technology be "transparent," meaning that an intelligent person walking up to the clock in three thousand years would be able to figure it out by studying it with the hands and eyes, the way you can track the sequential mechanisms of a

---

*00:00:39 The futility of my attempts at interpreting him reminded me of one of the series of Zen koans Hillis wrote satirizing the Artificial Intelligence Lab at MIT, where he worked for many years:

A disciple of another sect once came to AI researcher Gary Drescher as he was eating his morning meal.

"I would like to give you this personality test," said the outsider, "because I want you to be happy."

Drescher took the paper that was offered him and put it into the toaster, saying: "I wish the toaster to be happy, too."

Rube Goldberg machine. It has to be "figure out–able." That's a nice concept. In accordance with this principle, Danny has mandated that the clock be made entirely with Bronze Age technology: it has to have mechanical levers and counters and dials and power systems. It can't use electricity, for two reasons: first, electricity isn't really transparent—you can stare at a circuit board all day and not be able to tell how it works; second, as Danny is fond of saying, electricity is just one medium with which to do binary computing. He thinks about a future several millennia off where electricity has gone the way of eight-track cassettes and computing is done with neurons or DNA or something we can't even imagine today. He wants his clock still to work in that era. So he is resorting to technology that will always be transparent: simple tools.

Of course, that makes sense for Danny; he likes to build with physical technology, which is what he's been doing since he was a kid. But that choice is miffing other futurists. I have to paraphrase their point of view because none would talk to me on the record; they don't want to come off as being disrespectful. The gist of their complaint is that in reverting to Bronze Age technology, Hillis is looking to the past, not the future. If he believes in a postelectrical age, fine, but then build the clock in a postelectrical medium, not a preelectrical medium. In their opinion, by demonstrating the technology of the past, the clock will make us think about the past. Consider the Grand Canyon; in a way, it too is recording history, working as a sort of erosion clock measuring geological time. The vertical drop from the Grandview Overlook at the lip of the canyon to the Colorado River below measures eons. But when you stand there, the view makes you think about the past, about all the years that have been required for a river to cut a gorge that deep; it doesn't make you wonder about how deep the gorge will be in another million years. Similarly, the clock's Bronze Age technology is likely to make us think about the golden age of bronze, pardon the oxymoron. Two thousand years from now, if the clock is still standing, it's less likely to make millennium partyers think about the year 6000 than about what life was like in 2000 and wonder why in the world someone way back then would build such a thing.

This same conflict is being played out in Disney's Tomorrowland exhibit. Because it's just too costly to change Tomorrowland rides every year, the company has decided to exhibit historical visions of the future: a hundred years ago, what did we imagine would be going on in America in the year 2000? Fifty years ago, what did we imagine? Ten years? And so on. Ostensibly, it's about the future, but the important subtext is the past—the way visions of the future express the fears or manifest the hopes of the envisioner. It says more about who we were a hundred years ago, or fifty, or ten.

When I went to visit Hillis most recently, an Imagineer from the model shop had just delivered several rolling-ball clocks Hillis had designed. These were thick slabs of aluminum, two feet long by one foot wide. Carved down their faces were sharp-angled switchback grooves. Danny put a tungsten ball at the top of the groove and tipped the aluminum slab. The ball zigzagged down, chiming the time as it clinked from one track to the track below.

For four hundred years, mankind has been making rolling-ball clocks, which have always suffered because the grooved tracks that the ball rolled in have been of single consistent depth; if the ball ever picks up speed, its timing will go off slightly. Hillis made a rather simple adjustment to the design: by carving the depth of the tracks like the arced sweep of a pendulum, he ensured that when the ball speeds up, its momentum will carry it farther along the track into an increasing incline, thereby slowing it down. Thus the ball's speed self-corrects. The two rolling-ball clocks that Hillis showed me are the greatest rolling-ball clocks ever designed in more than four hundred years of trying.

They're cool, but are they important? They're certainly not very useful to anyone other than Danny. Here's one of our most visionary engineers, inventing something that would have been of use four centuries ago. No wonder fellow futurists are fretting.

Yet I have to censor myself. I have to remember that the point of Danny's work is not necessarily the practical use but its physicality. Hillis's rolling-ball clocks have a gratifying elegance that is sort of a tactile onomatopoeia. I pick up a slab and toss the ball in. It's enigmatic, provoking—it begs me to figure it out.

00:20:39 What All This Has to Do with Disney

Far less than people would like it to. Disney is paying Hillis's salary, but the clock is being overseen by a recently created non-profit organization, the Long Now Foundation, which has its offices in San Francisco's Presidio. Disney has made its machinists available to the foundation at cost. In exchange, Disney has the right to make a replica of the finished clock. Today, the project is at proof-of-concept stage—a prototype is slowly being engineered.

In the coming years, there will be articles galore published about Hillis's creation. Much of the speculation will investigate what it means for the Walt Disney Company, whose investors have offered great reserves of money because they see Disney, with its stranglehold over our children's imaginations, as having an infinitely sustainable resource. (Bambi will never go out of style.) Any indication of where Disney will be in 2030 will be scrutinized. And I doubt that the clock will be very encouraging. It isn't projected as a revenue source. Its budget isn't even a line item.

00:21:38 Whatever Happened to the Connection Machine

Last spring I went to visit Brewster Kahle, who worked with Danny on the Connection Machine. He now runs Alexa Internet and the Internet Archive out of an old white clapboard school-house in San Francisco's Presidio. Brewster walked me over to a building that was once a hospital where World War II soldiers whose limbs had been blown off would come to die—a fitting metaphor for what I was about to see. Brewster unlocked the door to the basement and walked me down the dusty staircase. The hallway walls were cement; the ceiling was a tangle of water pipes, air ducts, and coiled electrical lines. Brewster couldn't find the switch to the lone fluorescent tube bulb, but a little light leaked through the boarded-over windows. Shoved under the staircase and wrapped in cardboard was a Connection Machine 2. It stood as tall and wide and deep as the arm span of its designer, Tamiko Thiel. It was assembled like a Rubik's Cube of cubes, each small cube fronted by black smoky glass. Back in 1986, the Connection Machine was far and away the fastest computer the world had ever seen, but for several years now it hasn't even been worth plugging in. Brewster had bought it for old times' sake from Yale. It was more than happy to clear off the five-foot square of linoleum the machine had been occupying, and it jumped at his $500 offer.

The Connection Machine made possible simulations that had never been imaginable before: predicting global climate change, finding oil, visualizing what two galaxies colliding would look like. But in the end—and here I'm chopping three seasons of soap opera into one paragraph—the Connection Machine fell victim to its own brilliance. It was so far and away unique that it was relatively impractical to write software for. Danny's focus was diverted to corporate strategy. Things took several years to sort out, the way they always do: spin off divisions to whoever will take them, bring in some hard-nosed green-eyeshaded managers, and reemerge from Chapter 11 bankruptcy as a software company.

00:23:33 Whether One of Our Most Amazing Engineers Has Lost His Faith in High Technology

"It's a fair question," said Hillis when I one-twoed him with the evidence for such conclusion. During one of his staring-at-the-ceiling meditations, Hillis put his dilemma this way:

> We're in the middle of a phase transition:
> a butterfly flapping its wings at
> just the right moment could
> cause a storm to happen.
> —I'm trying to understand—
> I'm at a moment in my life—
> I don't know where to flap my wings.

So the clock may be intended to inspire us, but it's also possible (and not contradictory) that Hillis is subconsciously creating it to revive himself.

00:24:05 Why Hillis May Be Who He Is

The following elements of Hillis's childhood, to lesser or greater degrees, shaped who he is today:

- Danny's father, a biologist and physician, studied outbreaks of hepatitis, a disease often caused by feces in the water supply. One form, hepatitis A, will lay a child low for a week or so but can be fatal in adults. Danny grew up in various Third World countries (Burundi, Uganda, India, the Congo), witnessing the suffering of children.

- His father emphasized the importance of devoting oneself to problems that extend one's reach. His parents' friends were all scientists and medical doctors, immersing Danny in an environment that rewarded sheer intelligence. Where they lived, there was often no formal school to attend. Danny's mother taught him some things, but he was guided by his own curiosity.

- Most important, there wasn't always some older person to tell him what was impossible, such as when he read about transistors and electronics. In Calcutta there wasn't anything like a local Radio Shack at which to buy a hobby set, so at the age of twelve Hillis took some 10-point nails, some D-cell batteries, a hunk of plywood, and some swatches of screen door and, demonstrating the Swiss Family Robinson ingenuity that would later make him famous, built a computer that could play tic-tac-toe. Without resources, he had to solve problems from scratch, had to understand the problem from the very basics—an approach to problem solving to which he would always return.

- Calcutta. Danny was thirteen. His father introduced him to Mother Teresa, who told Danny that hunger could not be prevented or stopped but that she would devote every day of her life to relieving the inevitable suffering. Mother Teresa declined Danny's father's offer of assistance, fearing that aid from outsiders would absolve local Indian doctors from taking responsibility.

00:25:42 What Does It Mean For a Thing to Be Hillisesque

Quickly: Hillis's inventions are metatechnology—technology that has as its purpose changing the way we think about technology. Like metafiction or metaphysics, they accomplish this objective by pushing the definition of the medium. The Connection Machine shook up the study of the brain. It begged the question, When is a brain a brain and when is it still just a computer? Some of his fun inventions—such as his Tinkertoy computer— beg the question of whether an object is a game or a piece of mechanical art. He almost always uses unusual materials, simulating digital electronics with mechanics or simulating evolutionary biology with computers. In one chapter of the book he was writing when I met him, he described how a computer could be made of copper plumbing, with water running through the pipes rather than electricity running through wires.

Some of the deeply rooted assumptions about technology that his inventions alter:

- · That digital computing is necessarily electronic
- · That electronics are somehow nonphysical
- · That any machine is inherent to its medium
- · That technology is something to be afraid of

00:26:41 Is Silicon Valley's Horizon Really Too Short Term

It is kind of odd to criticize an industry that is so entirely invested in inventing the near future for being too caught up in the present. It's hard to blame the industry for paying too much attention to the bottom line when so many firms' bottom lines are running red in the hope that they'll go black in the future. Sure, individual people are motivated by money, but the cookies are making people work harder, which is bringing the future here faster. Hillis's criticism is not being taken very well in the Valley.

"The big danger of the industry is that by allowing these short-term economic considerations, it's the old hill-climbing problem," explains Douglas Carlston, chair of Brøderbund and one of the members of the Long Now Foundation's board of directors. "You keep climbing up that hill, but at some point you get to the top and look out and realize that not far away is an even taller hill. But you have to go down a valley to get to it. It's the local optimism problem. There's always a risk that the industry is not casting a large enough net." Carlston hopes the clock will inspire people to alter such habits.

According to Hillis, certain problems aren't solvable in three years, and it's people's nature not to work on problems they can't solve. If we can extend people's horizons, a whole range of challenges falls back into play. Just consider the headlock Microsoft has the industry in: venture capitalists funding only start-ups that avoid areas Microsoft has dominated, et cetera. For the foreseeable future, that won't change, and for a venture capitalist with a five-year portfolio it's a rational decision. But if we were to open our time frame to ten years, all sorts of post-Windows scenarios would become imaginable.

Danny wants to set an example, take a radical leap into the future. Building a ten-thousand-year clock is either the ultimate hubris or the ultimate humility, and it's so far out it's hard to tell.

00:27:52 Some Seemingly Unrelated Facts That Elucidate the Meaning of the Clock

· In 1163, the first foundation stone of what would become Notre Dame Cathedral in Paris was laid by Pope Alexander III. Among the master builders were Jean de Chelles and Pierre de Montreuil. Builders devoted their entire lives to the cathedral, as did their sons and grandsons and grandsons' grandsons, and so on; the cathedral was not completed by their descendants until the fourteenth century.

· In 1953, Walt Disney convinced his brother, Roy, to drum up the financing and let him build a theme park. Walt envisioned an exhibit called the "World of Tomorrow," with a rocket ship to the moon, a fun house with voice-activated appliances, and a mini–freeway system with minicars. At the time, the atomic bomb had the potential to obliterate the future, and our society's ability to see into the future was crippled. Technology was, at best, going to dehumanize the country. Tomorrowland changed all that; it gave a rosy picture of the future technology could bring us.

- In 1971, after more than a decade of space exploration, NASA released a fully illuminated photograph of Earth as a big blue marble against a black background. Though it was just a photograph—it had no more practical use than Danny's clock—as a symbol it was incredibly powerful. It helped rescale our minds to understand the fact that Earth is small and precious and vulnerable, not vast and infinitely plunderable. That simple photograph of Earth became the symbol of the environmental movement.

- In 1991, the U.S. Department of Energy assigned a panel of specialists the task of creating a warning sign, a message to the future, for the first permanent nuclear waste repository in the United States, near Carlsbad, New Mexico. By "permanent," the Environmental Protection Agency mandated ten thousand years. The Waste Isolation Pilot Plant had been twenty years in the design. By carving tunnels in salt beds that had been stable for 200 million years, the agency is counting on the natural creep of salt to refill the tunnels and seal the drums. Recently, the Department of Energy chose a plan: a thirty-three-foot-high soil berm with granite monuments inside its walls etched with pictographs and warnings in several languages. This berm will erode over time, gradually revealing radar reflectors or permanent magnets detectable by remote sensors. In case of further erosion, a granite danger kiosk will be buried underground.

00:31:04 Why It's So Rejuvenating for Danny Hillis to Work at Disney Imagineering

As a kid, promising Hillis a trip to Disneyland was the way his parents got him to make his bed, mop the floors, and mow the lawn. He earned merit points that could be spent on rides. But his most memorable visit was in 1984; he needed to write his Ph.D. dissertation about the Connection Machine to satisfy graduation requirements. He was living in a Boston loft with six other people and had recently founded Thinking Machines, so his life was crowded and noisy. One day he went to Logan International Airport and got onto the first plane, which happened to be going to Orlando, Florida. The next morning, from a resort hotel, he walked into Disney World, sat on a slatted-wood bench in front of the Cinderella Castle, and began working.

Kids came by with cotton candy stuck to their faces and wanted him to get it off. German tourists asked him to shoot their photograph with Donald Duck. Parades marched by, trumpets blasting and snare drums rattling. Distractions? Not at all.

In Disney parlance, the fountain in front of the Cinderella Castle is the panopticon—the place from which you can see everything. It was just what Danny needed to get his dissertation done. He wrote an entire chapter that first day and came back to the same spot the next day. In seven days, he wrote seven chapters in seven notebooks.

Hillis is a big kid at heart. "Adults are just children who have learned how to behave," he said to me several times. Playing has always been an important ingredient in his creativity. When he was an undergraduate, he designed toys for Milton Bradley and later helped design the first video game graphics chip. When he was at Thinking Machines, he held meetings in a tree house and drove a fire engine to work, a big-city Ford ladder truck at first, then a smaller twenty-five-year-old Dodge pumper truck purchased at auction. Danny knew some circus clowns, and when they came to town he would lead the parade to the circus in his fire engine. Danny also bought an Amphicar, one of a couple thousand built in the early 1960s. On sunny days he, Brewster Kahle, Richard Feynman, and Marvin Minsky would climb onto the vinyl bench seats and motor down Memorial Drive in Cambridge, discussing Zen Buddhism. Rather than cross the bridge, they'd turn off onto the grass, steer down the embankment, and plop onto the Charles River. Like the device that morphed Chitty Chitty Bang Bang, the Amphicar's propeller behind the rear axle would engage, the conversation would shift just as seamlessly to neural pathway computers, and the Amphicar would putter them up the Charles.

I think most creative minds would find Disneyland antithetical to creativity; most creative people's artistic process involves stripping away life's illusions and fantasies. Their art is about getting honest. Disneyland is a big, optimistic lie, a song we sing to ourselves to forget reality. In his collection of essays *Some Freaks*,

David Mamet makes the point that Disneyland is selling the superego, the sense that we are good and would never do anything wrong.

I've sometimes thought back to my day at Disneyland with Danny—a day I felt was such a failure because nothing happened, no conflict emerged, there was no dramatic tension. And of course that's the point: Danny was at peace in the theme park, his kids at his side. Here's a guy who spent his childhood witnessing the suffering of children—is it a wonder he feels most at peace with happy kids cavorting around him? Is it a wonder that It's a Small World, with its visions of rosy-cheeked kids around the world singing happily, is his favorite ride? Is it a wonder that as he reaches middle age, he needs to come back to the panopticon, the place from which he can see everything?

As Danny said, "I knew I was in the right place when, on one of my first days working, I asked for a parachute harness. And nobody questioned what I needed a parachute harness for. They just said, 'What size?' "

00:34:46 Specifically, One of Hillis's Visions of What the Millennium Clock Will Be Like

You're on the edge of a hot, dry desert, maybe an old lake bed between canyons hidden from the world. Or maybe you're in San Francisco's Presidio. Or maybe you're in the piñon forests above Santa Fe.*

---

*00:01:14 The Long Now Foundation's board of directors is having a difficult time making some crucial decisions, such as where to put the clock. They've got stacks of e-mail a yard high on the subject. Every time I visited Hillis, he had changed his mind again. The last time, he had absolved himself of the decision and said it was someone else's decision to make. If the decision of where to put the clock were one for just our lifetimes, the answer would come easily. But the very enormity of the consequences of the decision weighs on them; it's more permanent than any decision they've ever made before. Here they discern a difference between their process and what they see as going on in Silicon Valley today, where crucial decisions are made in the moment but lived with forever; for example, Windows still rides atop DOS. However, it is not at all clear how the board will ever make some crucial decisions if not under the threat of their self-imposed 2001 deadline.

In the distance—out in that desert, up some steps, or atop a hill—you see a pyramid. Not a huge pyramid, not big enough to make you say "Wow," but more of a curiosity, an invitation to explore. Maybe you're there as part of an annual ritual to cleanse your soul of another year's instant gratifications. Maybe you've been flown in for a corporate executive retreat and this is just a tune-up for some heavy whiteboard brainstorming assisted by $1,200-a-day creativity consultants. Maybe you're there on a pilgrimage, trying to recover from divorce or the loss of a parent, hoping to be able to see beyond the crisis of Now and into your own future. Maybe you're a tourist on a bus, and you just have to see what your Lonely Planet guidebook describes as a "Leary-esque experiment in postacid insight."

Hillis envisions a footpath to the pyramid. Every flagstone on that path represents a year of recorded history, or every step up another decade. It takes a while, longer than you anticipated, because the path winds back on itself like a meditation labyrinth. At first you're a little peeved at this deception, and you feel like cutting the corners to get there sooner, but other people are on the path too and peer pressure keeps you in line. Your superego interposes; you don't want to see yourself as being manipulated by peer pressure, so you convince yourself you're staying on the path because you actually like its meditative pace. You don't talk much, you observe the communal silence; it's like a church—nobody has to tell you to keep your voice low, it's understood. By the time you reach the end of the path with the pyramid overhead, you look back at your last few steps and realize that the final small portion of what turned out to be more than a mile-long path represents your entire life. You get the point that you're supposed to be humbled by this, but humility doesn't come easily.

You've brought at least two things: a brick and a flashlight. Every visitor adds a brick to the exterior of the pyramid. The point of this is to show you how much can be accomplished by accumulated labor; enough visitors each depositing their one brick has doubled the height of the pyramid in just a few years. Maybe you also brought a PowerBar. You take off your shoes because the person in front of you took off his shoes, as did the visitor in front of him. Someone tells you it's to avoid bringing dust into the pyramid. You enter the pyramid through the corner and turn on your flashlight. The passageway is only several feet wide, walled with stone, and to get in further you have to sneak through a small opening.*

Oozing out of the walls from every direction is a slow, deep heartbeat. It's as if you're inside an animal. But the tempo of this heartbeat is slower than your heartbeat, beating only about as often as you breathe. It slows your breathing, and this in turn slows your pulse. The air is brittle, dry, good for preservation, but it has that dry-ice tingle of air inside a throbbing nightclub. The tunnel stretches perhaps a hundred feet; you can't quite tell because it's dark. You aim your flashlight at the far end and see something huge sweep past the far opening. Whatever it is seems to sweep by in tune with that slow heartbeat. You inch forward, unsure of your footing. When you get to the end, you see that the sweeping thing is the base of a very tall pendulum† that reaches straight up so high that you can't really see the top.

You're free to explore. You begin to climb through a series of chambers, each one representing a different framework of time. Danny hopes visitors might spend the entire day inside the pyramid.

The first chamber is ordinary time, time as we're used to thinking about it. On the wall is an ordinary clock face with hour hands and minute hands. The next chamber is the phases of the moon. Working at moon speed, a round shield masks a half globe; the remaining visible portion waxes and wanes as the shield circles it. It takes a whole month to cycle. You go, "Uh, huh?" and move on to the next chamber, which is the year chamber. In here are the main clock's power systems. These are ten-

---

*00:00:18 Here Danny Hillis is showing his Disney touch—old Walt was vitally concerned with thresholds and sight lines, about creating a moment where you are very clearly entering his world, and once you are in it you cannot see out of it.
†00:00:18 In the National Museum of American History in Washington, D.C., there is a similar sixty-foot pendulum swinging from the ceiling, and Danny has stood there and watched its effect on people. The same families with kids who use the busts of the presidents as a slalom course, the same kids who tug on their dad's coat to go after examining the Declaration of Independence for three seconds, will come skidding to a halt below the pendulum. They'll stand there for several minutes, peacefully. "It seems to give people permission to slow down," Danny says.

foot-high double-helix contraptions. Inside the double helix is a weight that descends over the course of the year; as it descends, it powers the clock. Every year it needs to be rewound by turning a crank that pushes the weight back up the helix.

The next chamber has a huge thirty-foot-diameter millstone on the floor. This turns a full circle only once a lifetime, every seventy-eight years. You take an hour to gouge out your initials in the soft stone, and if you come back in ten years with your children you can show them how those initials have moved only a few feet. Eventually, millstones from previous generations will be tilted up against the walls. By now you've spent enough time inside that you're going to feel the need to use the toilet, and you figure you better find it, because you're not sure you can hold it for the next ten-thousand-year chamber.

On your way, you climb through the complex workings of the clock. There is a lot of big machinery and an occasional move-ment as a peg slides in or out or something turns. Now you are high enough up in the pyramid that you can look out at the full pendulum, and you look down at people entering the first cham-ber below. There's a slit in the roof where the sun comes in; di-rect light makes its way through the slit only when the sun is at noon height. Its rays are focused by lenses on a sandwich of brass and invar; the brass side absorbs the heat faster than the invar, it expands, and the sandwich bends just enough to click a gauge and make the clock resynchronize itself, in case it's lost or gained a few seconds in the preceding day.

Your brain doesn't want to go there, but you get the point: while you're here, you're supposed to think about your life. Not think about what you've got to get done that day, not what you've got to get done that year. But really think about the grand sweep of your life. Do you have a lifetime plan? Do you have any idea where you will be in ten years? Honestly, the answer is no, but a knee-jerk defensive response goes off in your head: "So what? I've never had a plan, and I seem to be doing just fine." Nobody's listening to you, though. Maybe you want to leave, but the group you came with seems perfectly content to stay awhile, so you sit there until the thought occurs to you, "Well, let's just say, to humor this place, that I did have a ten-year plan. What kind of stuff would be in that plan?" When you leave, there's another path. Every stone is a year into the future. By now you're kind of into it, or, more likely, in your mind you're crafting an intelligent comment you can make to your friends when you get to the end. Maybe you're thinking about how you'll describe the experience to people who haven't been there. You find yourself thinking that even though the experience wasn't riveting in the conventional sense, it was unique. Most important, you've been here, and you can say you've done it. The impact won't even hit you for quite some time. Maybe it will be years later, and you'll find yourself in a late-night, liquor-induced conversation where you're trying to explain how difficult it is to know whether you should marry the woman you're dating, gosh, it just seems such a permanent decision, and suddenly you find yourself talking about your visit to the clock, leaning on that visit as a metaphor to buy you time. . . .

00:41:40 Some Speculation on What's Next for Hillis

There is an inherent instability in the current situation, a tension between Hillis's fierce experimentalism and Disney's need to protect its brand name by avoiding risk. As much as Disney lets its Imagineers sniff the glue, they don't let them out of the shop without the approval of three layers of bureaucracy. Hillis is a doer. I foresee a day when Disney will not be able to talk him out of a project and he will have to take it elsewhere.

Coming to Disney was not "next" for him, it was in many ways a spiritual return. Similarly, the latest rumor is that Hillis is being recruited for the chief technology officer position at Sun Microsystems, that he and Scott McNealy and power broker John Doerr have been seen spinning in the same teacup on the Alice in Wonderland ride. If the rumor's true, and if anything comes of it, this too would be circular: three years ago, when the Connection Machine's viability was waning, its hardware team moved to Sun. Most of those engineers are still there.

Many of Hillis's friends think of him as a natural resource that must not be squandered. They consider him a one-man brain trust that is vital to our national interest. They would like to just let Danny be Danny, but they feel an almost moral responsibility to watch over him. That's why some are so pained by what they see as Hillis squandering his middle age at Disney on this monument to time when he could be engineering something really important. Others intuit that, regardless of whether the clock is important or not, his time at Disney is restorative. Whether it's by letting him have the childhood he didn't get growing up abroad or by insulating him from the financial worries he went through at Thinking Machines, Disney is an important step in his career.

When I first met Hillis, he had just arrived at Disney, and he was just beginning to accept the idea that his clock, if he ever built it, would best be hand-cranked by humans. Before that time he had been imagining devices that would never have to be touched by humans, never be reliant on human custodians— something that humans couldn't mess up, as in some ways they did with his Connection Machines. But Disneyland is the place that puts smiles on his twin sons' faces; the most important thing to come from his two years at Disney is that he has regained his faith in people. Now his thinking has come full circle: he insists that people must wind the clock. People have to have a role in its operation, or they will not care about it.

Danny's remounting faith in people makes it all worthwhile. Many believe that Danny will engineer something really useful for people only if he cares about people. In a generous twist of il-logic, they admit that the clock may be a waste of time but that maybe wasting time is really what he needs right now, and there-fore wasting time is not a waste of time.

One friend believes that Danny is sort of going back to school at Disney, learning the piece of curriculum he missed: pop culture.

I believe that's the right dynamic, just the wrong topic of study. At Disney, Hillis is learning enduringness. His failure to anticipate what makes something endure led to the obsolescence of the Connection Machine despite its brilliance. That riddled him, ate at him. So like a good engineer, he's gone out and learned from Disney, the company that has made a simple sketch of a mouse endure for seventy years. The clock is the manifestation of his fascination with enduringness.

00:44:39 What I Think

I've been spending as much time as possible in Silicon Valley lately, and one of the few conclusions I've drawn is that it does not seem to be as much fun as it once was. Mind-boggling, crazy things happen there—funny things—but few of the people who work there are remembering to enjoy themselves.*

Too much is at stake, and time is too short.

So though it may be unfair to criticize the technology industry for focusing on a too-near future, I believe it's fair to criticize it for relying too heavily on forwarded e-mail jokes and *Dilbert* for the daily smile. For me, personally, this is the greatest danger to the future of the industry, because if it stops being fun, our creativity will become formulaic and hackneyed.

Brewster Kahle tells a story of when Danny married his wife, who had a Porsche. Danny got hold of the Porsche and was immediately saying things like "Well, what can we do with a Porsche?" Not "Where can we drive?" or "Where can we be seen?" but "What can we do?" as in what kind of physics experiments can be done in a Porsche? They started debating whether a helium balloon in the passenger seat would move toward the windshield or toward the rear of the car when the sportster accelerated. Then they filled a balloon with helium and tested it. (Since the balloon is lighter than air, as the air mass gets shoved back into the seat, the balloon moves toward the windshield.)

Hillis is still finding brain-challenging ways to horse around. Lately, for fun, he's been trading foreign currency derivatives—oh, you know, just ordinary, routine stuff like yen-denominated deutsche mark futures.

Whether or not he ever gets his clock built, and whether or not the clock is taken seriously by society, Danny Hillis will always be a fascination for me. He is far and away the purest engineer I have ever met—nearly the Platonic form of engineer, if an engineer is defined as a person who makes things. Yet he is a philosopher as well, with a vast, cavernous mind that one could get lost in and never find the way back out of. He is the inventor of what was the world's fastest computer, yet now he is building what is ostensibly the world's slowest computer, a device that will tick only once a day. He can think like a glacier, devoting himself to a project that will last beyond his lifetime, yet he's a remark-

---

*00:00:17 There will always be those who insist that hard work is its own fun, and there are always those who have fun as a momentary stress releaser from long bouts of unfun, but those don't count.

ably in-the-moment person who seizes every opportunity to experience something new.* In all the debate about whether Hillis should build his clock, nobody seems to be bothering to doubt whether it actually can be done. Which is probably for the best. Hillis reminds me of Wallace and Gromit going down into their basement to build a rocket to the moon to get more cheese for crackers. Without anyone to tell them that's impossible, there's nothing to stop them from doing it. Hillis admits that he's often not really sure why he's building the clock, so he offers up attempts at explanation that are really just rationalizations of something he knows in his bones.

"The truth is," he says, "it just feels right."

---

*00:00:27 At one point in our meetings, Danny said that he had to research different nonpolluting ways of creating aerial fireworks or displays. As part of this, he needed to know how much sound a blimp engine made. So he asked me to go for a blimp ride, and we did. Typical Danny: he could have just called Goodyear and asked for the sound levels, but he will take any chance he gets to have a firsthand experience.

CHAPTER 8

IS THE
"Revolution!"
OVER?

SILICON VALLEY CHANGES so fast that no sooner am I done describing its many elements than I have to start in again for a fresh look. The sequel begins before the prequel's finished—already, it's time again to upgrade.

Let me tell you what Silicon Valley is like: the mountain edges of the valley rise up like the lip of a great big copper-bottomed frying pan of overpriced Revere Ware, and on the high heat of burning money everything and everyone in there melts into a boiling, spattering, frenetic stew. Boston is like a nicely arranged four-food-group meal on Sunday china, and Seattle is a huge hunk of Microsoft barbecue with a few thawed peas rolling off the paper plate, but Silicon Valley, California, is not just a stew, it's a stew that never comes off the gas heat. The juices meld, and the histories intertwine, and it's spiced up with high achievers from every nook of the world. Heat waffles off the ground, distorting it all into an earth-toned prism. Entangled superexpressways pass over industrial megaparks and shady 3BR/2BA ranch-style homes and provide occasional vistas of scorched tan acreage protected as natural habitats for scrappy, trash-can-scrounging coyotes. The tallest landmarks are power towers and phone poles. The real work is done in silence, sitting in cubicles, staring at screens. Everyone is attempting to make things that have not existed before. And though we could argue till dawn about the utility or significance of what they're creating, I believe that to create and risk failing is the essence of feeling alive—that in the moment of creation they shake off their anonymity and feel relevant to the sweep of the world.

Don't think for a moment that this stew can be re-created by throwing together some engineers, VCs, headhunters, and electronics stores, then drowning them all in money. Silicon Valley is special. Yes, the universities are excellent. Yes, California's labor laws let employees jump from one firm to another almost at will. Yes, the weather attracts big brains from cold climates, though most people who come here for the weather work so hard they rarely get to see the sunshine.

What those oft-cited "Silicon Valley advantage" theories don't convey is how evolved this place has become just from being on the high heat for fifty years. The competition has bred electronics stores the size of eight football fields, electronics stores open all night, electronics stores where you can do your laundry while shopping. There are VCs who invest only in video chips, VCs who funnel only foreign money, VCs who write books, VCs who are professors of sociology. There are headhunters who handle only Cobol programmers from Singapore, headhunters who specialize in luring toy company executives, and, I've recently learned, a headhunting firm that helps other headhunting firms hunt for headhunters. It's bizarre. Programmers are represented by agents, manual writers have three-book backlogs, and one of the fastest-growing companies writes software that is being sold to other software firms to help them manage their tech support. Let me repeat that in case you didn't get the full implication: there are so many software firms that just selling them software can make a company one of the fastest-growing software firms. It seems impossible mathematically, but it's not, and the reason is that high-tech companies are quick on the uptake with anything that makes them more efficient, which they'd better be, because this market is scary-competitive.

Meander into the Valley with me. Let's take a look at some of the highly evolved species that have shown up lately. Let's get a sense of why this economic engine can't be reproduced anywhere else. Let's see how, even if nobody believes they're a revolutionary anymore, the revolution goes on.

> **"One word: Adrenaline!"**
> **—The entire copy of an advertisement in The**
> **Stanford Daily recruiting engineers to a**
> **firm in Silicon Valley.**

Sunnyvale

At a party I meet a young guy with an urban lumberjack look, most notably a week's growth of stubble. His employer, Power-Agent, burned up $25 million in cash, shut its doors, and laid off all sixty employees. He's been hanging around the house for "almost three weeks—well, fifteen days," he clarifies, and he's starting to lose self-respect for being such a slob. This morning he went to the unemployment office at the Federal Building, which was so empty that only two of the fifteen teller windows were open. He got the picture and turned around. He figures he'll take a job next week. That's how he said it—not that he would start interviewing, not that he would get an offer, but that he would take one, as if job offers were weeklies stuffed into news racks on street corners and all you have to do was pick one up on the way to the café. It occurs to me that maybe he's already had job offers.

"Oh, sure," he confirms, chuckling a bit self-consciously, knowing darn well how lucky he is to be living here at this time. He's a business school graduate with a whole six months' experience in marketing. That his experience was with a firm that burned $25 million in venture capital and never made it to market hasn't seemed to hurt his marketability.

By the keg I meet a venture capitalist. He's just invested in an Internet start-up that has designed software that extracts résumé data from the monstrous résumé Web sites. That seems to me the definitive start-up for these times: one with a good solution to a very specific problem that didn't even exist a year ago. It's inordinately peculiar—can you really make money just extracting data off résumé sites? Sure, you can. It's amazing what you can make money doing here, and in that vein he tells me about the Cubicle Guy.

"Not cubicles," the Cubicle Guy insists when I sit down in his office. "Panel systems."

The Cubicle Guy traffics in used partitions. He buys them dirt cheap from companies going under or moving and resells them to new companies or growing ones. He profits from the churn. A recycled cubicle will run you a little more than two grand, slightly more than half the price of a new one. His business is booming. He wears a beeper because at any time he might be needed somewhere on the peninsula to make a bid.

"I'm not the only guy reselling panel systems. It's like ambulance chasing; the first lawyer on the scene gets the business. I watch the newspaper for layoffs. I watch stock prices for drops, anyone who might soon downsize. I talk to Realtors." So there is not only one Cubicle Guy in Silicon Valley, there is tooth-and-nail competition among several. That's how evolved it's become.

The Cubicle Guy is one of the quirkier parts of the institutionalized revolution, the support system that makes risk taking feel so unrisky. In order to challenge the status quo, you don't have to be so headstrong anymore, you don't have to be a rebel. You just have to have an idea. But you'd better act on your idea fast, because the same trends that made your idea pop into your head are making that same idea pop into competitors' heads. So there's a whole network of services, like the Cubicle Guy, to get you up to speed quickly. If I could co-opt a heuristic for the ease of starting a company here, it would be "plug and play."

"I know this lawyer," the Cubicle Guy says. "He's an associate at this firm. All they have to do to generate the legal documents for a start-up is run this single macro, which inserts the company name in all the appropriate places. Hit a button, out prints your company, sign on the dotted line." I've heard that story so many times, it's become an urban myth.

The Cubicle Guy takes me to his warehouse: 11,000 square feet, which isn't very big considering the size of his merchandise. "It's no trouble to move product once you've got it," he explains. The cubicles are cleaned here, then moved out.

A lot of the cubicles come back with gouge marks, graffiti, and slits between the cloth covering and the wallboard where secrets were hidden. Flyers and memos are still stapled on. These artifacts are pinned to one wall of the Cubicle Guy's warehouse, a private museum of Silicon Valley microsabotage. There are photos of girlfriends, laminated *Far Side* cartoons, positive job evaluations, worthless stock option contracts, a six-point reminder list of "Why I Work So Hard."

The phone on his hip rings, and the Cubicle Guy goes to work. "Are the panels sixty inches tall or seventy-two? Uh-huh. Brown as in oatmeal, or brown as in manila? Okay, do me a favor. Look at one of the T joints where three panels connect—is the connector piece more like a T, or are the three pegs equal in length? Uh-huh. That's probably Versys brand. . . ." He puts his hand over the phone. I give him a nod and let him go back to work.

It turns out that when you look into the matter, the height of a cubicle is a big deal these days. Six-foot walls protect privacy. Five-foot walls allow what's called "prairie dogging" and foster collaboration. The trend is toward the latter, says Primo Orpilla, who along with his architectural design partner Verda Alexander has carved out a niche giving workspaces the "pre-IPO look" that is so fashionable these days. Before any start-up office is designed, a meeting must be held with the workers to hammer out a consensus—on the height of cubicles. "You've got to get *buy-in*," Verda explains.

Their firm, O+a Design, is in such demand because this pre-IPO look is easy to get wrong. "It's a careful balance," says Orpilla. "On one hand, they don't want to look like they are burning too much cash on offices. On the other hand, a cool place to work really helps recruit talent."

They call their solution "comfort design," after the trend to comfort food. What is comfort design? Corner windows reserved for communal spaces with couches, rather than for offices for vice presidents. Any wall that can be made serpentine or tipped at an angle is better than a straight, flat wall. The interior surfaces of a building may be ripped away, exposing ducts, brick, rough timber—"Workers want to see the building's history," says Primo. Perhaps to balance the fly-by-night nature of their operation.

Primo makes it clear that Silicon Valley is a sea of cubicles, but not all cubicles are created equal. Rather than the conventional gray-fabric-covered walls, an O+a cube might have one wall surfaced entirely with whiteboard for dry-erase brainstorming, one surfaced with metal and refrigerator magnets, and a third made from tackboard to hang knickknacks on.

And I've got news for futurists who are picking the hottest technological innovations for the millennium. According to Verda, "Coming up with an affordable cubicle door is sort of the Holy Grail right now."

Cupertino

It's very hard to discern the extent to which people care about money. These are high achievers; they want to succeed, they want to win. For the highest achievers, money is an incidental by-product, a side effect—they get it whether they're motivated by it or not. It's as if Rogaine hair-growing cream, once it got into your system, also made your dick bigger. Who could tell why guys were rubbing it in?

I'll say this: money has less nuance in Silicon Valley than elsewhere. Everyone feels they deserve it every bit as much as the next guy. They all want to hit a walloping home run into the upper deck and then never have to think about money again, which is to say that the desired state is not to care about money, but to get to that state may require some caring.

That said, money doesn't impress. It's too ubiquitous to dazzle. And there are too many ways here to make a lucky bundle and never really have deserved it. Driving a Ferrari doesn't impress anybody but the heavy-on-the-eye-shadow secretaries perched on the bar stools at the Friday evening Black Angus happy hour.

The way to stand out is to make something that has a big impact on the course of technology. That's the dream. But there aren't that many slots available in the Hall of Fame, so the ordinary, everyday superachiever—a guy who's stood out his whole life, at least until he got here—often festers with confusion about his purpose.

There's a lot of money, sure. In the last few years, every mom and pop has woken up to the fact that a broad market index fund averaging a 12 percent return since 1961 is a better place to sock away savings than a money market account paying 3 percent, so institutional investors, who earn their keep by outdoing the stock market, are throwing money into higher-risk/higher-return scenarios, such as venture funds earmarked for Silicon Valley start-ups.

This leads to more money being spent tastelessly than at any other time in history. But the tastelessness is not an indicator of poor taste, it's an indicator of how little the money really matters to the spender. If you didn't care a lick who wins the Sunday football games but there's an office pool and you get a free betting card and you just willy-nilly check off the teams with cool mascots, does that indicate you have poor judgment? It just says you don't care.

Common, then, was a barbecue the other day at an Italian marbled manor—the owner had finally gotten around to hosting an open house for his friends. The meat served was super-premium shanks from a cow fed only corn and raised poolside, an élite cow that summered on the Cape and wintered in Vail. But the slabs of this delicious cow princess were served on flimsy paper plates, with 49¢-per-hundred plastic knives and weensy cake forks. When I had wrangled down my fill of meat, I went for a walk around the compound with a friend, and it was hard not to notice that the only furniture downstairs was a single black leather couch and a seventeen-inch TV propped up on a milk crate. The owner had moved in two years before, and the decor of his home just wasn't as interesting to him as creating the next generation of animation tools. He was going to spend his money on what he found tasteful or not spend it at all.

I sat down on the couch beside a woman who had a look on her face as if she was ready to go home. I admired her watch, a two-tone silver-and-gold Tag Heuer wristwatch I'd seen advertised in financial magazines. I believe they cost around $2,000. When she turned to me, I realized she'd had a few drinks.

"Oh, screw this watch," she slurred. "I saved my company's butt last year. I should have been given a bonus of at least twenty, thirty thousand dollars. Instead, I got a small raise and they tried to placate me with this watch." The firm hoped she would wear the watch with pride. Instead, she wears it to remind her never to trust the firm.

So there's the Rogaine thing: Does she want the money, or does she want the respect?

"If it weren't for the weather here," she says, "I'd go back to Michigan."

Mountain View

Someone who talks to people all the time about what they want is a twenty-six-year-old woman I'll call Claudia Gomez. She is what is known in the headhunting trade as a "ruser," meaning one who performs ruses, one who uses surreptitious methods to trick receptionists into giving out names and job descriptions of employees at Silicon Valley companies. She sells these names to research firms, which in turn sell them to headhunters. So hot is the black market for names out here that Claudia gets $40 for a salesperson and $80 for an engineer, and for a female engineer she gets $120, since every company wants to improve its diversity.

We are standing beside her car, which is parked at the corner of National and Fairchild, two streets named after semiconductor companies from the '60s. Every piece of available ground has been covered with asphalt, which, after several hours of sun, is hot enough to make my shoe soles gummy. Nearby, Freeway 101 thrums. The buildings here are tilt-ups, many of which were Superfund toxic waste clean up sites and not economic to reinhabit until the recent burst in rental value. Now the vacancy rate in this neighborhood is literally zero.

Claudia works her cellular phone. She dials the Netscape operator, asks for the Web site division. When she's connected, she says, "Hi, yeah, this is Sarah Velarde with the Lilith/Women in Rock Music Festival, and we'd like to give out free tickets to the concert at the Shoreline Amphitheater next week to any female programmers. Laurie Anderson wants to take a moment to recognize them, have the crowd cheer, that sort of thing." Claudia listens for a second. Even when communicating by phone, she talks with her hands. "Well, I'm supposed to send them the tickets directly. . . . Uh-huh. . . . Then how about I just put their names at Will Call?" She arranges to phone the next day to get the names of those who want to attend.

Other common ruses: posing as a reporter, bribing temp workers to photocopy employee directories and organizational

charts, posing as a conference organizer wishing to send literature to product managers, and pretending she's a Pac Bell tech-
nician stuck up on a telephone pole outside the building who
needs to verify extensions. One of her favorites is calling a company operator and saying, "Last night I was playing tennis and
got in a doubles game with a programmer from Netscape. I gave
him a ride home, but he left his tennis racquet in my car. Now I
can't remember his name. Dave or Don or something."

The big score comes when Claudia cold calls someone who is
on vacation. The voice mail message provides a jackpot of contacts: "I'm out until the fourteenth. If you have a marketing question, call Laura Abado, extension 328. If you have an advertising
question, call Marquez Padilla, extension 321 . . ."

Claudia arrived here from San Antonio six months ago. She's
not technically inclined, but there are still tons of upside for her
on this career track. Headhunters charge 30 percent of the first-
year "compensation package" of the employee they place. An average headhunter places one employee a month; in other words,
the average headhunter makes almost *four times* the annual income of the lavishly overpaid Silicon Valley worker bee. Is it any
wonder there are so many headhunters? Is it any wonder so many
options have to be passed around to make employees stay put?

After Claudia collects names, she'll cold call the people and if
she can get them to answer a few questions about what they're
looking for in an ideal job, she gets $50 more per person. This
is called profiling, and though headhunters might have a reputation for being sleazy, Claudia says that 99 percent of the people
she cold calls are willing to talk. Loyalty is not part of the equation anymore. Workers stick around because they're waiting
for options to vest and because they can't be perceived as job-
hoppers.

Two years ago, it was enough for workers just to be in the
game, to be a part of it, to hold some options and take their
chances. Their thinking was, "Hey, if the business got funding, it
must be worthwhile." Many start-ups went public or accepted a
buyout but never produced anything but vapor, and the experience gave their workers no lasting pride. If greed were all that was
motivating Silicon Valley, workers would be perfectly happy to
repeat the lucrative churn.

But that's not enough anymore. According to the Claudia

Gomezes whose job it is to ask people what they want, what people want more than anything is a business proposition that can succeed. Every headhunter has a story of a recent start-up that passed the test of venture capitalists but is being flunked by potential executive staff. Venture capitalists are fairly judicious, investing in maybe only a dozen deals a year, but job hunters choose a new firm only once every few years. Candidates have so many opportunities today that they can afford to give that choice the discriminating analysis it deserves. Prospective employees are doing their due diligence. They look for the ultimate endorsement of the business from the headhunter—taking part of the search fee in options. The cautious work part-time at night for a month before resigning from their current firm.

The traditional gatekeeper for high tech's start-up ideas has been financial capital. But that model has been subverted by a far scarcer resource: talent.

Nowhere is the labor market so twisted as in Silicon Valley. At the Shoreline Cineplex in Mountain View, before the lights go down and the previews roll, all the ad slides between movie trivia questions are for jobs. Outside every espresso shop stand shiny blue news racks stuffed with thick, free career magazines: zero percent editorial, 100 percent recruitment advertising. One of the best ways to get rid of a troublesome coworker is simply to give out his name to a few headhunters, who will quickly bombard the guy with so many offers that he will resign on his own within the month. In the ultimate perversion, companies hire headhunters to *telephone their own employees* (without identifying that's who they're really working for), in order to discover which ones are unhappy and vulnerable to being picked off. Do they fire these troublemakers? Odds are they'll be placated with a raise or a spontaneous performance bonus of two thousand stock options.

The newest phenomenon is closers—specialists contracted by a growing firm to pressure candidates to accept offers. They phone a candidate on the weekend or early in the morning, or take him to breakfast at Il Fornaio. "This is the perfect move for you," goes their script. "How are you feeling about it? You're our number one choice. I don't want to pressure you, but this job could get filled by someone else any moment."

Menlo Park

It's the last morning of summer, a Sunday, at the first annual SandHill Challenge, a soapbox derby competition being held to raise funds to combat teenage drunk driving. About fifty vehicles are waiting to race, two at a time, down the gentle quarter-mile grade. One vehicle is designed like a bread box, another like a missile. Someone in a Super Dave Osborne racing getup, complete with motorcycle helmet, is going to roll down the course on a high-backed, swivel-tilt office chair. It's Disney-movie fun. I'm half expecting to see a young Kurt Russell.

This event was dreamed up by Jamis MacNiven, the owner of Buck's restaurant in Woodside, which is *the* breakfast place for top-tier high-tech insiders, so most of the contestants are from that clique: venture capitalists, law firms, banks, and a few of the companies they finance. The contest is a nice metaphor for the pseudoaccessibility of the IPO market: officially, it's open to anybody who can raise the $1,000 minimum, but you have to be the kind of moneybags with a house in Woodside who drinks his coffee at Buck's to even know the event is going on.

You could spend a year at business school and not encounter so much wheeling and dealing. There are two teams with very similar designs, built on supersized skateboards. One has four skateboard trucks underneath; the other rides on a series of RollerBlade wheels. The latter team is a spin-off of the former. Says one driver, "We had a fight over the design, and rather than resolving it, we went our own way."

A lawyer is going around at the last minute donating money to several teams whose vehicles look fast: a go-cart with bicycle wheels, an aerodynamic teardrop covered in fiberglass, and so on. "I'm taking the Microsoft strategy today," he says, sliding his checkbook into the pocket of his Dockers. "I want to be a part of the winning car. In order for that to be true, the first conclusion was straightforward: don't design my own car. Instead, buy my way in." He laughs with menace.

The race begins with a fifty-foot running takeoff, like a bobsled launch. After that, it's just gravity power. Perhaps applying their business acumen rather than physics, everyone seems to agree that the fastest takeoff—the best early push—will deter-mine the winner. At the last minute, two teams merge so that the go-cart with bicycle wheels can be launched by a very athletic VC who, I learn, was a competitive decathlete two years ago. Even when they're having fun on a Sunday morning, competition is in these guys' bones.

All the vehicles are required to have brakes, but nobody's using them. A sharkmobile goes by. A Mars Sojourner screeches halfway down the track, then stalls—one of the wheels locked up. Super Dave Osborne attempts to steer with ski poles, but at his first plant he thrusts himself into a spin and careens into the shrubbery. The event raises more than $100,000.

The lawyer who was writing checks says, "This is a very, very characteristic moment for Silicon Valley. We've taken a lot of flak for not being political enough, for not being benefactors to social causes. But you can trick us into donating money just by making it competitive. It's gotta be a challenge. I remember when Larry Ellison wanted to give some money, I can't remember to whom. He couldn't just give the money. He challenged a world-class triathlete to a bar-dipping contest, and Larry did something like sixty-three bar dips, which is almost inhuman, about like doing five hundred push-ups."

On the whole, philanthropy seems sort of redundant—they're already giving seventy-hour weeks to the creation of new tech-nology meant to empower the world. That's not enough? That said, one's job is still put to the old-fashioned halo test: You've got to be improving society, or what's the point? But not everyone can design the Mac and liberate electrons. So a few tricks to pass-ing the test have evolved over time. The first is the libertarian view: you believe that the vigorous pursuit of self-interest leads to the most efficient allocation of resources, which ensures con-tinued development. The second is related but far more twisted. It's the workaholic value system: nothing good comes easily, so if it's a terrific challenge, it must be good. By this self-referential logic, any project that is totally consuming is worthwhile. The corollary to this is that if you're not sure your work is contribut-ing, you should work harder at it and soon it will. It follows that perhaps one of the reasons people here work so hard is that they're not really sure how their little piece of the jigsaw puzzle fits into the big picture of a better society. "Will society be any worse off," they ask themselves, "if this CGI script goes unwritten?"

"I predict that this event will be very, very big next year," another competitor proclaims. "There'll be a couple hundred entries. It'll raise over a million dollars. I'm sure of it. It has all the right ingredients to motivate people." He ticks them off on his fingers: "Competition. Gadgetry. Fun. An uncontroversial, good cause. In that order."

Downtown San Francisco

What happens when twenty or so newly minted supermillionaires get together and each of them brings at least $5 million of company stock to the party?

It's called an "exchange fund," and it's a way for those who've recently gone public to diversify their risk without yet paying the taxes due on their gains. Think of a potluck party, but rather than bringing melon ball salad, you bring five mil of Inktomi stock. These potluck contributions are wrapped up into one diversified security, and each contributor gets one twentieth of the proceeds. Voilà—diversification without taxation.

But don't look for explanations of exchange funds in the business pages of your local newspaper or in the business magazines on your local news racks. Ordinary people aren't supposed to know about these things. If you want to learn more, you've got to go to a place like Goldman Sachs's Private Client Services Group on the fiftieth floor of the Bank of America tower, and you've got to talk to a sweetly mischievous, twinkly-eyed seventh-generation Hawaiian in his mid-thirties named Allen Damon. He's another highly evolved creature who could not exist outside Silicon Valley. If you have more than $5 million in assets, he will sit you down in a room with a floor-to-ceiling window in which you can see south all the way to San Jose. He'll introduce you to the merry pranksters he works with, and then he'll run through the entire menu of financial desserts baked only for supermillionaires.

Investment banks tolerate a lot of bizarre behavior, but there are two things that will get you laughed at on the fiftieth floor of

Goldman Sachs, two boneheaded things that are a true embarrassment. Both have everything to do with paying taxes. The first: letting a short-term loss go long term, thereby missing a chance to offset the short-term loss with a short-term capital gain. The second: buying into a mutual fund. Mutual funds are optimized for and judged by their *pretax* performance, meaning that the fund manager couldn't care less about putting fundholders into the sorry position of having to send checks to the government. At Private Client Services, teaching you how to avoid getting laughed at is what they're about.

In the good old days, a supermillionaire could party alone, using a sleight of hand called the "short against the box." If you owned $5 million of Yahoo!, for example, you could put it on deposit with your broker (putting it into his "box"). Once your broker had it in his box and felt safe that he could take it from you at any time, there were all sorts of maneuvers he was willing to let you do: borrow against the collateral at low interest, short the full amount of the stock, or sell call options with strike prices right at the money, any of which gave you $5 million to reinvest in a diversified portfolio. But since you hadn't *actually* sold the stock to the broker (just put it into his box), you didn't have any capital gains to report.

Sadly, Congress felt no sympathy for the supermillionaire and did away with the short against the box in 1997. This congressional carpet bomb was extremely effective for all of about 0.8 seconds, after which the innovative folks at Goldman came up with the exchange fund and the TRACE. This acronym stands for Trust Automatic Exchange for Stock, and it involves crazy tricks such as a "collar in the perpetuity." Beyond that point Allen Damon's explanation gets too complicated for me, having something to do with selling both put and call options and then taking the whole soufflé public. The one part I do manage to catch is that TRACEs aren't worth the bother of doing all the paperwork in amounts less than $50 million. Which rules out all but about eighty people in the Valley.

But what if the newly minted supermillionaire just wants to sleep in his cubicle and doesn't care about all the money he's made? Damon admits that a lot of guys are not accustomed to having money. They feel both ashamed of and nervous about it. They're also very suspicious of Damon and his management fees. As a result, they often just want to let it sit there in their account. "There were guys like that at Forte Software who watched their stock drop from eighty dollars to six dollars." At another company, which Damon wouldn't name, some guys exercised their stock options at $42, so they owed capital gains taxes based on that price. But shortly thereafter the stock dropped to $10. "They had to sell all their stock just to cover the taxes due and still came up short," Damon says. "Tell me they don't care then. We've all got our horror stories. A decision to do nothing is just as much a decision as anything else. Inaction is action."

At Goldman Sachs Private Client Services, they breathe and think and eat in $5 million chunks. If you've recently made your first $20 million, you might feel a little bit sheepish about it for a while—*did I really deserve it?* But come to Goldman Sachs on the fiftieth floor, and you'll quickly realize that $20 million barely gets you a few rungs above oblivion. Twenty million dollars is nothing to brag about here, and certainly nothing to get worked up about. When you walk out of a room, nobody here whispers behind your back, "For having twenty mil, that guy almost seems *normal.*"

Because having twenty mil here *is* normal.

> **"You can't offer seventy-five percent of your company for twenty-five percent of ours when our company's been around for six years and you haven't even incorporated yours yet! That's not the way it's done!"**
> **—Overheard dialogue at an Indian buffet in Mountain View**

Mountain View

I go for a drive around Mountain View with one of the city planners who has been responsible, over the last five years, for meeting the needs of the economic boom, fueled by the hardware and software firms headquartered here: Sun Microsystems, U.S. Robotics, Silicon Graphics, Netscape. Barney Burke is a cuddly, devoted guy who gets a proud, patriotic flush across his face every time we turn the corner and come across another dirt-

and-girder development he's had a hand in. City planners take their cue from the local industry: they're not afraid to take risks, as they did in turning the hog farms, junkyards, and dump sites in the North Bayshore area, east of Highway 101, into 3 million square feet of premium office park. Another thing they have in common with the software business is last-minute, down-to-the-wire construction—invitations are already printed and mailed for the gala opening of the new library, which is only ten days away, but as we drive by the building, workers are still pouring cement over the rebar.

As we get onto an expressway, Barney spots a small vineyard he hasn't noticed before. "That won't last long," he says, salivating. When Barney gets back to the office, he'll look up the owners and make sure they aren't in the dark about how valuable their land has become.

Barney shows me one of the last working farms in Mountain View. Remarkably, this farm is located directly behind the Netscape headquarters, which has otherwise scarfed up every available office space it can buy or build. Barney points his finger at some of the tilt-up buildings nearby, tsk-tsking their single-story density. "That one won't last. That one, sure to go. This one too."

According to Barney, Silicon Valley is the epicenter of the new economy, and the epicenter of Silicon Valley—the place where it's all really happening—is here, the Land of Netscape.

It wasn't very impressive, this epicenter of the epicenter. It's not like being on Broadway in Manhattan, looking up at the Sony Trinitron. I could be outside any office park in the country. It's so anonymous it hurts.

Some Japanese tourists are taking one another's pictures in front of Netscape's sign, trying to get a fountain in the background.

Barney and I get to talking about the expensive costs of doing business here versus the benefits, primarily the proximity to smart people. I mention to Barney that I have an appointment to interview Eric Schmidt, the recently named CEO of network giant Novell, because I had heard he spends four days a week in Silicon Valley even though his company is headquartered in Utah, which not too long ago was judged to have more hard-working talent than here. Rather than picking up the train of discussion, Barney goes, "Oh, yeah, Eric Schmidt. Me and Eric and some other friends went to college together at Cal." Barney tells me a story of how the old friends flew in from the Midwest for a party Schmidt held last year and how Schmidt graciously sent a limo to the airport to bring them straight to the party. "He's that kind of guy, will go out of his way for an old friend."

We get out of the car and walk a hundred yards south. A noisy Caterpillar backhoe is digging up a train track that crosses the road east to west. To the west is the main railway running up the peninsula. To the east is Moffett Field. Eighteen-foot links of the railway are being lifted on forklifts into the bed of a dump truck. Dust is flying.

"This used to go by the nickname 'the missile track.' When the navy wanted to get something into Moffett Field that was too big to fit on a truck—say, a missile—they would load it onto this rail line and scoot it into Moffett. We're digging it up to make room for development. It's really the last vestige of the defense-budget economy, which used to dominate Mountain View."

As we walk along the track, Barney explains how when he first started work for the city, ten years ago, he would go into Printer's Ink bookstore, and the graffiti on the bathroom walls would say, "Bombs Away—Give me Star Wars pay!" Moffett Field was to Mountain View as Stanford University was to Palo Alto—the big institution that drove everything. Mountain View was traditionally the dorm for all the single aerospace engineers who worked at Lockheed.

In the early '90s, the end of the Cold War reshaped Silicon Valley. The defense cuts led to a recession in counties such as this one that had been dependent on defense money. Barney Burke on those bad years: "Oh, yeah, we got a little nervous around here. We felt it. There were even layoffs in the city planning office." As high tech weaned off the military gravy train, there were quite a few industry layoffs five years ago, and those layoffs killed the last vestiges of the ideal that employees should have loyalty to their company. Now workers are careful about looking out for themselves, wary of revolutionary language being just a management ploy to squeeze more work hours out of employees.

But there's still loyalty. I believe that Silicon Valley workers have a muscular faith in their industry, a deep optimism that they will be able to continue to find work for many more years.

They have loyalty to the whole process. Their need to see the altruism in their efforts is supplied by implicit deduction rather than explicit hype: the industry is good; I work in the industry; therefore, I am good. This halo by association, or the Big Umbrella, reinforces industry loyalty. Your company may burn its cash, it may get beat to market, or it may even lay you off with only a week's severance because the CFO discovers that some goof in the accounting department booked returnable wholesale shipments as fully sold, but you don't worry, because there are other companies willing to hire you. There will always be other companies willing to hire you.

> **Under all our desks are two boxes. One for colored paper, one for white paper. I was here late last night, and the janitor came through with one huge tub on wheels. He threw both my boxes into the same tub. When I asked him why, he said the paper goes out to a sorter, to whom it's no use to presort. He figured we are given two boxes because we need to think we're doing the right thing, whether it's useful or not.**
> **—E-mail from a friend at Microsoft**

San Carlos

B., a thirty-four-year-old, somewhat restless project leader at a company he doesn't want me to name, has been thinking about his plan for three months now. He's been waking up in the middle of the night, his mind playing through scenarios. During meetings at work, listening to executives drone on, he finds himself doodling diagrams on Post-it notes. Driving home, he lists the pros and cons of whether to put the plan into action.

B. is not thinking of another start-up. B. has been planning to murder one of the asshole programmers on his team.

"It'll look like an accident. Every year, five people in the Bay Area die on train tracks. He'll just be another statistic. I can't stand working with him anymore."

He takes me to the Holly Street Caltrain depot in San Carlos, where the act would take place. The area's under construction, without a boarding platform, but there's no fence or guardrail. "I take him out for Mexican food across the street. He has a few Dos Equis, his blood alcohol will make it look like an accident. The sun goes down at 7:45, right over those mountains, and the glare blocks the view of the passengers. We'll be standing at the north end of the depot. The southbound train comes in here at about twenty-five miles an hour. When it's halfway past us, a little push, he goes down . . ." B. still can't quite figure out how best to push a guy and reliably make him budge. The programmer weighs 180 pounds. To me, B.'s fighting weight appears to be about 155.

"One hundred sixty," he says. When my eyebrows go up he adds, "After a burrito, with a belly full of beer."

I think this situation needs a little deconstruction. First, B. will never, ever touch his programmer. It's just fun for him to think about; the planning relieves some of his tension.

In college B. was an avowed Communist and wrote his honors thesis on how teamwork was the ideal expression of man's nature. His hero was Ernest Borgnine, and to this day B. will recite scenes from movies where Borgnine sacrificed his life for the team—the throw-yourself-on-the-grenade signature plot device. So precious does B. hold team dynamics that when his stubborn programmer refuses even to attempt the work B. gives him, B.'s fuse blows. However, being a good manager, he can't vent at the office. Thus, the murder plot as a psychological release.

The other thing to consider here is that just a year ago, the company he doesn't want me to name bought B.'s Internet game tool start-up, earning him a couple million and making him a manager. That ain't an upper-deck home run, but for a mere game tool, that's as good as it gets. So B. is accustomed to the freewheeling environment of a start-up, and he's such a high achiever that ordinary office politics are intolerable.

So this is what you get in the Valley: incredibly successful people complaining all the way to the bank. Honeymoons are short.

Noah Ames (not his real name) is another one. He's CEO of a telephony software firm near here with thirty-five employees. By his own description, what he's been through deserves a movie, or at least a book: "I'm a seasoned veteran of the software wars. Boy, could I tell you some stories from the trenches." He's exhausted, though, and needs to get out. In another year, he figures, his company will be worth $6 million, but he can't wait another year, he's been at this too long: "I've spent too much of my damn life teth-ered to my company." He'd take any offer over a million dollars and walk.

Here's the kicker: Noah Ames, old man, is twenty-eight. He founded the company in late 1995—so long ago it's hard to re-member.

The big-picture future—the postrevolutionary future—isn't much on people's minds. Everyone's got a filing due next week or a development milestone or quarter-end sales quotas to worry about. There's a great sense that now is the time they will tell their grandchildren about, that today's fever may be the oppor-tunity of a lifetime. Just about everyone's working on Internet hardware or software, with very little attention being paid to what else might be worth inventing. Most people have a blue-print for what they'll be doing a year from now—they can read it to me off their business plans—but nobody has any idea what he'll be doing five years from now.

Noah Ames's telephony software might revolutionize the phone call, but having a revolutionary mind-set about it seems sort of silly. "The phone call will be revolutionized whether I'm a part of it or not," he explains. "There are dozens of Internet tele-phony firms. Nobody's the lone soldier anymore. I've got a friend who's twenty-four, and he's at his fourth start-up. How many revolutions can you join? It's like *Monty Python's Life of Brian:* you can't keep straight the People's Front of Judea from the Judean People's Front."

South of Market

The full force of the Microsoft PR hurricane has begun. Full-page spreads in the *Examiner*'s Sunday pink pages. Half-minute radio spots on Live 105. Billboards on the sides of Muni buses. Everywhere I go, advertisements beckon me to put some gusto into my weekend by taking a suggestion off Microsoft's enter-tainment listing Web site, SideWalk. These are no ordinary ad-vertisements; they are the carefully polished result of Micro-soft spending $700 a day on copywriters and $1,200 a day on art directors and $2,000 a day on test-marketing concepts until the socially awkward behemoth from Redmond looks truly cool.

Enigmatic, nuanced, and deep. They're good, these ads. Very good.

The next day, I get a call. It's a PR person. The counterattack has begun. She begs me to come visit the offices of an authentic, locally grown, by-the-bootstraps entertainment guide to San Francisco, a couple dozen employees in an antiearthquake-retrofitted warehouse with all five fingers on the real vibe of this buzzing city—employees still hungover from their voyages into last night's clubs, employees still hoarse from speaking up at their neighborhood political club. Who doesn't want to root for the little guy? Oh, this PR woman hooks me, hooks me good, because the question of whether Microsoft can do culture is a topic that never tires me. I hear gossip from Redmond about how Michael Kinsley is awkwardly out of place there—how, when he walks around campus, he doesn't know what to do with his hands: slip them into his pockets, let them swing at his sides, what? She gives me a time slot and an address, and at three that afternoon I go to take a look.

Here's what I found at CitySearch, this so-called little guy: Its investors include Goldman Sachs, AT&T, Compaq Computer, and various newspaper conglomerates. It has strategic partnerships with Silicon Graphics, Borland, and Informix. It has offices (and accompanying sites) in more than twenty metropolitan areas.

Getting rooted in the community used to be like making fine wine: it took a certain period of fermentation, followed by years of aging. But CitySearch has distilled the process down to a few fast months in what they describe as a SWAT-team approach. It aggressively hires local people to ring the doorbells of local merchants, convincing them to pay for a Web site in CitySearch's megalopolis. It can manufacture a grassroots presence according to well-honed timetables and sales quotas. When the site in Salt Lake City had success testing out radio spots featuring satisfied merchants, that type of advertising went national. This office's general manager, Scott Garell, spent his last four years learning brand marketing at Clorox, and he's applied every bit of his smarts here. I don't want to give a cynical impression of what CitySearch does—it isn't faking a "community" pose in the slightest, it's just that it has applied McDonald's franchise science to the high-tech garage start-up amazingly well. When I ask Garell what worries him so much that it keeps him up at night, he responds, "Funny you should ask that, because for a national sales meeting next week in Pasadena, I'm supposed to be moderating a panel on the topic of 'What Keeps You Up at Night?' "

Even motivational strategies for "fostering a passionate office culture" are tested in each city, and summary reports are written and sent up the chain of command. Then the most successful methods are implemented on a national basis. Thus, each office's democratically voted "overachiever of the month" is awarded with extra stock options, because that seems to work better than an "employee of the month" getting a ski weekend. If a skull-and-crossbones flag tested well, every office would be flying one.

That scene in *Barton Fink* keeps coming to mind, where Jack Lipnick, the studio boss, chastises Fink: "You think you're the only writer who can give me that Barton Fink feeling? I got twenty writers under contract that I can ask for a Fink-type thing from."

So that's Silicon Valley today. We don't need no stinking revolutionaries—we've got hordes of Generation Xers hooked on options churning out a revolution-type thing. We don't need you to stay up at night worrying about your business. We've convened a panel of expert worriers to handle that for you.

> **"Best Buy Furniture"**
> **—Decoy sign on Industrial Light & Magic's**
> **building in San Rafael. The sign keeps job**
> **seekers away.**

East Palo Alto

Be warned: if your imprint of Silicon Valley was soldered together in the 1980s, it's time to upgrade.

The legacy of Silicon Valley began with Bill Hewlett and David Packard, who founded Hewlett-Packard in Packard's garage. That was the old model, the classic tale of made-good entrepreneurism. They invented the products. They built the products. They sold the products. The company didn't change its name and it didn't sell out, and Hewlett and Packard spent their entire lives at their company.

Just eighteen months ago, the prototype for entrepreneurism was a guy like Dave Samuel. He had been at Oracle less than a year, having flown out from MIT on a junket and become entranced by the sunshine, but he felt stagnant inside the software behemoth. On January 11, 1996, Samuel had his idea: put music up on the Net. Four days later, he left Oracle and with two friends started work on TheDJPlayer in the basement of their rented house atop a hill in San Carlos. So far, it followed the classic scenario.

But things became nonlinear as soon as they released the product in June. TheDJ.com hadn't made a dime and had only a hundred listeners, but in no time they had offers from four companies to buy them out. "We hadn't stood up yet" is how Samuel puts it. If they'd achieved this much in half a year, how much more might they achieve in another year? It would be hard for them to keep their self-respect if they sold out so soon. And then there was the principle to fight for: telecommunications reform had just made it legal for radio station conglomerates to own several stations in the same market, which was going to mean less variety on the radio. What they were doing was important; they were building an audience for music that didn't have a chance against Mariah Carey.

So they did what is becoming increasingly difficult to do—they turned down the offers.

Not long after, it became time to find employee number 5. "It's been four of us, roommates, for the last year. Now we're using a headhunter and interviewing strangers. The chemistry's crucial. It's got to be the right person," Samuel told me.

Less than a week later, not only did they find the right person, they acquired his company. Josh Felser had been working on Internet radio as well and had developed some features Dave liked. TheDJ.com bought Josh's company, RadioCo, and the two men shared an office. The company has since been renamed Spinner.com. "I learned a little from the companies that had been trying to buy us," Dave Samuel said. This twenty-five-year-old CEO has already gotten wise to how things work: "Buy them before they've really stood up."

So there you go: Eat or be eaten. Even the little guys, the very little guys who are doing something very cool and important—the four-guys-in-a-garage start-ups—are playing the acquisition game.

That was late 1997. Today, though, there's a new evolution in the game. Forget nonlinear (selling a product that isn't even out of beta), we're talking *parallel entrepreneurism*. If venture capitalists can guarantee themselves at least one whopping success by spreading their risk over half a dozen companies, why can't an entrepreneur do the same?

When I caught up with Greg Slayton, he was leaning over the sink in his building's bathroom, washing his hands after urinating—and simultaneously talking on his cell phone. I guess having to pee is no excuse to stop working. He's one of the only nonsalesmen in the Valley who wears a suit, and I've never seen him without a baseball cap. Slayton is the CEO of the seventy-person MySoftware Company, which was about to be named one of the top-performing stocks of 1998, thanks to Greg's magic. This guy takes gung ho to a whole new level.

Before he'd come to Silicon Valley, Slayton had been involved in Third World economic development work in Malaysia for two years and Senegal for three more. Now, *that* was pressure: "When we made bad decisions, people died. If we picked the wrong town to drop food in and it was hijacked by guerrillas, people starved." For a year he ran an orphanage in Manila. "I think I'm the only entrepreneur in the Valley who used to fly bush planes and ride camels to work."

The fact that people like Greg are attracted to the Valley now says something about what's happened to it: it's no longer just for people who don't otherwise have a life. They're not here for the sunshine.

In his early years here, Greg too had his halcyon days of start-up fever: he cofounded a 3-D Web tools company called Worlds Inc. He raised his $17 million and as CFO steered the company to an $85 million valuation. He put in his fourteen-hour days. He was at the office the night of his wife's birthday. He gave it his heart and soul. But then, in a dispute with the CEO, he was fired.

"That was my baby," he says. "It really affected me." He says it's common for people who haven't experienced failure to develop a superman complex: if it's raining outside, they think, "I made it rain."

What he's done to manage his risk since then is spread it around. Though he puts 90 percent of his time into MySoftware, he asks rhetorically, "Why put all one's efforts into one bucket?" So he's cofounded a couple companies on the side. It takes him a while to think of them all. One's a high-tech management consulting firm, Synesis. One's a venture capital group. He sold another company he was involved in, Test Design, to a public firm, InTest, and now sits on the board of directors. And somewhere in the middle of all that he sold another firm he ran, Paragraf, to Silicon Graphics for $53 million. You get the idea: he's got things going all over town. You might think Greg Slayton was a start-up pimp if he didn't have the obvious evidence of having made MySoftware's investors 500 percent on their money this year.

This guy's got so much *can-do* it's blinding. He's got the *can-do* high beams on. Sometimes, with his get-friendly-fast joviality, you want to flash him back as if to signal, "Tone it down, Yankee."

Then, a few minutes later, he's digging through his Dayminder and out falls a business card for Slayton Capital, an angel fund, which all by itself has got him entangled in several more ventures.

"Oops. Almost forgot that one," he says.

Palo Alto

Edgar threatened to change everything. Edgar demanded that everything be 100 percent computerized. To the employees of R. R. Donnelley Financial in Palo Alto, the imminent entree of Edgar was Major League Baseball realignment, NAFTA, and a Martian invasion all rolled into one. At the water cooler and over the urinals, Edgar was all anyone talked about.

Edgar was the Securities and Exchange Commission's Electronic Data Gathering, Analysis, and Retrieval filing system, which went on-line two years ago. Before that time, Silicon Valley lawyers, underwriters, and issuers would meet at the plush offices of R. R. Donnelley, where they could make last-minute changes in their S1s and 10Qs before they were printed out and bound in black tape and thrown onto the red-eye flight to New York for a filing at the SEC offices the next morning. With Edgar up and running, anyone with a computer could file, and issuers would have no reason to keep coming to the R. R. Donnelley office.

But they kept coming anyway.

"They needed neutral turf for their negotiations," explains Reggie Ammons, the man who holds their hands through the process. A decade in California hasn't softened any of the accent Reggie developed growing up in Onley, Texas, 135 miles northwest of Dallas. His accent is three parts chaw-chewin', shit-kickin' old boy, one part grandfather-in-the-rocker storyteller, and two parts "Yeaus, Mastuh" obligingness. This oral cocktail connotes authenticity and history; just filling out SEC forms with him, you feel as if you're doing something grand. He's an upwardly mobile, supereducated bassackward swamp fella with manners so thick they stick to your teeth just talking to him. He's Bill Clinton in all the good ways, twenty years younger and plopped right down here in Silicon Valley.

As Reg tells it, lawyers want a prospectus to be a very conservative document to avoid unfulfilled expectations, while underwriters want it to market the shares. With the liability for a mistake enormous, their arguments over the precise language get quite intense. Neither side wants to meet at the other's offices— that would give the host an upper hand (this is probably something they've read in *The Art of War*). So every day they fill the drafting rooms and telephone rooms in this single-story, mock-Spanish building on California Avenue, where Reg takes care of them. They pace the hallways, chewing the ends of pens. There is a billiard table and a big-screen television and showers, and for anyone too weak or too frazzled to pull the customary all-nighter in what is normally a two-day process, there is a foldout bed.

At around 12:30 every afternoon, these people get nervous. They've got to get their S1 or their S4 or their 13G in to the SEC before 5:30 East Coast time, which is in less than two hours, so Reg Ammons gives a polite rap on the conference room door and says, "That's it, boys, you're done or you'll miss the deadline." The deadline's crucial, because there are very specific windows of opportunity in which underwriters want to make their initial public offerings—not in the week the employment figure comes out or on a day the Fed is meeting or just before the end of a quarter—and so sometimes if you miss the deadline you have to postpone the deal until another week or another month, and by then anything could happen.

Edgar was supposed to make all this obsolete, but in fact the opposite has occurred, because no law firm or underwriter wants to take the risk of making sure the filing is coded exactly the way the SEC wants it. So a crazy thing happens around two o'clock every day, as all the fire-breathing lawyers and steam-snorting venture capitalists gather around the computers where the e-mail is going out. They cross their fingers and sweat and try to make jokes, hoping that the damn electronic file gets properly pinged across the country. They watch that monitor as if it's a 49ers game in overtime.

The lesson is an ironic one: physical proximity is more important than ever, even in the very industry that is inventing the communications technologies that are supposed to make physical proximity irrelevant.

> **"They're slimy, but I like to feel part of the deal flow."**
> —*A friend's reply when I asked her why she lets headhunters take her to breakfast even though she's not looking for a job.*

San Jose

When Eric Schmidt took the job as CEO of Novell, which is based in Provo, Utah, he made it clear that he would not leave the Valley. Though he feels he has the best of both worlds by having staff both in Utah and here, as CEO he needs to be here. It's where the deals are cut. It's where the trade press is. It's where conflict occurs—and he needs to expose himself to the conflict, not to get isolated. Toward that end, he has broken ground on a new Novell headquarters in San Jose, which will consolidate a thousand employees currently scattered around the Valley. It's another example of the proximity thing: physical proximity for people is important, even in the company that invented corporate networks.

Schmidt speaks eloquently, passionately, persuasively. When I don't pick up his train of thought fast enough, he asks the next relevant question aloud himself, then answers it, which leads to another self-asked question, and so on. His parenthetical remarks can last a minute, and there are parenthetical remarks inside parenthetical remarks, but he never fails to come back to the open parentheses and close them. In this sense, speaking with him is calming—as when you pull a travel bag out of your closet and find an old favorite sweater you thought was lost. His voice has the smooth assuredness of a wee-hours BBC broadcaster. This seasoned technology officer from Sun Microsystems frequently calls himself a "freshman CEO," and he will mention how he asks lots of people for advice, but to the extent that one of the first responsibilities of a CEO is to be the company's front man to the press, he doesn't need any schooling.

Network technology is clearly where a lot of the most important innovations will be in the next five years, and Novell is the company that invented corporate networking. Schmidt's challenge has been to give the stable, dedicated corporate culture in Provo a fresh breath of Silicon Valley's aggressive, risk-taking style.

"At one of my first meetings at Novell, the topic was future operating system technology, and a key engineering executive stood up to ask, 'Do I have permission to be passionate?' I thought he was joking—I honestly laughed. I thought he was being funny. They need to know it's Okay."

He moved on to the next thought: "What is the right corporate culture? It has to be a good place to work but not necessarily a nice place to work. A good place to work is where dreams get fulfilled and interesting things go on. 'Nice' can be a cover-up for a lack of passion. At Novell, people are almost too polite.

"I have to give everyone a reason to believe. Why is Novell relevant? When people feel that they are relevant, that their work matters, they will do amazing things."

Schmidt is adamant that the revolutionary mind-set is still very much present in Silicon Valley. "Why do I work for this industry? It's because I believe that a small number of people can change the world through technology. That belief is incredibly seductive.

"Why do people who have more personal and business and financial success than is even conceivable keep working so hard? Any rational analysis would say it's time to retire, give your money away. It's because they're driven to change the world. That shared belief is what drives our passion. It's what drives me. On any given day, I feel I have failed if I haven't made progress along one of those initiatives.

"I've been around long enough now to give advice, and the advice I give is: Find a way to make a difference, and the rest will follow—personal success, promotions, financial gain."

I told him some of the stories that I'd been hearing, stories of disappointment and frustration, stories of people seemingly unable to enjoy their success, stories of people who didn't seem to be on the change-the-world bandwagon. What did he make of those?

He had a very interesting answer, one that suggested that as CEO he would harness discontent as yet another motivation to make good things happen. "Yes, people complain. The constant friction is an occupational hazard of the job. But I would be unhappy if people weren't whining. I want them to want more. You look around Silicon Valley, it's not too obvious that people are happy. They're incredibly stressed. Why is that? It's not because they work for me. They're stressed because they're naturally stressed. They're high achievers. The kind of mild dissatisfaction with what you have is a key prerequisite to success in this business."

He believes that the beauty of this industry is the paradigm changes that sweep through it every five years, giving people a whole new reason to get excited. It happened to him. "I had been at Sun for ten years. I was bored. It had got stagnant. Then I got interested in Mosaic technology, the Internet happened, and I got all excited again, so much so that I almost jumped to any number of start-ups. In other industries, that doesn't happen. In other industries, you get one sweeping change a lifetime."

Schmidt's analysis of the ideal corporate culture seems to fit Silicon Valley just fine: it's a good place to work but not a nice place to work.

"The Valley has a model," Schmidt says. "It's the total dedication model. You can't go halfway. It's binary."

South Park

Ron Johnson is a merry rock slab of muscle who wears pajama bottoms and T-shirts. Alison Chozen is a brainy hotty who could easily moonlight as a Victoria's Secret model. They love to finish each other's sentences. Listen to how this tag team talks, and you'd think they were high-tech entrepreneurs:

"Sometimes we're here late at night, trying to think of ideas. How can we improve on last year? We have to stay competitive—"

"—anything is possible. Put no barriers on your mind. Let it go. If you nurture and feed the mind, it's amazing what you can come up with—"

"—the next thing you know, we've promised something to a client, and we've put ourselves in a jam: we've got no idea how we are ever going to pull this off!"

The kinds of promises Alison and Ron make to clients are not for upgrades to software but usually for something a little more eye-catching. Such as camels.

"We'd promised a client two camels and suddenly it was a week away. We had to go out and find camels—"

"—but it turns out that if you make a five-thousand-dollar donation to the San Francisco Zoo, they'll let just about anything out of its cages for the night."

Alison and Ron are party planners with Mosaic Events Management, and they have developed quite a reputation in Silicon Valley for bashes that have a particular appeal to the high-tech crowd. "It's definitely different than for other industries," Alison says.

Ron picks up the thought: "At a high-tech party, usually nobody knows each other, and they're often very shy. So we need to provide something interactive, create an environment with games."

But you won't see a dance contest at a Mosaic party. In a tech crowd, there are usually not many dancers and often not many women with whom to dance. You won't see a casino night either.

Four years ago, that might have been enough, but the relentless pressure to innovate has affected the party circuit as much as it has the integrated circuit. "The trend is much more towards the physical," says Alison. So today they might roll out a hundred-yard-long Astroturf football field, complete with goalposts. Everyone will be given a reversible jersey, and the party will continue on the field as a helicopter lands and out jumps Boomer Esiason, ready to toss passes to a line of receivers. Roving novelty performers, like human condom men or hula hoop queens, roam the crowd. And there will always be a line to be a human dart.

To be a human dart, you slip into a head-to-toe Velcro suit, then squat into a butt bucket that is the firing device of a huge slingshot. Attached to either side of the butt bucket are huge rubber bands as thick as your wrist. Your team pulls you back until the bands are fully stretched, then releases you, and you fly straight through the air for twenty-five feet until you smack against a wall-sized foam target, also covered with Velcro—and there you stick. You are utterly incapable of pulling yourself off. You must be peeled off slowly by your teammates.

"Ninety percent of our business is repeat business," says Ron, and Alison finishes the thought: "Because we know their guests and we know what they want." What they want are climbing walls, trampolines, human foosball, bungee jumping. Basketball games in which the balloonish ball is four feet in diameter and the hoop is even bigger. You can get your picture taken draped in a ten-foot-long albino boa constrictor, which has yellowish skin and ruby red eyes.

The trends in food and drink are tough to keep up with too. "It's not enough just to serve ginkgo in the smoothies. You've got to have oxygen-infused cocktails for the mental boost." And while the trend around the country is toward comfort foods, in high tech it's still cutting edge.

"We can serve garlic mashed potatoes—" says Ron.

"—but only if we serve it in a martini glass," finishes Alison.

"We can do pasta—"

"—but only if we color it jet-black with squid ink."

The camels were for a Midnight at the Oasis Bedouin theme. Another time they promised two jaguars, which were flown in from Toronto.

"We've definitely picked up the value system of our clients—"

"—we've taken on their philosophy."

"It becomes not whether we *can* do it—"

"—but how we *will* do it."

Redwood City

I play soccer with a Peruvian I'll call Luis. He's just your basic office computer guy. He programs in C++, he does tech support.
He's never invented anything in particular, but the work has been
steady. For the last two years, he has been providing twenty-four-
hour, on-call tech support for an HMO corporate sales force.

Six weeks ago, Luis made an offer above the asking price
on a two-flat neotraditional near Stafford Park. Price: around
$550,000, and he'll have to make a monthly mortgage payment
of $3,845. His sister, brother, and parents will live upstairs from
him and his wife, but the elders are on SSI, his sister assembles
burritos at a taqueria, and his younger brother—who arrived
only three months ago—hauls office furniture. Their combined
incomes won't cover the property tax payments. When Luis told
me what he'd done, I was amazed—it seemed such a vote of confidence in this economy, in these high times, and from such an
unlikely person. Peru is a dysfunctional country, crippled by corruption, and I would think Luis would know too well how easy it
is for things to spiral the wrong way.

I helped the family move in. The brother ordered a pizza, and
with Luis as interpreter I learned the story of his father, an
adorable old potato of a guy. It turned out that he was a lawyer
who had handled some money for the rebel Communist group
Shining Path—eighteen years ago. Without quite realizing the
enormity of what he had done, he suddenly became one of the
most wanted men in Peru, and he hid in the Amazon jungle for
a year with the Shining Path.

I turned to Luis. "That's just amazing. In one generation, from
your father, a Communist revolutionary, to you joining the computer revolution."

Luis's moon-pie face wrinkled up, and his eyebrows pinched.
"What is this computer revolution?"

"You know, the way computers are changing the world."

"Revolution, though?"

I explained how there used to be an ethos in Silicon Valley that everyone was on a mission to transform our society, not just with the personal computer—the ultimate populist tool—but by creating decentralized models for the workplace and new religions based on self-enlightenment rather than church scriptures. We wanted to shake up the world. We called it a revolution. Ten, fifteen years ago, people felt the call to arms. I told him about the skull-and-crossbones flag flown over Apple during the development of the Macintosh.

This provoked a burst of laughter from Luis, and then he just had to translate for his father and brother, and they laughed too, and then Luis ran out to tell his wife and mother, who didn't laugh so hard until Luis made me repeat what I'd said, which he interpreted for the women, who stood there politely with their hands behind their backs, in matching rooster-print aprons. Then they laughed on cue, knowing what was expected of them.

A week later, after one of our soccer games, Luis shocked me with his latest news: "I quit my job. I'm going freelance."

"But you just bought your house!"

He nodded his head with full agreement, relishing the delicious improbability of it. "I know, I know, it sounds crazy."

"Why? You don't have any cash reserves. You just used them all on your down payment!"

"I'll find work."

I really couldn't believe it. I pressed him again: "Why?"

He shrugged. "If I don't use the extra bedroom in our flat as an office, my cousin will move in. My wife and I need our own flat. So it was quit my job or have a baby."

I thought about this and couldn't help laughing. "But how will you find work?" He'd been insulated inside the HMO for two years; his contacts were few. "How will people know to hire you?"

"Oh, the word will get out," he said with complete confidence, his head bobbing like a jack-in-the-box's, and that was that.

When I hunt for an anecdote about how good it's gotten in Silicon Valley lately, Luis stands out more than any story about absurd wealth ("My other car is a plane"), because absurd wealth has already happened—you went public, you made your $20 million, now what? Also, I think it's pretty easy to have faith in the far-off future, pretty easy to work at some research lab and believe that in 2010 cars will fly and computers will be wearable when you have a steady paycheck coming in each month. What's hardest is to have faith in the near future, to believe in the next eighteen months or, in Luis's case, the next thirty days.

As a soccer player, Luis is a midfielder. He isn't particularly athletic and doesn't hustle. But he has vision. When the ball comes to him, he has the ability to glance up at the field and instantly know what is about to happen—how the seemingly random twenty-two-player array will look in a moment's time. He will kick the ball to a spot behind the defense or into an open channel, where a teammate can run onto it. Luis can read the near future.

If it was a testimony to economic faith that Luis was willing to buy the house, how much more of a testimony was it that he was willing to entrust his mortgage payment to the vague notion that the people network would take care of him, that "the word will get out"? But that's how business is found these days in the smoothly working chaos of Silicon Valley: it's still important who you know, but the right person to know is never more than a few phone calls away. It's three degrees of separation. Everybody knows somebody who knows somebody, and, indeed, the word gets out.

Santa Clara

The questions remain when I look at the Valley to the south: Am I looking at another "steel city" Pittsburgh, the ground zero of an industry that is supplying a valuable technology to the whole world? Or am I looking at the future of the world itself—as the rest of the world adopts the technology being created in the Valley, will the rest of the world also adopt the Valley's work habits and campus parks and organizing principles? Are start-ups and the IPOs and the "total dedication model" not just a way of fostering new technology faster, but a blueprint for redesigning all our industrial paradigm institutions: schools, cities, nation-states? And is it possible, just possible, that if I get any more high-minded than I already am in this paragraph, my brain will explode?

Make no mistake: Silicon Valley is what it is because of its smallness. The fact that everybody knows everybody else is essential. This can't be reproduced nationwide. Sure, more people are coming here all the time, but those who've been here for a while have bigger Rolodexes. They have the advantage.

I had a Realtor down in Santa Clara show me a three-bedroom ranch home "priced to move" at half a million.

"Who can afford to buy a house now?" I exclaimed.

Then she told me how housing prices had gone up $1,000 a week this past year, with no end in sight.

She said, "At that rate, who can afford not to buy a house now?"

That's a pretty good assessment of Silicon Valley overall. It's evolved so much in the last five years that it seems pretty intimidating to get in this late in the game. But at the rapid rate at which it's evolving, can you afford *not* to get in?

"Do you want to sell Preparation H, or do you want to launch a new product category that will alter the balance of power in the world?"—was the pitch made by a venture capitalist, trying to convince a Stanford student not to take a competing offer from an online pharmacy.

"I hope it's not something to do with pets. Pets are so April."—was what I heard in the crowd before a Dot-Com's launch announcement.

I was at a party for a venture capital firm on Sand Hill Road, and after I had rolled a few games of bocce on their overly manicured lawn and gorged on the gooey selections from the oyster bar, I strolled out onto the back deck to watch the orange sun descend over the foothills. This half-mile stretch of real estate, from 2200 Sand Hill Road to 3400 Sand Hill Road, is now the priciest office space in the country. I had the sense—an unnerving, creeping sad sense—that we party-goers stank of being the new aristocracy, destined to inherit the future. Yes, I was bummed. It's far more fun and more interesting for the future to be up for grabs.

A lot of entrepreneurs here are into the science of Chaos Theory, which has found that truly alive systems exist only at what is called "the edge of chaos." Standing on that deck, I guess you could say I was afraid we were trending away from that truly alive time into the straitjacket of order.

The deck overlooked the parking lot. Most drivers ignored the valet service, either because they hated to be doted on or because they didn't want anyone touching their car. A "fancy" silver sports car purred into one of the slots below. I say "fancy" because I don't know my status items. It was a distinctively zippy/gaudy auto, giga-fancier than any of the BMWs and Audis that populated the lot. I was helped out by a few guys to my right, who one-upped each other.

"Look at that Ferrari."

"Spider."

"What is that, 1996 model year?"

"Yup. Probably bought it October, maybe November, 1995."

"1995!—that's pre-Internet!"

"That's old money!"

"Hah! Old Money!"

"What has that guy done lately!?"

"Driving his Big Dickmobile, trying to remind us he's important."

"Probably's afraid everyone's forgotten who he is."

The driver did get out shortly, and the guys didn't have any idea who he was.

My faith was restored. Chaos still reigned. Status in the Valley revolves around whatever is scarcest, and money isn't scarce. Status revolves around low employee numbers, founder stock, and hot deals. Try to rest on your laurels and you vanish.

No doubt somewhere else in the party someone was saying, "Look at Bronson out there on the patio. His book's been out months. What has he done lately?"

Silicon Valley is big enough and diverse enough that any writer can find what they set out to find. I love it for that. It wouldn't be interesting if it were simple to peg. You want to find that it's *insanely great* and heroic? There's evidence to support that. You want to find that it's lost its soul and ignited a bonfire of greed? The evidence is here. You want to find that it's controlled by a handful of Extremely Powerful Billionaires whose mere association with a new startup guarantees its success? That's here too.

The stories a writer chooses hold a mirror up to the writer as much as they do to the Valley. My philosophy has been that everyone's experience here is valid, from Mr. Fifty Million to Mr. Fifty Cents. I don't have conclusions so much as I endlessly retest the questions that I find important: Is there still opportunity here for the average person? Or are those chasing the American dream doing so in vain?

One of my favorite terms percolating in the Valley lately is *Dark Matter*. Dark Matter is what physicists theorize must exist, otherwise the very little matter that we do know about would collapse in on itself. As a metaphor, Dark Matter is all the stuff we rarely pay attention to but that we know exists; and as applied to the World Wide Web, Dark Matter refers to the jillions of ordinary people using it—creating their ten million personal Web pages, chatting about quilts on America Online, trading antique muffin tins back and forth on eBay. Eighty-five percent of Web traffic is outside of the Top 10 Web sites (on television, only 15 percent of viewership is outside the Top 10 channels). This new economy has rewarded those entrepreneurs who listen to the Dark Matter, not those who force their vision on it.

I had a Danish television crew following me around one day. The Nordic countries are obsessed with studying our economic engine because of its low impact on the environment and its dependence on highly educated workers, of which there is an oversupply in Scandinavia. I've found that Europeans get up to speed quickly on all the work-is-play side of the culture, but they're very wary of throwing money around so loosely—investing in mere ideas, et cetera. And they just can't comprehend the soaring stock prices. Those prices imply absurdly rosy forecasts for the future of these companies that have no track record. How can our investors have such faith? they ask me. Particularly when these companies are being run by people so young, with so little experience?

I said, "Well, let's look at another example. Do you have student loans in Denmark?"

They said that they didn't. Education is so valued in Denmark that the schools are entirely subsidized. It's free.

"Well, in America, we have this seemingly strange investment phenomenon. We'll take an ordinary eighteen-year-old high school graduate with:

1) no job history,
2) no demonstrated ability to make more than
   minimum wage,
3) no assets to pledge as collateral, and
4) on the way to college, so he or she won't pay back a penny
   for four years,

and nevertheless we believe that that individual is a good candidate for an investment of tens of thousands of dollars. Such a good investment, in fact, that we don't take an equity cut; our investment is in the form of a subordinated loan. That sounds like crazy economics. But millions of young Americans make it through life taking advantage of it, and it seems to work."

Here's the fundamental reason that I have faith in our economic future. I believe that we have fixed what was so wrong about our economy in the 1980s. The glory was in the wrong place. During those years, the great mass media culture said to college graduates, "Be one of the new breed—an information analyst. Be a lawyer, consultant, banker, accountant. Give advice or raise money for a living." We were promised that we'd never get bored or worry about commitment, because a new client walks in the door every day. It was in those professions that the money was being made, and so our brightest graduates followed the money. But who were we giving advice to and raising money for? I thought there was something fishy about it. It was like taking the most talented players off the football field and turning them into coaches. Economic growth was severely hampered because our smartest workers were out there giving advice about how to add value rather than doing it themselves. Our great inventions of the era were the junk bond, the LBO, telemarketing, and the science of 3 percent response-rate mass mailings.

The glory is now in taking the risk yourself. There's nothing cool anymore about being a mere advice-giver. There's nothing cool about a safe, steady six-figure income. It's cooler to be invested in than to invest, cooler to make news than to analyze news, cooler to be fully engaged than to consult those who are engaged. The talented are jumping back into the real game. Now *that's* the right way to create inventions of genuine value.